CASS LIBRARY OF INDUSTRIAL CLASSICS
No. 19

ENGLAND AND WALES

CASS LIBRARY OF INDUSTRIAL CLASSICS

No. 11.   Thomas Ellison

The Cotton Trade of Great Britain.   Including a history of the Liverpool Cotton Market and of the Liverpool Cotton Brokers' Association   (1886).
New Impression

No. 12.   W. Cooke Taylor

Notes of a Tour in the Manufacturing Districts of Lancashire   (1842).
With a new introduction by W. H. Chaloner.
Third Edition

No. 13.   Sir George Head

A Home Tour through the Manufacturing Districts in the summer of 1835   (1836).
With a new introduction by W. H. Chaloner.
Second Edition

No. 14.   James Bischoff

A Comprehensive History of the Woollen and Worsted Manufactures (1842).
New Impression   Two Volumes

No. 15.   John Holland

The History and Description of Fossil Fuel, The Collieries, and Coal Trade of Great Britain   (1835).
New Impression

No. 16.   Richard Guest

A Compendious History of the Cotton Manufacture   (1823).
New Impression   4to

No. 17.   G. I. H. Lloyd

The Cutlery Trades.   An historical essay in the economics of small-scale production   (1913).
New Impression

No. 18.   Archibald Prentice

History of the Anti-Corn-Law League   (1853).
With a new introduction by W. H. Chaloner.
Second Edition   Two volumes

ENGLAND AND WALES

J. G. KOHL

FRANK CASS & CO. LTD.

1968

Published by
FRANK CASS AND COMPANY LIMITED
67 Great Russell Street, London WC1

First edition   1844
New impression   1968

Printed in Great Britain by
Thomas Nelson (Printers) Ltd., London and Edinburgh

CONTENTS.

ENGLAND AND WALES.

ENGLAND AND WALES.

FROM LONDON TO BIRMINGHAM.

IT was by the Birmingham " Down Train" that I ventured to take my first timid steps into the English world. " Down Trains" are those that leave London, while those that proceed towards the metropolis are called " Up Trains." It is the same in most countries. The capital city of a nation seems to be always looked upon as occupying a more elevated position than the rest of the country; as standing high up on a kind of moral mountain.

It may sound somewhat strangely to talk of solitude in a Birmingham down train; yet, with hundreds of human beings, before me and behind me, in the same suite of carriages, there I sat quite alone and perhaps in no other situation does a man feel so entirely alone. He sees no one but himself, cannot change his place or arrest his rapid career, nor can he quit the solitude in which he feels himself confined. All he can do is to look into a map, to study the fields and houses that are running away from him; and now and then, if his ideas come to a stand still, he may take a book to wile away his time.

A bird flutters along upon our course, and above, the clouds follow in the same direction. The machinery of man has beaten ye in the race, ye denizens of air! The bird exhausted perches on a branch, and the clouds, though flying on the pinions of the wind, remain behind us.

But hold! We are at a station! What a stir, what a bustle we have here! I am no longer alone. A lady, a servant, and child, enter the carriage, and place themselves opposite to me. The lady's friends shake hands with her and take leave, with railroad speed. There is one comes running up with a basket of fruit for the juvenile traveller. Oh, how sweet are the fruits of friendship! thinks the stranger, to whom no one brings a greeting. Scarcely, however, was the train in motion again, when my fair travelling companion began to grieve and lament, lest her luggage should have been left behind. In the hurry of getting in and taking leave, she had not had time to look to her boxes. I consoled her as well as I could by telling her that the servants of the company were always very attentive to these matters, but she would not be tranquillised. She continued anxiously to stretch her head out of the window, and at last, to her great joy, succeeded in discovering, on the top of the carriage immediately behind us, the trunks she was in search of.

Her little girl was a constant source of entertainment to us all. A fruit or a flower sufficed to keep the child in good humour, but she was delighted with the cows and the sheep, the houses and the bridges, and all the rest of the et ceteras that were constantly flying away from us. Every time we came to a tunnel, she nestled her head, with all its curls, under her mother's shawl. She preferred the darkness of her own making, to that which was imposed upon her.

The sun shone brightly, so we had the shadow of the whole train running along by the side of us. We were much amused to see the guard (meaning his shadow) running along sometimes from one end of the train to the other; jumping from carriage to carriage, and nimbly climbing over the bales and boxes in his way. Sometimes he seemed to jump over the trees and haystacks and cottages by the roadside. I had a lively notion of Peter Schlemihl's shadow running away from him, and of the poor shadowless sufferer running after it.

A man passes the several stations along the line, without seeing any thing of them. He hears their names—Watford! Stratford! Hemel Hempstead! Northampton! but he may think himself particularly fortunate if he catch but a glance of one of their church steeples, or of two or three houses of their suburbs. When I saw the fine pointed spires of Coventry right before me, I flattered myself with the belief that of this interesting old town, at least, I should have a tolerable view. Vain hope! Scarcely had the spires shown themselves at our side when they were already gone. It was but a "peep" we had of Coventry, a place illustrious for the peeping propensities of one of its townsmen in days of yore.

At length, in all the glory of its lofty chimneys, its smoke and its dirt, there arose before us the town to which we had it in contemplation to devote a larger portion of our immediate attention. I mean the town which lies half-way between London and Liverpool, the town which Camden already calls *incolis infertum et incudibus resonans;* the town of Bromichham or Bremichham, a name probably derived from the Saxon words—*bram*, broom; and *ham*, home. At least there is some probability in this etymology, which, if correct, would imply a close affinity between the names of Birmingham and Bremen. The Latin name for Birmingham is no other than *Bremenium.*

BIRMINGHAM.

I arrived a little too late for the riots-season, for September had already begun, and the season for disturbances seems invariably fixed for July.* I saw nothing, therefore, of the Birmingham July days,—of which by the bye, Birmingham has far more than Paris, except the after throes, the complaints about dullness of business and want of credit, and then the queen's proclamations, everywhere posted up against the churches, and plastered over with mud.

When we inquire into the ancient history of manufacturing towns, we generally find that the first way in which they employed their industry, was in the manufacturing of arms. This was the case even with Manchester, where nothing now is made but woven stuffs, but where in the olden time, there existed only a few manufactories of arms and iron tools. This course of things appears natural enough; for most of the instruments employed in preparing the most delicate fabrics, not excepting silk and velvet, are of iron, and therefore it was natural that weavers and spinners should prefer to settle in places where the smiths and other workers in metal enjoyed some reputation. Sometimes, the new branches of industry almost superseded the old ones, as has been the case at Manchester; while other places have remained true to their original pursuits, as Birmingham for instance, where, from the earliest time, iron, copper, and brass were fashioned into form, and where the same avocations still continue, though now carried on upon a scale scarcely anticipated by the ancient inhabitants of the place.

All manufacturing industry connected with the fabrication of metals may be classed in the following divisions:—firstly, the forging of large heavy, or coarse articles, as iron ships, iron bridges, chain cables, &c. Secondly, large machines, whether of a coarse or a fine description; thirdly, what the English call " cutlery ware," including all kinds of cutting tools; and fourthly, the countless host of smaller articles, comprised by the English under the general name of " hardware."

Now, as iron is found, more or less, everywhere in England, and as manufacturing industry also is, more or less, disseminated through-

---

* The most serious riots in Birmingham occurred in 1791 and 1839. In the former year, the mob plundered the town for four days—from the 14th to the 17th of July—and the objects of popular fury were chiefly the houses of the dissenters. In the latter year, the interruption of business, and the supremacy of the populace, lasted a longer time, namely from the 4th till the 15th of July. The mischief done in the latter year, however, was less, though many persons of property were great sufferers, particularly certain silversmiths and jewellers, with whose costly wares (silver teapots, dishes, and candlesticks,) the windows of several obnoxious individuals were demolished. The mob stole but little, but destroyed the houses of several persons who had become objects of popular aversion. On this occasion it was not hatred of the dissenters, but the conspiracies of the chartists, that led to the disturbances. The year 1839 was followed by two years undistinguished by tumult; but in 1842 the month of July brought again some anxious days with it. Nevertheless, though from Birmingham, the head quarters of chartism, were thrown some of the principal firebrands by which, in the course of that summer, the English manufacturing districts were so often set in flames, still Birmingham itself, being well supplied with troops, remained tolerably quiet, and suffered upon the whole less than many other towns. When I arrived, on the 13th of September, I found order perfectly re-established.

out the country, these several branches of iron work are likewise found in full activity in all parts of England. Still, certain towns and districts may always be pointed out, as those in which one or other of these branches has been developed in an extraordinary degree. For the large and coarse ironworks there are the extensive foundries of South Wales, where the most productive iron mines in the kingdom are situated, and as the transport of so heavy a material would necessarily add greatly to the cost of this description of manufacture, the foundries are always established as near as possible to the mines.

For the making of machines, Lancashire, and Manchester in particular, take precedence of all other parts of the country; nevertheless, important establishments for manufacturing machines are also found in Leeds, Glasgow, and other towns.

The 70,000 souls that constitute the knife-grinding population of Sheffield, have the cutlery business, in a great measure, in their own hands.

All the remaining articles, large and small, into which iron is fashioned, as well as copper, brass, and other metals, all, however, of trifling importance compared to iron, are included in the general term of " hardware," for which Birmingham is, without comparison, the principal seat of manufacture.

Camden already speaks of the town as " resounding with ambosses," as if the whole place were busily engaged in forging horseshoes; but these ambosses and hammers, with which the ancestors of the good people of Birmingham were wont to overcome the resistance of the unpliant metal, have since been transformed into machines of such colossal dimensions, or, on the other hand, into such diminutive files, and polishing stones, that the old poetical expression can scarcely be looked on as applicable to the present state of things.

To give my readers some idea of the variety of occupations connected with the fabrication of metals, that are carried on here, I will take the Birmingham Directory of last year, in which I find an alphabetical list of the several trades of the town, with the number of individuals engaged in each. Under the letter B, I find the following:

Blacksmiths	48	Braziers	22
Bellfounders	11	British-plate-makers	20
Bellows-makers	15	Buckle-makers	8
Bit-makers	12	Button-manufacturers	100
Brassfounders	130	and this article is farther divided into gold	

button-makers, silver button-makers, metal button-makers, pearl button-makers, &c.

Under C, I find:—

Candlestick-makers	22	Coopers	45
Casters	30	Copper Companies	4
Candelabra-makers	20	Copper-plate printers	70

To show the extent to which the division of labour is carried, I turn to letter G, where I find the following enumeration of trades connected with the manufacture of guns:—

Gun manufacturers	22	Gun engravers	17
Gun barrel makers	25	Gun furniture polishers	10
Gun barrel ribbers	4	Gun forgers and filers	40
Gun breech forgers	6	Gun-stock makers	3

I was not surprised to find an enumeration of different descriptions of hammer makers, but I thought it certainly a striking instance of the division of labour, when I found that the making of inkstands formed a distinct branch of manufacture, and when I met in my Directory such trades as coffin nail makers, ring turners, dog collar makers, tooth pick case makers, fishing hook makers, stirrup makers, packing needle makers, &c. It must be admitted, however, that a man who spends all his life in making coffin nails or packing needles, must acquire an astonishing dexterity in his particular department.

It is of course, impossible for a traveller to see more than a very small number of the manufacturing establishments of Birmingham; but there are some that will amply reward the trouble of a visit, as a number of different works are often carried on simultaneously on the same premises, though each description of manufacture is in such cases kept carefully apart from the others. One establishment of this kind is that of Messrs. Collis and Co., in whose workshops a stranger may see hundreds of different descriptions of manufacture going on at the same time, and in whose show rooms he may be almost said to contemplate an exhibition of all the products of Birmingham industry. This establishment was originally founded by Sir Edward Thomason, a well known artist, who executed many admirable casts in bronze; medals, statues, urns, &c. One of his medals was shown me as the only one bearing reference to Napoleon that was ever executed in England. It was made on the occasion of his death, and bore only this inscription: "The Emperor Napoleon. Died at Rupert's Valley, St. Helena." Of course the medals relating to Wellington's victories are more numerous. Even the alphabet has in Birmingham been fashioned into medals, twenty-six of which are put up together in neat little boxes, and a large sale must be expected, for I saw great quantities of them piled up in the show-rooms. Of another description of small medals I likewise saw large quantities. These were called "Testamental Truth and Bible Truth medals," each of which bore the impress of some scene from sacred history. The whole, packed in a small box, formed a medallic catechism, by the aid of which, it is supposed, the children, while playing with their counters, may have the great truths of their religion duly impressed upon their minds.

As the people of Birmingham extend their speculations over the whole world, one may see in show-rooms of this description, articles, the utility of which is estimated only by the wild inhabitants of some distant and uncivilised land. Here, for instance I saw some strangely fashioned money, current among certain negro nations of Africa. South America, and America generally, are, however, the principal customers, and the constant study of the manufacturers is to find something that may please the tastes and fancies prevalent on the other side of the Atlantic. To carry on speculations of this description, an exact knowledge of the laws regulating the import duties of distant countries, is absolutely necessary. Thus, for instance, the import duties in Russia, on all metal wares, are regulated by weight. Candlesticks and other articles destined for that market are, in consequence, made hollow, and filled up after their arrival there. A great extent of ethnographical and geographical knowledge thus becomes indispensable to a Birmingham manufacturer. Even during my short stay I saw quite enough to be really astonished at the varied and extensive information possessed by the superior workmen, who, when I spoke to them of the early history of their several branches of art, showed themselves quite familiar with the fabrics of ancient Egypt and modern China.

The history of many branches of trade form important episodes in the history of Birmingham. Thirty years ago there were only two manufacturers of plated goods in the town; at present there are seventy, and each employs from ten to a hundred workmen. Fifteen years ago, the manufacture of *papier maché* was first introduced, I believe from France, but now this material may be seen fashioned in huge masses, with saws and plains. Tables, sofas, presses, and almost every article of ornamental furniture, are now made of paper, and are even said to have many advantages over the same articles made of wood. They are lighter, more easily cleaned, and less liable to break.

On the other hand, there are branches of trade, which, after having flourished for many years, have sunk into comparative insignificance. Among these may be instanced the manufacturing of buckles, the fabrication of which was carried on at Birmingham on such an immense scale, that when shoe-buckles suddenly went out of fashion in all Europe, many thousands of workmen, who had spent their lives in learning to make buckles, were thrown into the greatest distress. They sent a petition to George IV., then Prince of Wales, praying him to try the effect of his royal example, in bringing shoe-buckles into fashion again; but the current of fashion was too strong for even a prince to turn it, and the buckle makers were forced to seek other channels for the employment of their capital and industry.

Another article that, of late years, has risen to great importance in Birmingham, is that of steel-pens. I saw one establishment in which about a hundred workmen were engaged in the fabrication of an article apparently so insignificant. I heard of another, in which 250 people were employed, and where forty tons of steel were yearly converted into pens. A ton of steel produces 1,440,000 pens.

This manufacture, therefore, must every year send into the world no less than 57,000,000 of steel-pens, thus making the existence of 2,000,000 of geese superfluous.

Not the least remarkable places are the button-rooms, in which the different buttons for the army and navy, and for the liveries of private families, are manufactured in astonishing quantities. One button maker in Birmingham, I was told, had, on his premises, in 1834, no less than 10,000 different dies for livery buttons.

Although, of late years, the quantity of articles produced in Birmingham has been increased to so astonishing an extent, the quantity of metal worked up has certainly not been increased in any thing like a corresponding degree. This is owing to the superior lightness now given to so many things in daily use. Muskets and fowling-pieces are much less heavy than they used to be, and even steam-engines, without losing any thing of their power, have lost much of their former weight. A manufacturer of lamps in Birmingham told me, that there were some articles which he now made of about one-fourth the weight which he was accustomed to give them fifteen years ago.

One of the principal branches of Birmingham industry is the fabrication of fire-arms, and this town, whose tranquillity during the last war was not disturbed by the report of a single hostile gun, furnished, not only to England, but likewise to the enemies of England, more materials of war, and instruments for the destruction of human life, than all the other manufacturing cities of the world put together. Between 1804 and 1815, not less than 5,000,000 of muskets were made here; and, by a singular coincidence, this is said to be about the number of human beings destroyed in the course of Napoleon's wars.

All muskets manufactured at Birmingham must be submitted to a test imposed by government, which takes place in what is called the " proof-house." Muskets that have stood this test are stamped. I went to see this interesting proof-house. I was told that every musket was there filled with a charge five times as power-ful as that which it was expected to carry when in ordinary use. There are rooms in which the proofing cartridges are prepared, others in which the muskets are loaded, and a place, called " the hole," where they are discharged. This is managed in the following manner: the loaded muskets, 100 or 120 at a time, are placed side by side upon a low scaffolding, upon which it is possible to fasten them completely. Their mouths are turned towards the inner wall of the room, where the bullets fly into a heap of sand. The walls of the room are of great strength and thickness, and the doors and windows are strongly barricaded with iron. A train of powder is then laid, running over the touchhole of each piece, to a small opening, where it is fired. On the occasion of my visit, 120 mus-kets, intended for the navy, were tried. These are of larger calibre than those in use in the army. After the discharge had taken place,

a little time was allowed for the smoke to clear away before we
entered the proof-room, where we found that seven barrels had burst,
but that 113 had stood the test. The superintendent of the establishment told me, that sometimes as many as twenty out of a hundred would burst, but very often also fewer than seven. If we
take five or six per cent. as the average, it gives us a high idea of
the excellent workmanship of English gun-makers. We were told
that, not long ago, a workman, who had been detected in some
little peculation, found means to secret himself in the proof-room,
where he placed his body immediately in front of the battery. He
was found quite dead, and pierced by six bullets.

As every musket made at Birmingham must pass through this
room, it is easy to calculate the number made. I was told that,
on an average, 5000 were proofed every week, which would give
260,000 in a year. During the war, it is supposed, about 500,000
were made every year.

The various branches of industry carried on at Birmingham are
mostly conducted on a very small scale, when compared with those
of Manchester and other large towns. The consequence is, that
though, next to Manchester, Birmingham is the most populous of
all the manufacturing towns, containing nearly 200,000 inhabitants,
yet it is peculiarly uninviting and monotonous in its outward appearance. In Manchester you see large manufacturing establishments and collossal warehouses, on which no trifling degree of
architectural ornament has been expended, not to speak of the magnificent termini of some half dozen of railroads. Nothing of this
kind is to be seen at Birmingham. There the majority of the
manufacturers are men trading upon capitals of two or three thousand pounds, and often less, for the working of metals has not yet
set in motion any machines of such huge dimensions as are employed
for the spinning and weaving of cotton. Whether owing to this
cause or not, Birmingham, compared with Manchester, is evidently deficient in large buildings and public institutions. The
town covers a space of about nine English square miles, and the
greater part of this space is occupied by a mass of small, uniform,
and mean-looking houses, inhabited by the work-people. A large
portion of Birmingham might be described as a wilderness of houses,
all equally ugly, an ungainly mass, unbroken by a single building of
a pleasing exterior. The few public buildings that there are in the
town, lie close together, and all nearly in the centre. There we
beheld the principal churches, the town-hall, the schools, the chief
hotels, &c., all comprised within the space of less than half an English square mile; in the great suburban wilderness that has grown up
around the inner nucleus of the town, the only thing to interrupt the
general uniformity, is here and there a Methodist, an Independent,
or a Unitarian chapel. Some of this monotony may be owing to
the situation of Birmingham, in a large plain, unbroken by any picturesque object. The little rivulet, the Rea, and a few canals, creep

through the town, without contributing in any way to its embellishment. London has her Thames, Liverpool her Mersey, and Moscow and Rome have their mountains, where their inhabitants may at least breathe a fresher and a freer atmosphere. Birmingham has nothing of the kind, nothing but a dull, and endless succession of house after house, and street after street.

On leaving Birmingham you do not immediately get away from the regions of hardware. Many of the neighbouring towns devote themselves to the same branch of industry. Dudley, Walsall, Wednesbury, Wolverhampton, Bilston, Stourbridge, are all populous places, and all in the " hardware line." In the same way Manchester is surrounded by a cluster of cotton-spinning satellites. What may be the cause of this decided supremacy maintained by some one town in each of the manufacturing districts, I know not. Manchester contains 350,000 inhabitants, and none of the other towns in the cotton district has more than 50,000. Birmingham has 200,000, and none of her neighbours more than 30,000.

The value of all the hardware and cutlery exported from England during a succession of years, was as follows: in 1834, it amounted to 1,485,253lbs.; in 1835, to 1,833,043lbs.; in 1836, to 2,271,313lbs.; in 1837, to 1,460,808lbs.; in 1838, to 1,498,327lbs.; in 1839, to 1,828,521lbs.; in 1840, to 1,345,881lbs.; in 1841, to 1,693,900lbs. The principal customer for these goods was North America, which took somewhat more than one-half of the whole quantity exported, buying about nine times as much cutlery and hardware from England, as was bought by any other country in the world. These figures, however, would give but a faint idea of the whole quantity manufactured. The home consumption carries off more than double the quantity exported, and the whole amount of hardware and cutlery annually made in England can, therefore, be estimated at more than 4,500,000lbs. Nor even then have we the full amount of all the metallic fabrics made up in the country, the value of which, in 1840, was estimated at upwards of £16,000,000.

It must not be supposed, from what I have said of the want of external beauty, that Birmingham, a town of 200,000 inhabitants, and containing a vast amount of wealth, has not several splendid streets, and some distinguished buildings. Of the latter, those that most engross the attention of a stranger, are the town hall and the public school. The town hall is a magnificent copy of a Greek temple, and may fearlessly be placed by the side of the Glyptothek of Munich, or of the Magdalen Church at Paris. The style is magnificent and purely classical. Within is a hall capable of containing 9000 persons, and said to be the largest room in England. The building is made use of, partly for the great musical festivals given at Birmingham, as at other of the music-loving manufacturing towns, and partly for public meetings, whether held for religious, political, or local objects. The platform is so arranged, that a good speaker may easily make himself audible from it in every part of the hall.

Sometimes large banquets have been held here, when there has been abundant room for 1000 persons to sit down to table. When concerts are given in this hall, seats may be arranged for 3600. At the great political meetings, at which as many as 9000 are said to have been present, almost every body must stand, for on those occasions the seats are generally removed.

Another admirable building, and perhaps unique in its kind, is King Edward's Endowed School, a handsome specimen of the gothic style. Of these endowed schools there are many in England. Under this name are comprised the whole scholastic establishments, endowed by various kings with certain funds for their support, and still conducted upon the plan originally laid down for their guidance. Thus the Birmingham school is still governed by the old charter granted by Edward VI. in 1552. Edward VI. established several schools of the same kind, and endowed them either with lands or money, according to their own choice. The Birmingham school chose land, and its annual income, in consequence of the augmentation in the value of land, has gradually increased from 31*l*. to 7000*l*. Another school established near Birmingham, at the same time, less prudently chose to have an annual sum of money, and its revenues at the present day are 15*l*. a-year, as they were three hundred years ago.

The new building for the Birmingham school was completed in 1838, and is certainly the handsomest erection of the kind in England, not excepting Eton. It is built in what the English call the Tudor Gothic style, and presents a large handsome parallelogram divided into two courts, by a broad handsome gothic corridor. What struck me most on entering this school, was to find, for the 450 pupils who received instruction ·there, only two school-rooms, or more properly speaking school-halls. One of these is for the commercial school, and the other for the classical school. In the former 200, and in the latter 250 boys received their education, scholars of eight and eighteen years old sitting together in the same room. For the head master there was a large handsome gothic cathedra, whence he could easily overlook the whole room, and for the under masters there were seats of a similar character, whence they could survey and keep in order their several divisions. My visit happened during the school-time, and the head master conducted me from class to class, that is to say, from one great chair to another. I told him, it would be impossible for me or for any German teacher, to give instruction under such circumstances. He, however, maintained that there were many advantages connected with this system. He said it was more easy for the director to control and guide the whole establishment; that the arbitrary conduct of individual teachers was prevented, one acting as a check upon the other; and that the boys felt themselves more to be members of a large community, than when divided into small classes, where none knew what was going on except in his own room.

There is no doubt, however, that the arrangement has a material effect in forcing English teachers to adopt a system of instruction different from that which prevails in German schools. In an English school, the pupil is necessarily thrown more upon his own resources, and the master does little more than hear the lessons which the boy has learned; any thing like a free discourse or exposition from the teacher to his class, as is customary in Germany, is quite impossible.

A few of the pupils, Evans, Westcott, Purton, and a few others, had recently established a periodical under the title of *King Edward the Sixth's Magazine*, and presented me with the first number, in which I found several short essays on " human happiness," on " schools," and " academies," an account of a " schoolboy's dream," &c.; I must confess, however, that I found little to please me in the collection. Similar periodicals, I am told, exist at other English schools, but I cannot believe their effect to be a beneficial one. At school we ought to receive instruction, and not attempt to set ourselves up as public instructors. Such publications, I am convinced, tend rather to foster vanity than to excite useful emulation.

Among the numberless Nelson statues to be seen in so many English towns, Birmingham has the smallest. It is merely of the size of life, and stands in an open place called the Bullring. The simple unpretending character of the popular hero is perfectly well expressed. His meagre wrinkled cheeks are presented to us as they were *in natura*. His plain hair hangs down low upon his forehead, and the empty sleeve, to mark the loss of his right arm, is fastened to the breast of the coat. The whole seemed to me somewhat too natural, though the work of Westmacott, one of the best living English sculptors. I question the good taste of calling attention so pointedly to the loss of a limb. Suppose a general or admiral had lost both his legs or both his arms in a battle, would any one think of erecting a legless statue of him in a public place?

This statue, small as it is, is the only one, literally the only statue that Birmingham can boast of! A city of 200,000 living specimens of humanity, and only one marble man among them! In Rome and Athens there was probably a statue or a monument for every fifty inhabitants; but even in cities of more modern date, as Berlin or St. Petersburg, there will scarcely be less than a statue for every 4000 inhabitants. It may be questioned whether in the whole world, another town of equal extent and importance could be found, so destitute of public monuments as Birmingham. Not only Liverpool, Manchester, and Glasgow, but even Newcastle, Bristol, and Hull, have more of embellishment to boast of, to say nothing of such magnificent cities as Dublin and Edinburgh. Birmingham and Leeds appear to me, among all the large towns of England, to be the two most destitute of taste, ornament, and enjoyment. As far as the useful arts are concerned, Birmingham may be a paradise, but with respect to the fine arts it is a very desert. Of this I had occasion to

convince myself at the theatre, where I made the discovery that even
one of Shakespeare's masterpieces may be so played as to become
wearisome. The piece was the *Merchant of Venice*, but every part
was so exaggerated and distorted, that at last I could not look at the
stage without positive feelings of disgust. To say the truth, however, I have never seen any thing much deserving of praise at any of
the English theatres out of London. Of the theatre itself there is as
little to be said as of the performance, but it must be badly built, for
on the walls I saw an order from the police, prohibiting the standing
on the benches in the gallery, a man having lately fallen into the pit
in consequence of doing so. Another placard put up about the
theatre, offered a reward of five guineas for the discovery of the
person who a few nights before had thrown a quart bottle from the
gallery into the pit.

THE WORKHOUSE AND THE TRAMPERS.

The workhouse at Birmingham was the first institution of the
kind in England that I had an opportunity of seeing, and I was surprised at the defective and antiquated system of its arrangement. I
speak, indeed, after only one visit, and can therefore only describe
the disagreeable impressions made upon me during that visit; still
the defects were so palpable, and in themselves so important, that
should even many of the virtues and advantages of the institution
have remained concealed from me, still the evils that I saw were
quite enough to neutralise the good that I may not have been aware
of. In the first place the building stands in the middle of the town,
wedged in among a mass of other buildings; but this is the case in
England with many institutions of the kind in the large towns, which
have grown so rapidly, that people have not been able to get out of
town fast enough with buildings of this kind, for which fresh air is
so desirable. In the next place, being the only institution of the
sort in Birmingham, the workhouse is much too small. It provides
a shelter for 500 adults, and 300 children, and it can require little
rhetoric to show how very inadequate such a provision must be for a
town of 200,000 inhabitants, of whom thousands have sometimes
been without bread at once. These defects have been of late recognised, and a larger building is about to be erected in the vicinity
of the town; still the fact must remain upon record, that, so late as
1843, Birmingham, with a vast number of poor requiring relief, and
a vast amount of wealth very competent to afford all the relief required, had only a very inefficient and very insufficient institution
for the administration of that relief.

I was particularly struck by the crowded appearance of every part
of the building, by the want of information and coarseness of manners shown by all the persons employed about the place, by the strict
and rough manner in which the poor were treated, by the deficiency

of neatness and order, and lastly by the union of so many different things in one institution and under the same direction. Besides the principal division of the building, set apart for the pauper inmates, there was a wing for the education of poor children, and another for the treatment of the sick. Here were a school and a hospital under the same roof with a poor house, and if my memory does not deceive me, a separate part of the house was used for the confinement of lunatics! In most of the large towns of England these antiquated parish workhouses have become matter of history, and exist no longer; for this very reason, it may be the better worth while to cast a glance at those which still remain.

The paupers are divided into two classes,—the "in poor" and the "out poor,"—of whom the former are lodged in the house, and the latter, without residing there, receive periodical relief from it. Of the former, on an average, there were every week 476, each of whom, as the governor told me, cost two shillings and tenpence, including building repairs, salaries of officers, &c. Each of these poor, accordingly, cost the town about fifty of our dollars a year. In addition to these, there were always in the house, on an average, 277 children, and the out poor averaged, one week with another, 2182. The expense to Birmingham of this relief given to the poor, amounts in the year to about 41,000*l.*, and as the rate payers in a population of 200,000, do not probably much exceed 40,000, it may be calculated that every independent townsman of Birmingham pays twenty shillings to the maintenance of the poor. The real amount of the poor rates, however, is more than double this (88,000*l.*), but this is owing to the circumstance that many other expenses of the town are charged to the poor rates, including many of the expenses of the police, the cost for the registration of births, and deaths, &c.

One of the customary divisions of these old workhouses is the "Tramp room," as it is called, a room in which an asylum is given for the night to the paupers who are wandering through the country. I found there a few wretched beings, women covered with rags, who had spent the night in the place. Notwithstanding the filthy condition of the room, I was about to enter, when some of my friends pulled me back, and warned me that by doing so I should expose myself to contagious diseases, and to every description of vermin. These trampers, vagrants, migatory depredators, "and travellers," for there is a close affinity between them, are a peculiar class in England, and abound, more than anywhere else, in the manufacturing districts, where, during the late years of depression, they have augmented most astonishingly in numbers. From the reports of the constabulary force commissioners, it appears, that many of the poor in the large towns are constantly tramping about, living a life of professed vagrancy, and making a precarious income, sometimes by begging and selling trifling articles, and sometimes by various frauds and occasional depredations. In many parts of the reports I have just alluded to, the witnesses examined, admitted that they had started from this or that town, " expressly to travel about, and live by robbing." Birmingham and Sheffield are said to be the towns from which, in particular, great numbers of trampers are continually starting. This is partly owing to the circumstance that the articles manufactured at those two places are light, of general use, and therefore well calculated for hawking about the country.

Besides the tramp rooms of the workhouses, there are lodging houses in almost every town, large and small, and even in many villages, where the wandering poor can obtain shelter for the night for a few pence. In so small a place as Chester, according to the reports mentioned above, there are no less than 150 such houses, and in many towns there are night asylums, supported by the public, and where the relief given is confined as much as possible to the deserving poor.

It is in consequence of the great number of distressed and often depraved wanderers that are continually starting from these manufacturing towns, that the country about them has become so notorious for highway robberies. According to the evidence given before the commissioners, by several commercial travellers of considerable experience, England would appear, in the year 1839, to have been surpassed only by Spain and Italy, in the insecurity of the public highroads.

STAFFORD.

Leaving the "metropolis of the inland counties" by the Grand Junction Railway, the power of steam seemed in a few moments to have transported us to all the charms of an English rural residence, in the centre of Staffordshire, and close to the chief town of that county. I was delighted to have a clear view of the sky again. In Birmingham you can form no speculation on the weather. The rain is not felt till it has worked its way through the smoke, and the sun shows himself only as a yellow patch. Sunrise and sunset, stars and moonlight, are things unknown. It is easily understood why the English, having such towns, should be so passionately fond of rural life, that even those whose avocations bind them to the town, all endeavour to have their residences as far away from it, as their means will allow.

I now, for the first time, became acquainted with the admirable arrangement of an English country household,—with the tranquillity and the thorough comfort of an English rural residence; and I now began to understand how our way of life must appear to English people a mere make-shift, a state of existence in which they observe numberless wants and deficiences, of which we, in general, remain perfectly unconscious. I spent a few days most agreeably in a circle of esteemed friends, and made several excursions into the various departments of the household, and to several interesting places in the neighbourhood, to an old castle, to several farmers' houses, and to the town of Stafford. In the house itself I was particularly interested by the neat kitchen, with its manifold arrangements for boiling and roasting the daily bread of the family, with its hot closets, heated by steam, to warm plates and keep the viands from cooling. Then there was the tidy dairy, glittering again with its snow white Staffordshire ware, while each vessel containing milk was constantly kept cool by a stream of spring water flowing around it. Nor did I fail to admire the cleanly pantry nor the airy larder with its excellent arrangements for the preservation of the food deposited there ; nor the orderly scullery, in which the plates and dishes were cleaned. Many of these things are with us made a part of the kitchen, whereas in England they have their separate places. In an English household, the more you enter into details, the more you see to admire. Even in the house of a substantial farmer, these little accessories to domestic comfort are not wanting, and if fitted up with less luxury than in the mansions of the wealthy, the same order and neatness usually prevails in both. At the first farm house I visited, every piece of bacon was found wrapped up separately in paper, as a protection against flies. What farmer in Germany would have dreamt of such a precaution ? The floors and staircases of the house were neatly carpeted, and the rooms were patterns of tidiness. In the farmer's own room hung a map of the county. He regaled us hospitably with primrose wine, currant wine, and other native delicacies, described by Goldsmith in his Vicar of Wakefield. In the garden were roses and other flowers, tended with as much care as if a scientific gardener had formed a part of his establishment. In his rick yard he showed us the abundance of the preceding harvest, and explained to us the way in which the straw and hay are cut out of these compact ricks. The English have large knives for the purpose, with which they make perpendicular cuts into one of these ricks, and bring out pieces as regularly shaped as could be taken out of a loaf of bread with a carving knife. This farmer threshed his corn only with machines; in his stable he showed us some " lovely little pigs," and in his own person he presented an excellent specimen of what is usually called a " jolly fellow," having a cheerful, well-fed, well-contented, " well to do" look about every part of him.

It is really astonishing how full these well cultivated parts of England are of large and small country seats. In the course of a little excursion that we made to a neighbouring château, Chartley Park, to see some wild cattle kept there, we passed at least a dozen handsome seats, including Ingestrie, the property of the Talbot family, and Tixall, belonging to a Clifford. The latter is celebrated for one of the handsomest sets of stables in England, built entirely of stone and iron, at an expense of 15,000l.

Chartley Park is an ancient seat of the Lords Ferrer. The wild cattle kept there are a part of the original British breed. We went with one of the keepers into the park, and found the animals collected in one place, nearly as much tamed as ourselves by the coldness and severity of the weather. They were always tolerably tame,

we were told, in autumn and winter, when there was little grass for
them to feed on ; but in spring, when the fresh herbage came up,
they were as wild as deer, and often dangerous. In colour and marks
they were all exactly alike, all being white, with black noses and
ears. Not one of them had a spot on his body to break the uniformity. If by any chance a calf is born with his body differently
marked, the event is looked upon as boding a disaster to the Ferrer
family. The number kept at Chartley Park, on the occasion of
my visit was thirteen, and they have never been able, it appears,
to increase them beyond twenty. At Christmas, when it is customary in England to make presents of game, poultry, and other
eatable articles, the Lords Ferrer sometimes shoot one of their wild
cows, and send the most delicate parts to their favoured friends.
For this purpose, when I was there, they had recently separated a
cow from the herd, and were endeavouring to fatten the creature
by keeping her away from her calf, on a more confined piece of
ground. To milk them is impossible, and if confined in a cow-
house, they sicken and die in a short time. They are mostly kept
in the wildest part of the park, called Chartley Moss, where they
are sometimes hunted. They are not large, but very neatly built,
and seem to have much more intelligence than our tame cattle.

Stafford itself is a small town, containing only about 1200 inhabitants. What most interested me there was the county prison, where
a number of prisoners were at the time confined, in consequence of
the late riots. For Staffordshire, in the first place, includes the
very remarkable district called the Potteries, in which many thousands of excitable beings are busily employed in making crockery
and digging up coals; and in the second place, the industrial territory of Birmingham stretches a good way into Staffordshire, in
which are situated Wolverhampton, Walsall, Dudley, and other
towns busied in the manufacture of hardware. Some of these districts having been the chief scenes of the disturbances that had
occurred a few months previously, the county prison was crowded.
Originally the building had been calculated for 150 prisoners, but
with the growth of the neighbouring towns, the increase of crime
had more than held pace, and from time to time it had been found
necessary to enlarge the prison. The present building, the governor
told us, could conveniently contain about 500 persons, but the
number then confined there amounted to 750, the largest number
ever known to have been there at the same time. The riots had
brought 220 prisoners within the walls, including twenty female
rioters. In consequence of the crowded state of the prison, extraordinary measures of precaution had been taken. Soldiers had been
quartered in the town, and sentinels were posted about the prison,
a measure not at all customary in ordinary times. In the rooms of
the persons employed about the prison we found muskets and pis-
tols ready for use, and upon the wall which enclosed the whole

building, loose stones had been laid, that these might fall down and alarm the guard, if an attempt were made to escape by throwing a rope over the wall. Within the walls of this prison I saw a cemetery of a kind completely novel to me. It was a piece of ground in which had been buried, side by side, a number of criminals who had been executed. I was told, at the same time, that it was customary in England to inter within the prison walls, criminals who had suffered the extreme penalty of the law.

FROM STAFFORD TO THE POTTERIES.

Again entrusting myself to the railroad, I was deposited in the neighbourhood of Butterton, a small antique country seat, with a mansion of the Elizabethian order of architecture, situated in the pleasantest part of the north of Staffordshire. Here also I spent a few days, during which I saw some of the interesting objects in the neighbourhood. Among these were, first, a very handsome but not a very important object, namely, Trentham, the celebrated seat of one of the richest men in England, the Duke of Sutherland; and secondly, a very important and very useful, but not a very handsome one, namely, the district of the Potteries. I determined to reserve the most important matter for a future visit, and, hiring a fly, drove to Trentheim, *i. e.* Home on the Trent,—a river the name of which some old English writers attempt to derive from the French word *trente*, because thirty tributary streams pour their waters into the Trent, and because it contains thirty species of fish.

Trentham is beautifully situated. The most ornamental side is turned towards a magnificent terrace of flowers, beyond which is a handsome piece of water, and beyond that the picturesque wilderness of the upper valley of the Trent. The garden terrace is adorned by some beautiful bronze statues of stags, tastefully grouped with other sculptures among the flower beds. The interior of the house is splendidly fitted up; but all these are things so frequently to be seen in England, that I found nothing sufficiently eminent to deserve a detailed mention in a country which has its Warwick Castles to boast of. I saw nothing at all unique in its kind, in all the " fuchsia bed-rooms," " butterfly dressing-rooms," " bird drawing-rooms," " bird sitting-rooms," " honeysuckle-room," the " rosebud-room," or his grace's private rooms. Trentham, as the housekeeper told us, is not properly speaking a " show-house," nevertheless, every corner of it was shown us. In each bedroom I observed a Bible and a Prayer-book lay on the table. With us there is seldom more than one Bible in a house, while in England we thus find one man the owner of several hundred copies. On board of ships and steamboats there are also generally several copies of the Holy Scriptures for the use of the passengers, and in many hotels in England a Testament or Prayer-book lies in almost every room. This may afford some idea of the immense consumption there must be in the country for this class of books. Indeed, I should not be surprised to learn that England alone possessed more copies of the Bible than all the other countries in Europe together.

On the ground where Trentham now stands, there stood formerly a convent, the residence of the royal and sainted Virgin Verburga. Of the walls of the ancient convent not a trace remains, yet something better has survived than an ancient piece of masonry; namely, an old " priory dole," in virtue of which every traveller who knocks at the gate is relieved with bread and beer, and I was assured that several hundreds often applied for the dole in the course of the day. A lodge not far from the principal entrance, has been fitted up for the distribution of the dole; and as many of the poor, since the spread of temperance, decline the beer, a spring of water, neatly enclosed in marble, has been provided expressly for the use of the abstemious.

Staffordshire borders on Cheshire, and in the same way that the hardware trade of Birmingham has extended itself over a large part of South Staffordshire, so the manufacturing of Cheshire cheese may be said to have its ramifications in North Staffordshire. On our return from Trentham to Butterton, we visited one of these cheese factories, kept by a farmer who had forty cows constantly kept for this purpose only. He told us he expected to get three and a half hundred weight of cheese from each cow in the course of a year, and then he showed us his cheese room, in which several hundred delicate Cheshire cheeses were lying, each weighing from sixty to seventy pounds. Here also I was doomed to hear complaints of the badness of trade. The farmer did not know what he should do this year with all his cheeses, for which he was not able to get more than forty-five shillings a hundred weight.

THE POTTERIES.

Each of the principal branches of English manufacture has appropriated to itself some particular town or district, and, following this example, the makers of earthenware have chosen for themselves a small locality, within which there is more crockeryware made than in all the rest of the kingdom. This district, situated in the northern part of Staffordshire, and comprising several small towns and villages, lying so close to each other that they might almost be said to form only one, is called the Pottery District, or the Staffordshire Potteries, or sometimes more briefly the Potteries.

The places comprised within the Potteries are: Tunstall, Burslem, Sneyd, Rushton, Grange, Hanley, Shelton, Penkhull, Boothen, Stoke, Fenton, Vivian, Longton, Laneend, Etruria, and a few small villages. The most important of these places are Burslem, Hanley, Stoke, and Laneend. They all lie close together, like so many cherries on one stalk, and extend down the valley of the Trent a distance of about seven English miles, that being the distance between the two extremities of the land of crockery,—Tunstall and Laneend. They are all included within the one parliamentary borough, and as the members are described as sitting for Stoke-upon-Trent, the whole district is sometimes called the borough of Stoke-upon-Trent. The population of this remarkable district has increased fifteenfold within the last hundred years. In 1738, the population of the whole did not exceed 4000, in 1838 it was upwards of 70,000, and nearly all of them more or less connected with the making of crockery.

Camden, in his "Britannia," makes no mention either of the Potteries generally, or of any of the places that are now included within that name. Nevertheless, it is known, that, two hundred years ago, earthenware goods were manufactured at Burslem, particularly a kind of butter pots; but these must have been of a very rude kind, for we hear that an old Burslem butter pot, large enough to contain fourteen pounds of butter, was sure not to weigh less itself than six pounds. The fact is, that, as the looms in use at Manchester and Leeds, till about the middle of the last century, were but little better than those with which the ancient Romans wove their cloth, so the pottery kilns continued till nearly about the same time, to be constructed according to the ancient fashion. About the middle of the last century it was that the Wedgwoods began to bestir themselves in the potteries, at the same time that the Arkwrights revolutionised the looms; it was a remarkable time, for, almost simultaneously, great reformers and improving geniuses sprung up in all the chief branches of English manufacture, and made the rivulets of national prosperity swell on a sudden into broad and stately streams.

Josiah Wedgwood was the name of the great man whose excellent taste gave grace and beauty to the earthenware of Staffordshire, and at the same time so materially improved its intrinsic excellence, that the article has become one in general use in every part of the civilised world, and continues, in most countries, to be still known by his name. He it was who first gave a classical form to our teapots, our coffee cups, our sugar basins, and our water jugs. He it was that scattered flowers over them, and graced them with Greek and Etrurian figures, with endless varieties of colour, that his chemical knowledge enabled him to produce and render permanent. In the place of the old heavy butterpots, that had remained unchanged for centuries, appeared vases and bowls of all imaginable sizes, forms, and colours, and suited for an endless variety of uses. In his celebrated establishment, which he called Etruria, and which, when completed in 1771, was the largest earthenware manufactory that the world had ever seen, he introduced and effected all his reforms; and these in time found imitators, several establishments similar to that of Etruria having successively been organised.

The ancestors of Josiah Wedgwood had long been settled as potters at Burslem. In 1743 an old man of the same name died there who had made his fortune by making crockery, so much so that his two sons were able to retire from trade, and live in independence. The celebrated Josiah, who died in 1795, was, I believe, their cousin. The family still play a prominent part in the potteries, and when, in 1832, the borough of Stoke-upon-Trent first obtained the privilege of sending representatives to the House of Commons, it was a Mr. Josiah Wedgwood who was the first member elected by the new constituency.

In the olden time, that is to say about a hundred years ago, when every potter had his own little establishment, in which he worked diligently, assisted by a few journeymen, the people in this part of the country had no knowledge of political combinations, of trades' unions, of socialism, chartism, riots, or strikes. Each dug the clay from before his own house, shaped the earth into a pot, dried it under his own shed, or, perhaps, for greater expedition, in the smoke-house, and then sold the produce of his workmanship at the markets of Utoxeter or Newcastle-under-Lyme. Every industrious man could obtain his living, and that contented him. When, however, the population increased in so astonishing a degree—when hundreds came to work together in the same establishment—when the small villages swelled into towns, and approached so closely to each other as nearly to form only one great community—when the spirit of improvement and invention set even the potters thinking—when the general equality among potters was disturbed, by some of them becoming masters of millions, while the majority were depressed to the condition of workmen; then politics crept in among them, and combinations and conspiracies began to be formed, even as among the cotton spinners of Lancashire, the woollen weavers of Yorkshire, the cutlers of Sheffield, the hardware-makers of Birmingham, and the colliers of Newcastle, as, in short, among all the workmen of England, who are packed together in certain districts as closely as bees in hives.

The first associations among the potters took place about the beginning of the present century, when military associations were formed for the defence of the country against the *Armée de l'Angleterre*, with which Napoleon threatened to invade England. Associations of a different character, animated by a spirit of hostility to the British government, arose on the occasion of the continental blockade, when the retaliatory measures of England led to difficulties with the Americans, the best customers of the potters, whose meetings, petitions, and deputations, contributed not a little to induce the British government to withdraw measures so prejudicial to the American trade.

After the peace with France, at the time when the German students began to enter into patriotic unions, political clubs and radical meetings were organised in all the manufacturing districts, the potteries not excepted, and the burden of taxation, and the defects of the representative system, were eagerly discussed, and parliamentary reform loudly called for. Simultaneously with these political combinations, there arose others, known by the name of "Trades' Unions," which were directed against the master manufacturers, and the effects of these unions showed themselves in the events of 1836 and 1842. In the former of those years, a formidable association was organised in the Potteries, with a view to raise the rate of wages, and to regulate them according to the interest of the workmen. They had their union lodge, their committee, and their secretary, and they quitted their work at every establishment where the terms they prescribed were not submitted to. The men thus thrown out of employment were maintained, as is usual on such occasions, by small weekly advances from the lodge.

Some of the masters allowed themselves to be dictated to by the union, but others organised a counter-combination, which they called the Chamber of Commerce, where they had their weekly meetings. The result of their deliberations was to close their establishments altogether, for several months, well assured that the poorer workmen, unable longer to carry on this system of hostilities, would by that time be willing enough to return to the old terms. If the poor fellows did but know that there was a natural price for labour, determined by competition, under which the employers dare not go without injuring themselves, as little as the men can force their masters to go beyond it, such melancholy scenes could scarcely occur; scenes from which no one derives advantage, and least of all the workmen. I have seen many Chartist, and Anti-Bread Tax lectures advertised in the manufacturing districts, but I never heard of any lectures given with a view to convey correct information to the people on the influences that regulate the natural price of labour, and yet of all information there is none which it is of more importance for the poor workmen to receive.

For a long time the people in the surrounding country had missed the cloud of smoke that had been wont to hang suspended over the district of the potteries, when the works were all in full activity. I was therefore the more gratified, as I approached the place, to see that the accustomed cloud was not wanting, and that it appeared of a most satisfactory thickness, as it floated over the beautiful landscape of the Trent valley. On approaching from Newcastle-under-Lyme, Burslem and Hanley are seen lying somewhat high, and the view that presents itself is unique in its kind. A stranger might be tempted to believe he saw a vast line of fortifications rising before him. The surrounding hills are all crowned with the lofty columns and the huge pyramids of the chimneys, and with the great rounded furnaces, of which dozens are often seen close together, looking like colossal bomb-mortars. The high roofs of the drying houses, the magnificent warehouses, and the massy walls that encloses the whole great establishment, or "workhouse bank," with the piles of clay, flints, bones, cinders, and other matters, serve rather to strengthen the illusion. Nor does the scene lose in interest as you proceed through the district. Between the great workhouse banks lie scattered the small houses of the shopkeepers, the workmen, the painters, the engravers, the colourmen, and others, while here and there the intervals are filled up by churches and chapels, or by the stately houses of those who have grown rich by pottery,—the Wedgwoods, Spodes, Wieldons, Parkers, Davenports, &c., all people who from potters have become *millionaires*, and from *millionaires*, members of parliament, high sheriffs, and proprietors of stately mansions and broad lands. From one place to another you pass along roads constructed with as much care as the floor of a ball-room. Nor are means of communication of a higher order wanting. A large canal traverses the district, and a magnificent system of railroad places it in immediate communication with Manchester, Birmingham, Liverpool, London, &c., thus enabling the potters to forward their wares to the best markets, and at the same time to receive the ponderous raw material required by them: their coals, of which they burn 8000 tons a week; their China clay, of which they receive yearly 7000 tons from Cornwall; their soapstone, of which the same county furnishes them 5000 tons; the flints, of which incalculable quanties come to them from Ireland and Wales; the gold, of which they are said to consume every year to the amount of 33,000*l.*; besides the clay from Devonshire, and the bones and many other articles which are supplied to them from all parts of England.

My first visit was paid to a large establishment at Burslem, that of Aslock, which comprises no less than twenty large porcelain furnaces. Some houses confine themselves to earthenware, some to porcelain, while others work in both. It is in earthenware alone, however, that they excel, for their porcelain is inferior to that of Dresden and Berlin, and of course much more so to that of Paris. Their painting on porcelain indeed is so far inferior to ours, that comparison is entirely out of the question. Most of those to whom I spoke admitted this inferiority, but maintained, on the other hand, that "in flower, lace, and wicker work, none could beat them." This point I will not take it upon me to decide, but I certainly did see some exquisite specimens in this department of art. I saw the most delicate baskets, filled with beautiful flowers, all of white unglazed china clay, and all so true to nature, and so admirably executed, that it is difficult to imagine the workmanship could be surpassed. One man had undertaken to make a bird of paradise in porcelain, and had laboured to give to the clay all the delicacy and beauty of the natural plumage. The clay had been spun out into long feathers, some of them an ell in length, and certainly he must have had an astonishing knowledge of the material he worked with, and must have been able to calculate with great precision the effect of the heat, to draw out such thin long feathers, that neither bent under the manipulation, nor broke while in the furnace.

The town-house of Burslem was full of soldiers, and sentinels were mounting guard in every public place. The people stood and stared at the red uniforms, and nearly the same scene presented itself in the other places comprised within the district. Burslem was one of the places which played the most prominent part during the riots, and I saw the ruins of a house that had been destroyed, belonging to a clergyman, who had never interfered either with chartism or the regulation of wages. Individuals, however, when their civil passions are excited, are often blind in their fury, and wreak their vengeance on those who have least of all done any thing to offend them; and shall we look for greater wisdom from a mob? Nevertheless, the reports that went abroad of the destruction effected here, were grossly exaggerated. The chief injury had evidently been done to the windows, for in addition to the house just mentioned I saw only the ruins of one other that had been demolished. The collision of the people with the soldiers at Burslem has been represented as a grand battle, and in some English prints I have seen it described so pictorially. In one I saw the people composed of men, women, and children, in rags, marching along on one side, with a huge flag, on which are inscribed the words " Give us bread," and to this petition the soldiers are replying by hurling cannon balls at the people instead of loaves. One artilleryman wears the features of Wellington, another those of Peel, and the latter is seen trampling on a paper bearing the words " The people's rights." Now while I was at Burslem I inquired into all the particulars of this affair, and saw the street where it occurred. The poor, hungry, misguided multitude, composed chiefly of silk and cotton weavers from Lancashire, reinforced by malcontents from among the collieries and potteries, came on and had advanced as far as Burslem, without encountering any resistance, stopping the works everywhere as they marched along. Their intention was to proceed on to London, and there force the parliament and ministry to the desired concessions. All these high-flown designs were scattered to the wind on the appearance of a handful of soldiers. The mob, as they advanced, became aware that they had military in front of them, and conceived the plan of dividing themselves into two bodies, and outflanking the soldiers. In doing this they only weakened themselves. The body that entered Burslem found its advance stopped by the armed gentry and yeomanry of the county, while the main body, reduced by the absence of so many of their companions, fled in confusion on the first attack of the soldiery. One life, there is no doubt, was lost during this attack, and many were hurt, of whom, it is probable, some died of their wounds; but the number of these is not known, as the rioters carried off all their wounded, and had them attended to in private, that the law might not lay its hands upon them. On this occasion, as in Birmingham in 1838, and re-

cently in Wales, it was seen how greatly an English mob stands in
awe of shedding blood, and how easily it allows itself to be dispersed
by a few soldiers. Had a French mob, with plans and views similar
to those of the populace at Burslem, found themselves opposed to
soldiers, the issue would have been of a much more sanguinary character. Whence comes this? Nobody will dream of attributing
cowardice to the English as a national characteristic.

Omnibuses ply at all hours between the different places belonging
to the Potteries, and I did not fail to take advantage of these con-
veyances to visit all the most important points. The carriages were
generally crowded with workmen, clerks, and artists; engravers with
their copper-plates or pictures under their arms, or painters armed
with rolls of paper, containing, probably new designs. Not only
were the carriages filled, but they might fairly be said to be hung
with passengers, for many seemed satisfied if they could but cling
with one foot and one hand. The great object is to save time, and
the omnibuses always drive fast. Comfort is quite a secondary
consideration. When I started for Hanley, the driver seated himself on my lap, and then asked me whether I was comfortable. I
was not a little surprised, among the outside passengers, to find a
wealthy manufacturer from Manchester; the masters, therefore, are
not above riding in the same carriages with the workmen.

In Hanley I saw a large magazine of earthenware, with which I
was much better pleased than with the porcelain show-rooms that I
had just before visited. English earthenware is, in fact, one of the
finest and most complete articles in the world; and if all other things
were equally perfect, this would be a world of perfection indeed. We know little of English earthenware in Germany, beyond tea-pots and milk-jugs, partly because we are content to put
up with things of an inferior quality, and partly because many of
the articles in common use in England have not yet become matters
necessity to us. It would be difficult to enumerate all the articles
here manufactured of clay. There are tea and coffee services of all
imaginable sizes and kinds, ornamented in the most varied manner,
and yet always with good taste. Then there are endless varieties of
vessels, large and small, pitchers, jugs, dishes, bowls, basins, and
every kind of apparatus for washing, and for bathing the feet and
the different parts of the body, articles with which an English sleeping-room is usually so richly furnished, and of which the uninitiated
stranger is often, at a loss to divine the use. All these things in
England are not only handsomely ornamented, but are also made
large. The English complain, and not without reason, of the
diminutive size of most of the apparatus of our bed-rooms.

We must not forget the neat vessels made for the English dairies,
nor the wine-coolers, the butter-coolers, and the water-coolers. The
latter, admirably suited to the purpose they are intended for, are
chiefly made for the East and West Indies. I was told that the
clay used for these cooling vessels was not to be found in any part

of England, except in the vicinity of the Potteries. An article, not at all known to us, but for which there has lately been a very great demand in England, is known by the name of "tesselated tiles." These are small thin tiles, elegantly formed, either square or six-sided, and are used for paving halls, and particularly for churches, where they are used at present in astonishing quantities. They are of a red colour, ornamented with yellow or black designs. The floors of almost all the new churches in England are paved with them. Sometimes the designs on the several tiles are made to correspond, and in that case large pictures may be represented, or the tiles may be made to imitate the pattern of a rich carpet. A floor thus paved might not inaptly be said to be covered with a stone carpet. It forms really a very elegant species of mosaic, and is unquestionably the least expensive that has yet been invented.

In some of the workshops I was much interested by the simplicity of the manner in which the little wreaths of flowers and other ornaments were fastened to the articles they were intended for. These little ornaments, often of a different colour from the vessels to which they are about to be attached, are, of course, moulded apart. They are then taken up quite dry and laid loosely on the places to which it is meant they should adhere. A workman then comes, and with a pencil, filled apparently with water, moistens the parts and places the ornaments in the desired position. This moisture, quickly imbibed by the clay, makes the parts adhere firmly, and all this is done with astonishing rapidity; but every thing is done twice as fast in England as it is with us, for in no other country is the principle so well understood, that to save time is to save money.

The copper-plate printing, on one of these large establishments, is also carried on upon an astonishing scale. Many thousand copies are often taken from one plate, and for this purpose a remarkably thin paper is used, that the ink of the engraving may be the more readily transferred to the clay, and that the paper may all the more easily be rubbed off. The paper-makers form no unimportant class of the population of the Potteries.

All these things I saw with great convenience in the enormous warehouses of Mr. Copeland and Mr. Minton, probably the two greatest manufacturers of crockery in the world, for they told me that each of them had from 800 to 900 persons in his employment.

If we compare the common earthenware of England, with that of the French and Germans, or of any other nation, it appears not only excellent in quality, but also highly ornamental and unsurpassably beautiful. The common French and German earthenware, is comparatively ugly, coarse, and misshapen. On the other hand, English porcelain, as I have already remarked, particularly those articles in which beauty and elegance are the main points aimed at, are far behind those of the continent. I believe there is something characteristic of the English in this. In articles of ordinary use, the English seem better than we, to know how to combine excellence of quality with outward elegance and beauty, whereas in those articles in which grace and beauty alone are to be kept in view, the English are never equally successful. Their tools, their furniture, their machines, their knives and scissors, their bread, and their joints of meat, are not only excellent, vigorous and nutritious, but also beautifully formed, and not to be at all surpassed; whereas their pictures, their sculptures, their pasties, and their cakes, and in short every thing in which fancy takes precedence of usefulness, are far behind ours in excellence. Look, not merely at the earthenware of the French, but at their tools, and their implements of gardening and agriculture. They are all strikingly rude and little suited to the purposes they are intended for. Even the common bread in France is inferior to that used in England. On the other hand, how much loftier flights of fancy are displayed by the French in works of art.

Mac Culloch estimates the value of the earthenware and china annually manufactured in England at 2,300,000*l*. Of this, the Potteries alone furnish to the amount of about 1,600,000*l*. Spackman calculates that the earthenware, china, and glass together, amount annually to 4,991,126*l*., or about five millions, of which, in 1840, four millions were consumed, and about one million exported. Of earthenware of all sorts, exclusive of glass, the exports are somewhat over half a million, and if we deduct this from 2,300,000*l*., about 1,800,000*l*. will remain, to represent the amount of crockery consumed by the English themselves. The rise and fall in the exports of earthenware (exclusive of glass) during a period of seven years, are shown in the following table:

1834	493,382	1838	651,344
1835	520,421	1839	771,173
1836	837,774	1840	574,600
1837	563,237		

From these fluctuations, however, no distinct conclusions are to be drawn respecting the real prosperity of the manufacture, for sometimes over production has led English merchants, as they themselves express it, " to force a market," by sending abroad large quantities of goods on speculation, to be sold for what they will bring, in the hope that people will accustom themselves to the new merchandise, and afterwards become regular customers for it.

CHESTER.

Upon our German railroads, over the entrance to a tunnel, we have frequently neat and appropriate inscriptions. Thus, over the tunnel on the Austrian railroad from Vienna to Baden stand the words *recta sequi* (follow the right course, or go ahead) in golden letters. The fashion is unknown in England, where tunnels are things of much too ordinary occurrence to be deemed deserving of inscriptions. On the railroad from Leipzig to Dresden, at every station

where the train stops, young girls and lads present themselves with
heaps of sandwiches, and little packages of cherries and strawberries,
and glasses filled with beer, and cups with bouillon; for the people
calculate with tolerable accuracy, that whenever a train stops, it
will bring with it a hundred or so of hungry and thirsty travellers,
well disposed to satify their appetites. This commendable railroad
fashion is also wanting in England. It is customary on the continent to speak of the English as great eaters, but it would seem that,
in Germany, we, at all events, feel the desire to eat more frequently.
At none of the stations in England have I seen refreshments handed
to the travellers; there are merely refreshment rooms at the principal
stations, where the train stops a few minutes longer than at the
others. On my leaving Butterton to proceed towards Liverpool,
Crew was the first place where I could get any thing to eat. Another disagreeable characteristic of an English compared with a German railroad, is that whereas at a station on the latter, all these
little gastronomic luxuries are to be had for a penny, or at most
twopence, nothing is to be obtained on the former for less than sixpence. A sandwich, a glass of wine, a piece of cake, or a plate of
fruit,—each cost sixpence. Even for a glass of porter at Crew I
was charged sixpence. It was Dublin porter (Guiness's) which,
although made on the other side of the English Channel, has obtained so much favour in England of late years, as almost to beat
the London manufacture.

At this same station I made the acquaintance of a gentleman who
was in some way or other connected with the *Times* newspaper.
He confirmed to me a fact which I had heard before, but which I
had found it difficult to believe, and which is calculated to afford
some idea of the gigantic scale on which the operations of that paper
are carried on. The matter stands thus: American and Transatlantic
news, often of great importance for England, are generally received
in Liverpool sooner than in any other part of England. The agents
of the *Times* in Liverpool, on such occasions, if they deem the news
of sufficient importance, are authorised to forward it to London by
a special train, which from Liverpool to London costs 100*l*. These
special trains are rarely used, except by the government, by the
most eminent mercantile houses, and lastly by the London newspapers. The utmost that can be gained by such a special train, is
to receive a piece of news six hours earlier that it could have come
by the ordinary train. I asked how often it might happen in the
course of the year that such a train might be forwarded. This the
gentleman who gave me the information was unable to say, but he
thought it must happen at least once a month.

Midway between Crew and Liverpool lies Chester, a town of
much more ancient fame than Liverpool itself. Indeed it may be
considered as the mother of Liverpool, for at a time when nothing
was yet known of Liverpool commerce on the Mersey, the fame of
Chester, and her trade on the Dee, was widely spread in Germany,

Spain, and France. In time, however, the navigation of the Dee was injured by the accumulation of sand in its bed. Camden already remarks that the sea was receding there,—and thus the trade of Chester got aground, and Liverpool, as lying nearer to the sea, began to flourish. To be sure, it may be taken as a general rule, that when new commercial relations develop themselves, new towns spring up into prosperity. Old towns, even where their local advantages are equal, are sure to be wedded to their old routine, are some time before they are able to assimilate themselves to new circumstances, do not immediately trust to the new prospects opening before them, and therefore fail to draw profit from the speculations to which those prospects invite. Chester belonged to the middle ages; to the Hanseatic and the Venetian system of cities, but when the commerce of America and the world began to develop itself, Liverpool quickly outstripped her more ancient rival.

Chester, more particularly West Chester, derives its name from the Roman *castrum*, like Winchester, Worcester, Leicester, Dorchester, Chichester, and like our German Cassels. Chester was the usual station of the twentieth Roman legion, and there are few cities in England where, if the Roman soldiers were to return, they would sooner find themselves at home, for it belongs to the small and continually lessening number of those that have preserved an appearance of antiquity. The plan of the city is the simplest that I know. Its walls form a parallelogram, and the two main streets intersect each other at right angles, dividing the parallelogram into four equal quarters, and then extend somewhat beyond the walls. From these main streets a number of bye streets run off on both sides. On the walls is a footpath, with room for two or three persons to pass each other, so that one may walk completely round the city. Indeed these city walls, two miles in circumference, form the chief promenade of the townspeople. According to tradition, they were built by Cymbeline, in the century before the birth of Christ. Of course they have undergone many alterations since then, and in later times they have been much reduced in height, and converted to their present purpose of a public walk five feet in breadth; and a curious promenade it is; sometimes up hill, and sometimes down; at one point closely wedged in between houses, while at another the narrow path passes under some ancient watch-tower; here it runs under a gateway, and there we must descend a flight of steps, because the wall has been cleared away to make room for a street; now we pass behind the venerable cathedral, and now in front of the spacious old castle, which has been converted into a military barrack. There is only one other town in England that can boast of an equally singular public walk, namely, York, which is surrounded by just such another old wall.

To say the truth, Chester is the very town for curious promenades, for it contains walks even more curious than the wall I have endea-

voured to describe. These are " the Rows," as they are called. They are long covered passages, running parallel with the streets, through the first floors of the houses. The thing is not very easy to describe. Let the reader imagine the front wall of the first floor of each house to have been taken away, leaving that part of the house completely open towards the street, the upper part being supported by pillars or beams. Let him then imagine the side-walls also to have been pierced through, to allow a continuous passage along the first floors of all the houses. How the people of Chester came, in this way, to spoil their best floor in so many of their houses, is a matter that was never made perfectly clear to me. We have also a number of towns in Germany, particularly in Silesia and the Austrian dominions, where covered passages, for the accommodation of the public, have been made to run through or round private houses; but then these passages or galleries are always on the ground floor, and on a level with the street. Some English antiquarians will have it, that these rows were intended as a means of defence, Chester being exposed to frequent attacks, from the Welsh on one side, and from the Scots on the other, when, after the city walls had been forced, the citizens were able to defend themselves in these Rows. In support of this theory, it has been asserted, that in all the battles which, during the civil wars in England, occurred in Chester, the party in possession of " the Rows" almost invariably obtained the victory.

It must not be imagined that these Rows form a very regular or uniform gallery. On the contrary, it varies according to the size or circumstances of each house through which it passes. Sometimes, when passing through a small house, the ceiling is so low that one finds it necessary to doff the hat, while in others one passes through a space as lofty as a saloon. In one house the Row lies lower than in the preceding, and one has, in consequence to go down a step or two, and perhaps, a house or two farther, one or two steps have to be mounted again. In one house a handsome new fashioned iron railing fronts the street, in another only a mean wooden paling. In some stately houses, the supporting columns are strong and adorned with handsome antique ornaments, in others the wooden piles appear time worn, and one hurries past them apprehensive that the whole concern must topple down before long. The ground floors, over which the Rows pass, are inhabited by a humble class of tradesmen, but it is at the back of the Rows themselves that the principle shops are to be found. This may give an idea of how lively and varied a scene is generally to be seen there. Indeed the Rows are generally full of people, either making their little purchases in the shops, or mounting to these boarded floors, to avoid the disagreeable pavement of the streets.

Perhaps these rows may be in some way connected with another singularity pointed out to me at Chester. The streets do not, as in other towns, run along the surface of the ground, but have been cut

into it, and that, moreover, into a solid rock.   The rows are in reality
on a level with the surface of the ground, and the carriages rolling
along below them are passing through a kind of artificial ravine.
The back wall of the ground floor is everywhere formed by the solid
rock, and the court-yards of the houses, their kitchens, and back-
buildings lie generally ten or twelve feet higher than the street.   The
English historians and antiquaries have given themselves a great deal
of trouble about this matter, without having ever been able to assign
a rational hypothesis as to the motives which could have induced the
ancient settlers in Chester to undertake so colossal a work as to hollow out all their streets.   For my part, I own myself unable to sug-
gest either a reasonable motive or an unreasonable one.

    Chester, the reader will by this time be aware, has other pecu-
liarities besides its walls, and certainly among the curiosities of the
town, not the least curious, to a German, presents itself at the cathedral, where the first tomb to which his attention will be directed,
is, he will be told, the tomb of the German emperor, Henry IV.
The Chester people, who have invented such singular streets, and
such singular side walks, have taken it very positively into their
heads that this famous German emperor, of whose death a very different history is told in his own country, did retire to Chester when
wearied of the continual disturbances in his own dominions; and
that the people of Chester took care of him to the end of his days,
after which they buried him in their cathedral, and erected a monument to his memory.   I told the man that showed me over the cathedral that I doubted the truth of the whole story.   He replied,
that there were some people in the town who believed it as little as
I did, "but for my part," he continued, "I have not the slightest
doubt about it, for why should they print it in the books if it were
not true?"   The monument itself, I must not forget to observe, is
more richly ornamented than any other in the cathedral, and a handsome inscription is there to confirm the popular tradition.   Now there
is nothing very inconceivable in people abandoning themselves to
historical errors, in their traditions and popular tales; but I own I
am at a loss to understand, how such an historical error can force its
way into broad daylight within the walls of an eminent cathedral,
to be there chiselled in stone and wrought in iron.   This unfortunate
emperor, as our authentic records inform us, died at Liège, on the
7th of August, 1106, after having been deprived of the crown by
his son Henry V.   Otbert, bishop of Liège, caused the body at first
to be interred in the cathedral, but as the emperor had died under
sentence of excommunication, the bishop, in obedience to the commands of the papal legate, had the body taken up again, and deposited, unburied, on a small island of the Meuse, where, history
further tells us, a pious monk sung penitential psalms night and day
for the emperor's soul.   Henry V. had the body brought to Spire,
and buried there in St. Mary's church; but the fanatical bishop of

that city would not allow repose to the imperial remains, which were taken up and placed in an unconsecrated chapel, where they remained for five years longer above the ground. Then only, the sentence of excommunication having been recalled, the bones of the unfortunate emperor were interred with great solemnity in the cathedral of Spire. Even there they were, however, disturbed, for towards the end of the seventeenth century, when the French desolated the palatinate, the bones of Henry were again torn from their resting-place. They have since been replaced there, and a monument is in the course of being raised over them, though not so magnificent a one as the English have raised at Chester over the grave of our emperor's counterfeit.

Now, in every tradition there is wont to be some truth, and, if so, the next question is, where is the truth that appertains to this famous Chester tradition? The following were not impossible:

Firstly: That the emperor, after his dethronement, and the ill-treatment he had received from his son, fled down the Meuse to England, and that the person who died at Liège was not the emperor at all; or,

Secondly: That a stranger, an impostor, availing himself of the stormy end and obscure death of the emperor, went over to England, and there to excite pity and extort support, gave himself out for the unfortunate emperor.

If neither of these suppositions can be shown to be correct, the question remains, who was this Henry IV. who was honoured at Chester with the title of Emperor of Germany, and whence came he to be taken for that emperor? This is a question which it will probably be as difficult to answer as that respecting the identity of the man with the iron mask.

Although the cathedral of Chester is not to be ranked among the first churches of England, it is a celebrated and a highly interesting one. It must, nevertheless, be placed in the second class, along with those of Carlisle and Dublin. It is built of a red sandstone, which must be very soft, for many of the architectonic decorations have been so completely defaced, that they look like the half-melted architectural fancies in the saltworks of Wieliczka.

Chester, quaint and interesting as the city is, is less visited by tourists on its own account, than for the sake of Eaton Hall, the brilliant seat of the Marquis of Westminster, situated in the valley of the Dee, a few miles above the town. It is one of the most celebrated among the country seats of the English nobility, and as the park begins as soon as one leaves Chester, the whole walk to. the house passes through the marquis's grounds. There are several entrances to the park, and all these, as is customary in English parks, have large gates, with dwellings, called "lodges," on each side, for the park and gate-keepers. These lodges are, in general, very neatly decorated, are surrounded by small flower beds, and usually built in a style to harmonise with that of the mansion.   At Eaton Hall, the lodges, like the principal building, are all of gothic architecture, and often of such extent and splendour that they might themselves be taken for handsome country houses.   One of these lodges,—the New Lodge,—is a copy of St. Augustine's Abbey at Canterbury; another represents the gateway of a large gothic castle, with turrets and battlements, and a third is taken from some other original.   The new lodge alone cost 10,000l.   From these lodges the road passes several miles through the park to the palace itself.

The building is as long and capacious as any of the largest English cathedrals.   It measures 500 feet in length, that is to say the main building, for if the stables and other dependents are included, the whole presents a mass of gothic architecture of 700 feet long.

Eaton Hall is what is called a " show house;" which means that the owner gives permission to his upper servants to show the building to every stranger, when he is himself away, and the consequence is that a crowd of visiters, at such times are continually pouring in and out, to gape at the profuse splendour everywhere displayed. The house, with its innumerable eight-cornered turrets, its ornamented columns, its spires and battlements, looks like a vast, wealthy, old English abbey.   Between the columns were numberless shields bearing the arms of the Grosvenor family, and of the various families to which the Grosvenors have become allied by marriage, and whose arms they have thereby, according to English custom, become authorised to quarter with their own.   There are noble families in England who have an endless number of these quarterings.   In Earl Spencer's coat of arms I counted no less than 163 such quarterings, including a whole Noah's ark, full of lions, bears, eagles, dogs, stags, boars, wolves, foxes, and dragons; besides the heads of oxen and negroes, the feathers of ostriches, the wings of what you please, together with stars, swords, shells, crescents, and other heraldic emblems.   Such a coat of arms may be said to bear some affinity to the great house of the Grosvenors, for besides the above-named heraldic shields, there were a number of heads and other decorations sculptured along the walls, as is often seen in our gothic cathedrals. The window-frames are of cast-iron, and elegantly decorated with gothic figuring, and the whole house is surrounded by a massive gothic railing, also of cast-iron.

As a number of architects and painters, such as Messrs. Porden, Gummon, Jones, and Harrison; besides gilders, cabinet-makers, turners, carvers, and other artists, have taxed their ingenuity to furnish and decorate this magnificent palace with all the richness and profusion possible, it would be a difficult undertaking to give a detailed account of all that the inventive genius of these gentlemen has produced and collected.   Let the reader give a free rein to his imagination, and picture to himself as much luxury and splendour as his fancy can conjure up, and he will scarcely go far beyond the mark. To me the chief fault of the place was, that it was too full, too crowded with ornament; in one point,—the gilding, of which there is an astonishing profusion in every room,—I think the artists have decidedly gone beyond the line of discretion.

The largest and most splendid room in the whole house is the library, which looks as if a monarch had converted his coronation hall to that use. It contains an interesting collection of books, manuscripts, and antiques, among which again are distributed a number of the most luxurious divans, sophas, and armchairs; for in the country houses of the English nobility, the library always ranks among the customary sitting-rooms of the family, even when it does not happen to be the one most frequented.

In the centre room, the saloon, is a large organ, an instrument often seen in English country-houses. Of wonderful chimney-pieces, fine statues, remarkable specimens of carving, valuable pictures, and other matters of the same kind, there is, of course, no lack, and there are many things, which if seen alone would be studied and admired, but which here, amid the mass of objects, lose their individuality to the intoxicated eye.

It was my misfortune, moreover, to visit the place in company with some gentlemen who had just returned from the Doncaster races, and who had been attracted, less by their admiration of the fine arts, than by their desire to see fine horses. The late lord had been a celebrated breeder of horses, and Eaton Hall had in consequence become famed on every· race-course in England, and still continues to be so, for the admirable horses reared there. The present marquis has several times carried off the chief prize at Doncaster, a prize often worth more than a 1000*l.*, and many an aristocratic breeder of horses is as proud of carrying off the crown at Doncaster, though only once in his life, as was ever a Greek youth of having been crowned as victor in the Olympic games.

Among the most celebrated horses shown me at Eaton Hall, were Launcelot, a crowned victor; Touchstone, one of the most far famed and most highly prized stallions in the country; and Pantaloon, another courser of high distinction. Launcelot reposes at present on his laurels, for he is now so fat and corpulent, as my connoisseurs told me, that he would not be able to run 100 yards according to the prescribed rules of the art. My unscientific eye could not indeed discover any greater appearance of fatness about Launcelot than about the other horses, but my companions assured me that the animal had fat upon his lungs, and would therefore not have breath enough to run a race. I took a liking to Launcelot, on account of an intimacy between him and a cat. The two creatures were almost inseparable, the cat always sleeping either on the horse's back, or in his manger, and the portraits of the two have even been published in a print, the original picture being preserved in the hall. The grooms told me when Launcelot returned from a walk or from the paddock, to re-enter his stable, the black cat would come jumping eagerly from manger to manger, and from the back of one valuable horse to that of another, to resume her accustomed place near her friend.

One of the most valued mares bred at Eaton Hall was Violante, who died a few years ago. I asked the stud-groom (with us he would at least have been *Stuterei Inspector*, or Superintendent of the Stud), where the monument was that had been erected to so distinguished an animal. " What monument?" he exclaimed; " we erect no monuments here to horses; when they die they all go to the dogs."—" And Violante like the rest?"—" Aye, to be sure."—There seemed to me to be something hard in this, something unfeeling. If we were to make so much of our horses in Germany during their lifetime, as is done in England, we should show some marks of kindness to them after death. In many parts of Germany I have seen monuments erected to horses and dogs, and other favourite animals. To us there appears a feeling of delicacy and humanity in this, but the English, I believe, look upon it as something profane, something degrading to humanity. Touchstone we found in his paddock. These paddocks are handsome pieces of pasture ground, surrounded by high walls, and for the stud we were now visiting there were no less than twelve such paddocks. For Touchstone, the groom told us 4000 guineas had been *refused*, the customary expression of an English groom, who would always rather say how much has been *refused*, than how much has been offered for a horse. I wish I could adequately describe the enthusiasm manifested by my sporting friends, on being introduced to Touchstone, or that I could even give the words in which their enthusiasm found a vent when the creature trotted up to us, and standing before us, looked at us with such an intelligent expression, that one might almost have imagined it understood the fine speeches addressed to it. The groom was particularly eloquent about the " sweet temper" of the animal. " Oh, there's nothing like him for sweet temper." This is a commendation I have so often heard from English grooms, when speaking of their horses, that I suppose it is considered an essential characteristic of a distinguished horse, as among the Arabs also, a mild disposition is particularly admired in a fine horse.

Other horses were shown us, of which we were told that they had already been entered for races to be run in 1844 and 1845, for horses in England are often engaged for races a great way off, as ladies in Vienna engage their partners for many balls in advance. Young horses are sometimes advertised to be sold by auction, as " yearlings with their engagements;" and as these engagements have often necessitated the payment of stakes of 25*l.* and upwards, and open a prospect to the " Oaks," the " Derby," and the " Doncaster Cup," the value of the animal is considerably enhanced in consequence.

In an establishment of this sort in England, the stud-groom and the training-groom are the two most important personages. We had them both in attendance on us, and it appeared to me that the stud-groom assumed a considerable degree of superiority over his colleague in office, telling us, that if the " breeder" showed any want of judgment in properly crossing the races, all the " trainer's" pains would be thrown away, for fleetness, beauty, courage, and emulation, could never be instilled into a horse, unless he had them in his blood. The training-groom, an experienced veteran in his art, refused to admit the absolute truth of all this, maintaining that without a good education, to develop and confirm these good qualities in the horse, the breeder's pains would be equally useless, for the entire race would degenerate in a short time.

The gardens and grounds about Eaton Hall are delightful, the beautiful river traverses them, and at a short distance are seen the Welsh mountains, among which it takes its rise. The park extends to the borders of Wales. The Grosvenors are an old Norman family, and their chief, the Marquis of Westminster, belongs to the fortunate class of English noblemen, a class including the Dukes of Sutherland and Northumberland, to whom common report, on what grounds I know not, attributes the possession of incomes of 300,000*l.*, or 350,000*l.* a year. Of the Marquis of Westminster I was moreover told, that in a few years his income would be materially increased, for the ground on which stands Grosvenor-square and many of the adjoining streets, belongs to him, and many of the building leases will be falling in, in a short time, when a number of valuable houses will fall into his hands. Here I would notice a small distinction between the high nobility of England and Germany. The officers in the employment of an English noble of high rank and great wealth, know nothing of the endless titles lavished on the functionaries in the service of a Lichtenstein or a Schwarzenberg, who have their administrators, chief administrators, councillors, councillors of agriculture, court councillors, &c. &c. &c. An English duke or a marquis has seldom any officer higher than an agent in his service, but the places of these untitled agents are often worth more than 2000*l.* a year.

LIVERPOOL.

I went on that same evening to Liverpool, and at ten o'clock arrived on the " Cheshire shore," on the south side of the Mersey, opposite to the great town itself. This " Cheshire shore" has risen and flourished simultaneously with Liverpool, and rural houses of entertainment, and villages rich in country seats have been gradually scattered along the river side, serving to the townspeople as watering-places, and as places of residence and amusement. The town receives, likewise, a large portion of its supplies from this side of the river. The broad Mersey lies between the Liverpool people and the Cheshire shore, which for that very reason, probably, is a greater favourite with them as a

place of recreation. To each little place on the opposite side of the
Mersey, a steamboat plies from Liverpool as a ferry. At certain
hours of the day, about twelve of these ferry steamers assemble at
the same wharf to take in their several cargoes, and at a given signal
they all start, scattering themselves in different directions over the
Mersey, like a pack of cards over a table.

We arrived at the chief of these ferries called Birkenhead, where
we and our luggage were packed with railroad speed into a steamer,
and within view of the widely spreading and brightly illuminated
Liverpool, we glided swiftly over the dark waters of the Mersey.
Every moment the echo of the noise made by our paddles as they
struck the water, announced that we were passing some stately
vessel lying at anchor. These echoes increased in number as we
proceeded, and traversing a forest of masts, among which lamps and
lanterns were glittering like so many glow-worms in a grove, we
speedily reached our landing-place, and the neighbouring hotel to
which we were consigned.

Chester boasts that, though she be nothing now, her glory and
greatness stand recorded in the works of the most ancient writers;
Liverpool, on the contrary, prides herself upon the fact that no
author of bygone days makes mention of her glory, but that what
she now is, has been the work of a generation still living. If Liverpool is spoken of in any ancient book, it is perhaps to say that the
place probably derives its name from the marsh or pool lying near
it. In 1561, Liverpool contained only 7 streets, 138 cottages, and
690 inhabitants. Towards the middle of the seventeenth century
the town began to grow into importance, and now it may be looked
on as the second commercial town in the world. As its growth
still continues, there are not wanting prophets who foretell that it
will some day rank as the first.

In 1801 Liverpool contained 77,708 Inhabitants.
        1821   „   „   118,972   „
        1831   „   „   165,221   „
        1841   „   „   224,954   „

The population has accordingly trebled in forty years, and several places lying in the vicinity, and almost belonging to Liverpool,
have, in the meantime, increased in an equal proportion. Everton,
Kirkdale, West Derby, and Toxteth Park, contained, in 1821, a joint
population of 22,103 inhabitants. Now the number is 71,009.
If we add these to the population of Liverpool, and the 13,000 seamen belonging to the town, but absent on voyages, and not therefore included in the census, we shall have 309,000 inhabitants.

The revenue derived from the Liverpool custom-house amounts
to one-fourth of the entire customs revenue of the United Kingdom.
The harbour receives annually 16,000 vessels from the different
parts of the world, and these vessels carry away with them 2,400,000
tons, or, 48,000,000 cwts. of merchandise. The vessels belonging
to the port are in number about 10,000, forming one-twelfth of the

entire British mercantile marine—coasters, of course, included; and, notwithstanding the badness of the times, so loudly complained of, I had sufficient proof that the shipping of Liverpool must still be on the increase in the zeal with which the workmen were labouring night and day at the completion of a new dock calculated for the reception of 200 vessels, a dock which of itself, in any German commercial town, would have been looked on as a colossal undertaking, as forming of itself a magnificent harbour, but which here was only one among a dozen.

Some branches of the Liverpool trade, particularly those influenced by the unfortunate state of things in America, have indeed suffered seriously of late years, but there are others which even lately have been growing in prosperity, and among these I may particularly mention the trade with the East Indies. To India, including China, the South Sea, the Cape of Good Hope, the Indian Archipelago, Arabia, and all Africa, except the Mediterranean ports, there sailed from Liverpool:

In 1840......................234 vessels carrying 90,350 tons, and 4402 seamen.
    1841......................266   ,,   ,,   115,106   ,,   5161

Being an increase of.., 32   ,,   ,,   24,756   ,,   759

This shows an increase of 20 per cent. in one year, and though only in one branch of the trade, yet in one of the most valuable and most interesting.

Let us compare the increase in the Indian trade of Liverpool with that observed at the same time in London, Bristol, Hull, and the other ports of Great Britain.

		London.	Bristol and Hull.	Glasgow and the remaining ports.
Number of Ships...	1840............	512............	12................	155
	1841............	530............	20................	190
Tonnage	1840............	205,453............	7716................	56,048
	1841............	213,407............	7272................	72,822
Seamen	1840............	12,210............	392................	2,950
	1841............	12,101............	372................	3,758

From these tables it results that the East Indian trade of Great Britian employed shipping in 1841 to the amount of 408,607 tons, and that of this shipping nearly one-fourth sailed from the port of Liverpool, and more than one-half from London; secondly that in the Indian trade of London, in 1841, as compared with the preceding year, there was an increase of only three per cent., while in that of Liverpool there was an augmentation of 24 per cent.

As Odessa's trade increased with the increasing cultivation of the Steppes, and as New York and New Orleans rose in proportion as the interior of the United States became more thickly settled, so has the growing prosperity of Liverpool been dependent on the development of the manufacturing districts. Manchester has been the nurse of Liverpool, and in proportion as Manchester, out of the old Mancunium, grew into its present vast dimensions, so, step by step, did Liverpool advance simultaneously in wealth, population, and activity.

The corresponding progress of the two cities will be seen on com-
paring the following statement of the increase of population of Manchester and Salford (the two form in fact one town) with that
already given of Liverpool.

1801	118,000	1831	275,000
1811	142,000	1841	354,000
1821	193,000		

The chief source of the commercial prosperity of England is not
to be sought in the amount of her exports of her own raw produce,
but rather in her exports of the raw produce of other countries, after
that raw produce has been worked up by native industry.   Thus, in
1842, the native raw produce exported, (including coals, metal, salt,
wool, &c.) amounted in value to 6,606,652*l*.   In the same year the
exports of the manufactures of cotton, wool, silk, linen, metal, and
earthenware, amounted to 36,527,999*l*. To this amount must be added
about 6,000,000*l*. for a long list of manufactured articles of minor
importance, such as soap, candles, leather, refined sugar, beer, &c.
We have, therefore, an exportation of about 7,000,000*l*. of raw
British produce, and an exportation of upwards of 42,000,000*l*. of
British manufactures.   Now the districts that furnish these manufactures are all much nearer to Liverpool than to London, which has
not a single manufacturing district of any importance in its vicinity.
From Manchester, the centre of the great cotton district, Liverpool
is only thirty miles distant, and London 170 miles.   To Leeds, the
centre of the woollen district ; to the Potteries ; and to Sheffield, the
great emporium for knife and scissors-grinding, Liverpool is much
nearer than London.   Even Birmingham is nearer to the Mersey
than the Thames.   With all these manufacturing districts, Liverpool
is closely connected by canals and railroads, so as to be able to receive
merchandise thence, with greater facility than London can.   Let us
now cast a glance at the countries whither the great mass of these
goods are conveyed.   North and South America here assume a
position which makes all the other countries appear comparatively
unimportant.   I do not happen at the moment to have a table showing the countries to which the exports went in 1842, but I have such
a table for 1839, which, as we are now dealing chiefly in round
numbers, will answer my purpose sufficiently well.   In 1839 then I
find the exports to all countries in the world, amounted to 53,233,000*l*.
Of these were exported to the principle customers of Great Britain,

To the United States of North America	£8,839,000
British West Indies	3,986,000
„ North American Colonies	3,047,000
Brazil	2,650,000
Chile	1,103,000
The Foreign West Indies	891,000
Rio de la Plata	710,000
Mexico	660,000
Peru	635,000
Hayti	392,000
Columbia	267,000
Making to North and South America	**£23,180,000**

Nearly one-half, therefore, of all the British manufactures exported in that year went to America. Now Liverpool lies considerably nearer to America than London does, so much so that the duration of a passage from the United States may, on an average, be calculated to occupy six days less to Liverpool than to London. Next to America, the principal customers of England are Germany, Holland, and the countries on the Baltic and the Mediterranean; with respect to these London is, of course, more advantageously situated than Liverpool.* It is to the foreign customers of England that the foregoing remarks chiefly apply, but we must not lose sight of the important fact, that the best customer for the produce of English industry is England herself. It is impossible to estimate very accurately how far the home consumption of England exceeds her exportation to foreign countries, but there are some articles respecting which there exist authentic returns showing the home consumption to amount to twice, thrice, or even four times the exportation to all parts of the world. In articles of raw produce the home consumption is even larger in proportion than this, amounting to twenty or thirty times the exportation; and with respect to agricultural produce, there is probably no exportation at all. Spackman estimates the entire produce of English industry at an annual amount of 514,000,000l. sterling. Assuming this to be correct, it would appear that the exportation (50,000,000l.) amounted to little more than one-tenth of the home consumption. In these 514,000,000l. it is true, are included articles of produce that never become objects of trade, such as the agricultural produce and manufactures that are consumed on the spot where they are grown or made; but when the diversity displayed in the local industry of different parts of England is considered, when it is remembered that one district grows corn, and another is devoted almost exclusively to pasture, while the limits within which are confined the various branches of manufacturing activity are yet more strictly marked out, it follows that the quantity consumed on the spot where it is produced must be very trifling, and that by far the greater part of the above named 514,000,000l. must become an object of domestic trade and internal intercourse. The commercial city, therefore, that enjoys the position best suited for commanding and carrying on this domestic trade, must have immense advantages over every other commercial town.

First, however, let me mention one or two points calculated to throw a light on the importance of the domestic compared with the foreign trade of Great Britain. The earthenware manufactured in England annually, according to Mac Culloch, is estimated to amount in value to 2,300,000l. of which only to the extent of 600,000l. is exported. The whole remainder, to the value of 1,700,000l., is con-

* Hull has of late years run away with a large portion of the commerce formerly carried on by London to the northern countries of Europe.—*Tr.*

sumed at home, and becomes an object of inland commerce. We
are in possession of detailed information relative to the linen exported from Ireland. From these returns it appears that the average exportation to foreign countries, during a series of years
amounted to three or four millions of yards, while the average exportation to England and Scotland, at the same time was between
forty and fifty millions of yards. In the next place, as the United
Kingdom may be said to be composed of a number of islands, and
those much intersected by the sea, the greater part of the domestic
trade of the country is carried on by means of small vessels(coasters),
the traffic on the common roads, on canals, and on railroads, standing in a much less proportion when compared to the coasting trade
than in any other country. According to the statistic tables of
Spackman, 19,710 vessels, carrying 3,392,626 tons, cleared out in
1841 for foreign countries, from the several ports of the United
Kingdom; in the same year, 146,127 coasting vessels, carrying
11,417,991 tons, cleared out for all British ports. The tonnage
of the vessels employed in the coasting or domestic trade of Great
Britain, was more than three times as large as the tonnage employed in the foreign trade, and the same proportion will be found
to apply to other years. When to this we add the traffic on railroads and canals, some idea may be obtained of the vast magnitude
of the domestic commerce of England.

Now when we come to examine the geographical position of
Liverpool, we find it situated almost in the centre of this great
domestic trade, all the extreme points of the United Kingdom lying
nearly at an equal distance from that centre. London, on the contrary, lies itself at one of the extremities of the kingdom. The central situation of Liverpool makes it the place to which the great
bulk of the merchandise intended to serve as an aliment to the inland trade will naturally be directed, there to await the demand
that may manifest itself in this or that part of the country. The
trade between England and Ireland, for instance, naturally takes
its chief course over Liverpool. Dublin lies as conveniently to the
west as Manchester does to the east of Liverpool; and if Liverpool
and Manchester are united, or brought near to one another by an
admirable railroad, Dublin and Liverpool are not less intimately
connected by an admirably organised system of steam navigation.
Indeed, so conveniently for the trade with Ireland is Liverpool situated, that the Irish is the most ancient branch of trade it can boast
of, and the gradual extension of the Irish trade has not failed to
exercise its influence on the growth of Liverpool, in the same manner as the increasing prosperity of Manchester has stimulated the
prosperity of Liverpool. The great increase in the Irish trade dates
from the introduction of steam navigation in 1820, since which
time Liverpool has thrown a net of steam-boats about Ireland,
where the Liverpool vessels are in every part those which carry on
the chief commerce. It would no doubt be highly interesting to

know the entire amount of the British inland trade carried on through Liverpool, particularly the Irish trade, and then to compare it with the inland trade carried on through the other commercial towns; but for such an inquiry, I believe, there exist no data in any English statistical work. The inland trade of Liverpool must, however, be enormous, as may be inferred from one item which I will mention. In a local work on Ireland I find it stated, that the cattle alone exported from Ireland to Liverpool amounts to a yearly value of about 7,000,000*l.*

Next to the trade with Ireland, the most ancient branch of Liverpool's commerce, one which most materially contributed to advance the prosperity of the place, was the detestable trade in human flesh. This trade commenced in 1709, when the first ship sailed from Liverpool to Africa for a cargo of slaves. In 1730, fifteen vessels were already engaged in this disgraceful traffic, and in 1765 no less than eighty-six vessels, which were supposed to convey 25,720 poor negro slaves every year from Africa to the West Indies, whence they brought back 10,000 chests of sugar to England, and at that time more than half the vessels engaged in the African trade were owned by Liverpool. In the year when the slave trade was abolished, Liverpool had 126 ships engaged in it, and though immediately on the abolition the African and West Indian trade manifested at first some decline, yet both have since very greatly increased, so that it may be assumed that, on the whole, the commerce of Liverpool has not suffered any material loss from the abolition of the slave trade.

It follows from what I have stated, that Liverpool enjoys in the first place a really commanding position, in reference to the home trade of Great Britain, and that it possesses many advantages over London and other ports, for carrying on the foreign trade with those countries which happen to be the best customers of England. Liverpool is still a young city, and has probably not yet availed herself of all the advantages of her position. This town may yet rise to an importance far beyond that which it has yet reached.

Among the great cities of the world, of first or second rank, there is no other so exclusively devoted to commerce. Every house in Liverpool is either a counting-house, a warehouse, a shop, or a house that in one way or other is either an instrument or the result of trade. The great buildings and institutions of the town are a custom-house, an exchange, a set of docks, a railway station, or something else that is intended, directly or indirectly, to be serviceable to commerce, and the inhabitants are nearly to a man traders or the servants of traders. Not even the authorities of the county reside at Liverpool, for the county town is Lancaster.

Trivial as the name and object of such a building may appear in the eyes of philosophers, the custom-house of Liverpool is really a wonderful pile, and the enthusiast for the fine arts will not fail to admire it, however worthless or odious may appear to him the business transacted there. To me it seems that this building is not merely the first of its kind in the world, and incomparably the finest of any kind in Liverpool, but that it deserves even to rank with St. Paul's Church and with other architectural marvels of the first order. If a stranger were placed in the front of the pile, without knowing where he was, he would certainly be apt to believe that there, at the least, must be held the meetings of a senate, to whose consultations the welfare of a mighty empire was committed. It is not merely the extent of the building (500 feet by 100) that commands our admiration, but the simplicity of the style harmonises so beautifully with that extent. The Ionic columns which support the porticoes of the centre and of the two wings, are fifty feet in height. The whole was finished in eleven years, and government alone contributed 150,000*l.* to the expenses of the building. It is unquestionably one of the most magnificent pieces of architecture that our age has produced; and if it has not acquired as much fame as the Isaac's church in St. Petersburg, or the Museum in Berlin, or the Glyptothek, the Pinakothek, or the Walhalla, in Bavaria, or the church of St. Magdalen in Paris, or other colossal piles of modern erection, the reason must be the comparatively vulgar use to which it is applied. Not that it is confined to the purpose which its name would seem to indicate; for not only the business of the customs is carried on there, but also that of the excise, the stamps, and the post-office, together with all that relates to the harbour and docks. In short, all the public offices in Liverpool connected with trade are comprised within the walls of the custom-house.

To give some idea of the amount of business transacted within this building, I will merely mention the amount received annually for customs, which exceeds four millions and a half sterling, or about thirty millions of our dollars. In 1840, the amount was 4,607,326*l.* or about a hundred thousand dollars a day. This was equal to one-fifth of the customs paid by the whole of the United Kingdom, to two-fifths of those paid by London, and to more than was paid by all the custom-houses of Scotland and Ireland put together.

Close to the custom-house lie the docks, and these offer to the stranger a spectacle of commercial bustle, and a multitude of splendid harbour and marine works, unequalled, I believe, in the world, not even excepting those of London. Some of the London docks are perhaps larger than any of those of Liverpool, and may therefore afford accommodation to a larger number of vessels; but, in the first place, they are fewer in number, and not being destined for such various branches of trade, offer not the same variegated scenes as those of Liverpool; and secondly, being at a distance from the central part of the town, they do not afford the same convenience to the merchant. London was already a great town before she began to think of her present commercial importance, whereas Liverpool, her trade, and her docks, grew up together. In London, when docks came to be thought of, it was impossible to clear away half a town, so they had to be placed somewhat out of the way; but in Liverpool, a convenient site was from the first left for the docks, and the custom-house, the exchange, and the merchants' counting-houses, grouped themselves about them. In London, a merchant when he wants to send an order to his ship in the docks, must often send his clerk down by the railroad; in Liverpool, a merchant might almost make himself heard in the docks, out of his counting-house window.

The whole length of the river side at Liverpool is filled up with docks. To have an idea of the grandeur of these works, taken as a whole, the reader must imagine a length of three English miles running along the river, and this occupied, in a breadth of from 250 to 500 yards, with all descriptions of harbour works; with basins cut into the rock, and then lined with solid masonry; with admirable quays surrounding these basins; with entrance docks and canals, provided with various kinds of locks, and crossed by handsome iron bridges, or by wooden pathways. He must next imagine the whole length of three miles armed with a lofty wall, whose imposing greatness can be properly admired only at low water; these basins filled with ships, the quays crowded by busy workmen, engaged in loading and unloading merchandise, with the imposing warehouses, and the really elegant residences of the officers of the docks.

It would be difficult to state the precise number of all the basins and other artificial harbours for the reception of large and small vessels, but, including those belonging to the canals, there are certainly more than forty. Of the docks, properly so called, there are about sixteen. When in these docks, the vessels have the advantage of an unvarying depth of water, and great facilities for loading and unloading, and for effecting all necessary repairs. Most of the docks are intended for the use of a particular class of ships. Thus the Brunswick Dock is for vessels laden with timber from America; the Queen's Dock for West Indian, Baltic, and Dutch vessels; the Coburg Dock for the large class of sea-going steamers; the King's Dock for the tobacco vessels from the West Indies and North America; and the Prince's Dock, the most magnificent of all, for ships from India and China, and for the largest class of American vessels. Each dock is differently arranged, with a view to the accommodation of the class of vessels for which it is intended. Thus at the Brunswick Dock the quays are particularly calculated for the unloading of timber, and often one side of the dock is arranged for loading and the other for unloading.

The graving docks are a particular class of small docks, intended for caulking and other repairs.

To each dock is attached what is called a basin, into which, as it is generally in direct communication with the Mersey, vessels may enter at every period of the tide, and through which all vessels must pass before they can enter the docks themselves. These basins are a sort of preliminary docks ready at all times to afford shelter, while the docks themselves, where it is required that the water should always remain at the same level, can be opened only at high water.

Astonishment and admiration are awakened in no ordinary degree, at the contemplation of the bulwarks which man has here erected against ocean; of locks often fifty feet high, with which he regulates ebb and flood in his docks; sea-gates, often seventy feet wide, of the most magnificent and solid workmanship; and the immense reservoirs which he has dug into the rocks, for the reception of his vessels. The Prince's Dock, the largest of all, cost 561,019*l*., and more than half of this sum was expended in wages to the men employed in digging, excavating, &c. The expense of the whole of the works along the Mersey quay is incalculable, but must have amounted to many millions; and it is not merely the extent of these works that deserves our admiration, but also the short time within which they have been completed. Most of the docks have been constructed during the last thirty years. The first ever built in England was begun in 1708, but this great ancestor of all the docks of Great Britain no longer exists, the custom-house having been erected on its site. If all Germany would but consent to expend on the cathedral of Cologne, as much as the single town of Liverpool has expended on her docks, the noble pile would soon stand complete in all its details, to the admiration of centuries, and to the honour of God.

In general, it is impossible to judge the real magnitude of the work expended on one of these docks, as they are mostly filled with ships and water, but it is when we happen to see one of them empty that we are surprised at their depth and capaciousness. I saw the Salthouse Dock empty. It had been found not to be deep enough, and there had been a wish to correct the irregularity of its form. These alterations were proceeding, at the time of my visit, with great rapidity, it being deemed desirable that the whole should be finished before the autumn. To accelerate the works they proceeded night and day, relays of workmen relieving each other every twelve hours. The men who work at night, slept by day, breakfasted at eight in the evening, and had an hour allowed them, from midnight till one, for their dinner. At eight in the morning they were relieved by the day party. On Saturdays the night party worked only till midnight, and resumed their work on Monday morning at one o'clock, the hour from midnight being, as usual, allowed them for dinner. This night-work presented a spectacle unique in its kind. The entire cavity, in some places at least fifty feet deep, and covering at least five acres of ground, was filled with numberless torches, lights, and fires, and 300 workmen were busily engaged,—hacking, digging, and breaking and exploding the rock. In five weeks, it was hoped, the dock would be ready for the reception of vessels.

On looking more closely into the details of these docks we see how admirably the English have arranged every little matter connected with these great commercial institutions, and how imperfect most of these things continue to be in other countries. At certain distances round all the docks are large, broad-headed, cast iron posts to which the vessels are made fast. Now it seems almost incredible that in so old a commercial city as Bremen there should still be public walks where the trees have continued to be applied to this use for I know not how many centuries. The patient promenaders of the German city, as they stroll along the Neustadtsdeich, have, for centuries, been accustomed to jump over the ropes, in which their legs are in momentary danger of becoming entangled, as in so many snares, and yet, to the present day, it seems never to have suggested itself to these good people, that for so serious an inconvenience so easy a remedy might be found. In the next place, every dock is surrounded by iron cranes, on each of which is marked the weight it is able to lift, as thus: "Not to lift more than two tons." Now certainly, it seems natural that before people make use of a machine intended to raise heavy weights, they should know the weight it is capable of lifting, but I know seaport towns enough were so self-suggesting a precaution is never dreamt of. Close to the edge of the quays are large long sheds, under which the merchandise can be sheltered immediately on leaving the vessel, and from which it can be packed into the waggons that are to carry it away. These sheds have side walls, consisting either of wooden boards or of canvass stretched on iron rollers. These side walls are moveable, and are generally put out of the way when the weather is at all favourable; but they can quickly be restored to their places should a storm or heavy rain come on, when the sheds are, for the time being, converted into small warehouses, sheltered on every side.

It is to the Prince's Dock one must go, to see all these arrangements in the greatest perfection, or to contemplate the finest among the vessels that visit Liverpool. Among those most admired are the American packet ships, and particularly the British and North American Royal Mail Steamships, the *Acadia*, the *Britannia*, the *Columbia*, &c.—specimens of architecture quite as wonderful as many a temple or custom-house. I visited the *Caledonia*, of which the crew was so numerous, that at a draper's shop I saw the uniform of a *Caledonia* seaman exhibited as a regular article of sale. These vessels are rated at 1200 tuns, and their steam-engines are of 440 horse power. They are all precisely alike, having been built after the same model. They carry the mail to Halifax and Boston, generally performing the voyage to America in fourteen-and-a-half days, and the voyage home in eleven or twelve days. The quickest voyage hitherto performed was that of the *Britannia*, in July, 1841, when she ran from Halifax to Liverpool in nine days and a half. These beautiful vessels lie somewhat out of the way in the Coburg Dock. In the other docks may be seen other steamers, such as the boats of the Glasgow line, those of the Dublin line, the Isle of Man line, the Cork line, &c.

In consequence of this regular and rapid communication with America, Liverpool has become the principal point of departure for that continent, not only for England but for all Europe, the main ferry to unite the old world and the new. The same circumstance has made Liverpool the principal port of embarkation for emigrants, who are certain, at all times, to find opportunities there for Canada and the United States, more so than even in London. In the month of April, 1842, no less than 13,055 persons embarked at Liverpool for the United States, and 1945, to the British North American colonies, making in all 15,000. This is more than emigrate from Germany, by the way of Bremen, in a whole year. From the whole United Kingdom, the emigration amounts, on an average, to about 100,000 individuals a year; in 1841, the number was 118,592, of whom 72,104 were from England, 32,428 from Ireland, and 14,060 from Scotland, but many, no doubt, of those who went from England were Irish and Scotch, who had come to Liverpool as the most convenient port of embarkation. Of these emigrants, 45,017 went to the United States, 38,114 to Canada, 28,724 to Australia, and 3901 to New Zealand.

A spectacle particularly calculated to awaken interest, is the sight of a noble vessel, which, after bravely struggling with the storm and the other perils of the sea, now, with her broken ribs and limbs, reposes quietly in harbour. In Liverpool, where there are always a thousand or two of vessels in the docks, it can seldom happen, that one or other of them has not her tale to tell of some imminent danger recently encountered. Such a vessel I saw in the *Laurel*, which I found lying in one of the graving docks. On her way from Canada, and when still a thousand miles from Liverpool, she had encountered an iceberg, that had broken her bowsprit, and knocked in one of her sides. She would infallibly have sunk, but that her cargo (timber) kept her afloat. It struck me as something strange to hear English sailors making use of the German expression " icebergs," but it is the customary word, " ice-mountains" being never used.

Many of the extensive warehouses in which goods are deposited (in bond) till the duty has been paid, receive all descriptions of merchandise, but others are set aside for particular articles. Of these the tobacco warehouse, near the King's Dock, is the largest of all. This building goes on increasing in extent, to make room for the increased masses of this merchandise for which accommodation is required, to the sorrow and vexation of many an English housewife, who would fain keep the atmosphere of her house clear of the poisonous fumes of the tobacco leaf. Behind this warehouse, along the quay, is a promenade, and a similar one exists behind the Prince's Dock. These " marine parades" are genuine Liverpool promenades. Their trees are masts; their flower beds and parterres are groups of tar barrels, tea chests, and tobacco casks; the occasional vistas that open, carry the eye along rows of warehouses, and the view ranges over the broad green meadows of the Mersey, with the blue ocean and its sportive billows melting away in the distant mist.

Such of the tobacco as has been spoiled, or is not considered by the merchant to be worth the duty, together with the "scraps" that are swept together, are burned in a stove constructed for the purpose. I found a very old feeble man in attendance on this stove, so feeble that I could not help expressing some surprise at his not having been pensioned and relieved from active duty. I meant no offence by the remark, yet he seemed almost to have been offended by it, answering—"Allow me to say, sir, as long as I can do a man's duty, I will stay here." If every public officer would think and act in the same way, our governments would have fewer pensions to pay.

Few of the houses near the docks are inhabited, most of them being either warehouses or counting-houses, and one house often contains many counting-houses, the names of the different firms being painted on the sides of the doors. The streets are constantly filled with long caravans of waggons laden with merchandise, like the narrow streets of that part of London which lies between St. Paul's and the Thames; but this warehouse quarter of Liverpool is much more elegant and convenient than that of London, where, on account of the narrowness of the streets, constant stoppages are occurring.

In the vicinity of the docks are situated various establishments for the manufacture of articles required for the equipment of vessels, such as rope-walks and the like. Among others, a vast machine established by the Liverpool corporation, for the testing of chain cables. I saw a chain tested, whose links were not above two inches in diameter, and this comparatively thin chain was subjected to a pressure of sixty tons.

I also visited the establishment of a sail-maker, but, as it was a Monday, not a very busy day either in Liverpool or in any part of England, I found most of the workmen absent. "They had not time on Saturday evening," observed one of the directors of the concern, in an ironical tone, "to spend the whole of their week's earnings; and as they could do little that way on Sunday, they must have their Monday into the bargain." A great deal of canvass is exported, and, to give it a more attractive look, it is generally bleached. "We Liverpool people, however, prefer bleaching our canvass at sea, as the bleaching on shore always weakens it." The Liverpool people, I found, considered their sails to be very superior to those made at London. In sails also, I here learned, there is such a thing as mutation of fashion; so of late years it has become customary to introduce a narrow blue stripe into the sails, and the innovation has found great favour in the eyes of sailors. I wanted to have some idea of the quantity of canvass required to equip a large vessel, and to gratify my curiosity the books were referred to,

when it appeared that a new vessel of 500 tons that had lately
been fitted out, had required 4841 yards of canvass to make her
a complete set of sails; and that 3300 yards had been used up for
the sails of a smaller vessel of 340 tons. The fragments that are cut
off are sold as rags to the paper-makers, at the rate of twenty
guineas a ton (equal to $2\frac{1}{3}d.$ a pound), and when the rags are
mixed with rope ends the price is from twelve to thirteen guineas
a ton. If a poor Parisian *chiffonnier* could be transported from his
muddy streets to a place so rich in rags, how eagerly would he
strike his iron hook into the tempting mass! How rich, how happy
would he feel! As happy as Napoleon in Germany, when he was
hooking one principality after another into his great basket.

When I said Liverpool was no manufacturing town, I made an
assertion, it will be seen, that must not be taken without some qua-
lification. Besides the establishments to which I have already
alluded, there are large manufactories of steamboats and steam-
engines, anchor smiths, chain smiths, oil mills, sugar refineries, large
bakehouses for making ships' biscuits and others; but all these are
industries immediately connected with commerce and shipping, or
with the immediate wants of the town itself. There is but one
manufactory, in the common acceptation of the term, namely, a factory for spinning cotton, which is consequently looked upon as a
little curiosity in its way. One of the largest and most interesting
of the establishments to which I have alluded, is that of Messrs.
Fawcett and Preston, for the construction of cannon and of large
marine steam engines. Some idea may be formed of the importance of the concern, when we are told that the house undertakes the execution of such orders as 300 pieces of heavy ordnance
for the King of Holland. Steam-engines are made here of more than
500 horse power. Their largest was of 520, the engines of the
steamers on the Boston line of 440, and the largest employed in
any manufactory in Manchester of 300 horse-power. I saw a cy-
linder, eighteen feet in circumference, making for a steam frigate.
Sugar-mills for the West Indies and Brazil are also made at these
works. Having, however, seen steam-engine manufactories of even
superior arrangement at Manchester, I will postpone, for the present, my description of such a one.

To see how many things are now made of iron in England, one
must visit one of the iron warehouses, as, for instance, that of Coal-
brookdale, at this place. Tables, sofas, vases, inkstands, and an
endless variety of articles fashioned into the most graceful forms,
may there be seen. Liverpool, however, is scarcely richer in iron
than in gold and silver, which are everywhere displayed in manifold
forms in the shop windows. For my own part, were I to begin to
wish, my wish would be a very modest one, for I would wish only
to be master of all the dust of Liverpool—not forgetting, of course,
the gold and silver dust, which may here be seen displayed most
temptingly in bowls in the windows, like the many-coloured bon-

bons in the window of a Parisian confectioner. It is owing to this wealthy city of Liverpool (not, of course, forgetting Manchester), that Lancashire is reckoned, after Middlesex, the wealthiest county in England. From the report of the Poor-Law Commissioners, the real property of England and Wales (that is to say, the houses and lands alone), appears to be worth 62,540,000*l.* a year; hereof, 7,293,369*l.* fall to the share of Middlesex, and 5,266,606*l.* to that of Lancashire. These sums, in 1815, were respectively, 51,898,423*l.*, 5,595,537*l.*, and 3,087,774*l.*, showing a much greater proportionate increase in the northern than in the metropolitan county. How much greater, however, would the proportionate increase appear, if the accumulated capitals and the mighty steam-engines that have been erected, were taken into the account.

The Liverpool Exchange may also well be termed " a magnificent pile of masonry, a splendid range of buildings." The most interesting room in connection with it is the news-room, where merchants meet to transact business, and to read the papers. It looks like an immense school-room, for a vast quantity of newspapers are here displayed upon a number of small desks, over which the pupils of Mercury may be seen diligently engaged in their studies. In Liverpool alone there now appear ten weekly newspapers. The three principal ones are Conservative, five are Liberal, and two confine themselves to mercantile matters.

In the centre of the Exchange stands the Nelson monument, in which are represented—his death, his victory, and his reward; the joy and sorrow of Britannia; the combat of the soldiers, and the subjugation of the foe. This monument alone was enough to convince me, how much more difficult it is to erect a classical, tasteful group of this kind, than to criticise it when erected. There is quite enough to criticise about the Nelson monument, though it has cost 9000*l.* The English, as I have already said, seem unable to represent the merely beautiful in its ideal sublimity; but for matters of real utility, their embellishments are remarkably beautiful, classical, and well suited. To take only the railroad terminus at Liverpool— what pomp, what architectural adornment does it not display! A noble façade built of solid stone, rich in columns and in handsome gateways, fit to compare with the triumphal arches of Athens, Berlin, and Paris. Few of our German railroads are adorned with any of these magnificent propylæi, yet it is but right that we should pass through a triumphal arch to the triumph of science. A friend, himself connected with the railroad, showed me the admirable details of its management. At this terminus, I found, a number of railroad companies had their separate offices: the Grand Junction Company, the North Union Company, and several others.

Among the carriages that run on English railroads are some entirely unknown to us; for instance, the bullion waggons, intended for the conveyance of money, and of gold and silver bars. These carriages are chiefly used by the Bank of England, the Mint, the private banking-houses, and the great bullion merchants. With most of the trains, the Post Office has two carriages, or rather flying offices, with huge nets at the side, to receive the letter bags at the stations where the train does not stop. The bullion waggons do not occur on all the railroads, but only on the principal lines, as those between London and Liverpool, and Liverpool and Manchester. As nearly a million of pigs and cattle arrive annually from Ireland in Liverpool, it may naturally be supposed that the cattle waggons must play an important part on all the railroads radiating from that town.

Liverpool stands everywhere upon a rocky bottom, and as its docks and cemeteries have been cut into the rock, so have the tunnels of its railroad been bored through it. Immediately behind the terminus, which stands in the heart of the town, the railroad disappears, and does not emerge again to the light of day till after it has run a distance of 2230 yards. We went as far as the Edgehill station, which offers the most bustling scene of any, for thence branches off another tunnel, which also runs 2300 yards under the town to the docks, and is intended for the conveyance of merchandise. Two large steam engines are at work at this station, dragging immense masses of goods and passengers out of the two huge caverns. The dock tunnel terminates in Liverpool at Wapping, close by the docks. I went there likewise to see the empty waggons shooting forth on their return. They come down the tunnel from Edgehill merely impelled by their own weight, and day and night the engine continues at its never ending work.

The railroad between Liverpool and Manchester, as most of my readers are probably aware, was the first constructed in England for the conveyance of passengers by locomotives impelled by steam, and the experience gained upon this railroad, since 1830, has been of the greatest value to all the other railroads in the kingdom. Experiments have been made here with all kinds of rails, substructions, engines, and carriages, and, in little more than ten years, such have been the improvements effected, that the trains run the thirty-one miles between Manchester and Liverpool in half an hour, whereas originally they required an hour and a half, and the consumption of coal, formerly from twenty to thirty pounds a mile, has been reduced to twelve or eighteen pounds. The rails have, meanwhile, become much stronger and heavier than they were. At first they weighed thirty-four pounds per yard, now from sixty to seventy. The engines also have become heavier and more powerful, weighing at first only ten tons, whereas at present they weigh from fifteen to sixteen. The largest weighs seventeen tons.

It is but little, in general, that the public at large know of the history and development of railroads, for the rapidity with which we are impelled over them, and the hurry and bustle of the people employed there, leave but little time to gather information; and the many prohibitions to which one is subjected at the several stations, have the effect of throwing a kind of mystery about the thing.

There are people enough who travel thousands of miles by railroad, without having any thing like a rational idea of the present condition of this great invention, or of the immense improvements that have been made or are still in rapid progress. We travelling authors of modern times are, usually, very concise on the matter of railroads, whereas when we travelled with our two grays and a postilion we used to have an astonishing deal to tell about the merits and defects of our equipage. Not even in England have I found a well written work on railroads; not, at least, a work in which the attempt was made to give an adequate account of the early history of this yet growing giant.

Perhaps the largest of all the excavations, made into the rock at Liverpool, is the St. James's Cemetery, extending over a surface of 44,000 square ells. It was originally a stone quarry, and a more fitting site for a burying ground could not easily be imagined, for the place looks like a gigantic grave, though magnificently decked out with walks and parterres, with trees and flowers. This cemetery resembles the Valley of Jehosaphat near Jerusalem. On one side rise the steep, hewn, rocky walls, along which run terrace walks. The vaults or catacombs are hewn into the rock itself. The other side is less abrupt, beautifully planted, and the most delightful garden walks lead into the valley of the dead, already filled with a multitude of graves and monuments. The principal way leads through a tunnel under the rock, an allusion, perhaps, to the narrow gate by which we enter the fields of Paradise. On the summit of a steep rock is an oratory, a tasteful building in the Doric style, and in the centre of the grounds stands a monument to Mr. Huskisson, the martyr of railroads, the lamented of his country. This is unquestionably the most beautiful cemetery I have seen, and its appearance is the more remarkable, as it lies in the middle of the town, and is surrounded, on every side, by broad streets and high buildings. For the poor, in this cemetery, there are deep square pits, hewn deep into the rock, in which the coffins are placed in order, slightly covered with earth, but the hole is not filled up until it has received its due complement of dead.

This great rendezvous of the dead lay half way to an assembly of certain living beings, in whom we are disposed to take considerable interest, because, with many points of resemblance to us, they are still essentially different creatures,—I mean to the Liverpool Zoological Garden. Any thing new that makes its appearance in London, is quickly imitated in Liverpool. Thus I already saw the bright flame of the Bude light burning here, in one of the public places, though it was only a short time before that I had seen a similar light in London tried as an experiment. So also Liverpool had already its Centrifugal Railway, and an artificial field of ice, for skating on in summer, such as had recently been established in London, was spoken of as about to be opened at Liverpool. Liverpool is generally the first provincial town in England to adopt any novelty that appears in London, it was not, therefore, to be expected that Liverpool should be without its Zoological Garden, seeing that several English towns have institutions of the kind.

I never visited a zoological garden in England, without seeing some animal that I had never seen before, or without witnessing some scene completely new to me. These gardens, however, are less intended for the promotion of science than of recreation. They are the favourite promenades, are beautifully laid out, and music, illumination, and refreshment rooms are never wanting. The lions roar an accompaniment to the orchestra, and when the animals are fed, there's almost sure to be a fight between the tigers or hyenas, a spectacle particularly attractive to an English public. I witnessed here a very interesting battle of the kind between two hyenas, and all the promenaders in the garden crowded to the show. The quarrel began thus. Like most of the animals, the hyenas began to be very restless as the usual feeding time approached, and went round and round each other, like two horses in an oilmill, grumbling and gnashing their teeth all the while. One was considerably larger and stronger than the other, and the smaller fellow of the two, seemed to have his imagination very much excited beforehand by the prospect of the handsome joint about to be served up to him. Perhaps he feared his more vigorous companion might have some unlawful designs upon the said joint, and perhaps the occurrence of former appropriations of the kind might be fresh in his recollection. Be this as it may, the little fellow was decidedly in an ill humour, and at last, setting his hair on end, withdrew into a corner of the cage, and sat grinning and showing his teeth at the big one, who continued his rotatory promenade for some time longer, till at last some remark of the little one's, unintelligible to me, seemed to give particular offence, and the big fellow suddenly stood still, set his hair also on end, and howled and grinned most potently. The explosion was at last brought about by one of the spectators throwing a stone at the head of the smaller hyena. The creature may have supposed the insult to have come from his companion ; at all events, the two were at close fight with one another in an instant. The blood of the odious creatures soon began to flow, and the combative little champion soon got the worst of it, so much so, that I apprehended he would soon lose his life under the feet of his more powerful antagonist. The keepers, however, were not long in making their appearance. They separated the combatants, and laid a stick between them. Immediately the two animals withdrew respectfully to the opposite corners of their cage, ogling the innocent and motionless stick with such submissive looks as the frogs in the fable are said to have cast on the log that Jupiter gave them for a king. When the keepers were gone, the creatures crept forward a little, and timidly smelt the stick from their respective sides, and at the two opposite ends, but neither ventured to overstep the barrier, and trembling evidently all over, they continued at a peaceful distance, and as quiet as mice, till they received their food. In a German menagerie these two animals would long ago have been separated; in England they are left together, that the public may now and then be diverted with a spectacle such as I have described.

The elephants in this garden were as tame as in India, and walked about, led by their keepers, to draw water for themselves from a pond. As the elephant was returning with his water, the keeper made him kneel down, and some children who were present with their parents got upon his back, whereupon he trotted away with his little load. Such are the juvenile diversions of those who are hereafter to rule India and Africa. The one elephant was a male, Rajah by name, and the son of Sultan, one of the finest elephants of Calcutta; the other was a female, and her name Poodah. The two lived together in great domestic happiness, and their's, I was assured, was the first case in Europe of a pair of elephants living quietly with one another.

No part of an English zoological garden is more frequently visited than are the monkey cages, and to say the truth, the comic gestures of the monkeys are so varied and so entertaining, that they afford an inexhaustible fund of amusement. They have this advantage over most animals, that they never seem to lose their spirits in captivity, but skip as restlessly and as extravagantly about their cages, as though they were still in their forests. The consequence is that in one of these little houses, filled with some dozens of monkeys, scenes may every day be witnessed of a truly African or American character. "Visitors are requested not to tease the animals," is posted up in large letters at every cage, nevertheless, the creatures are teased incessantly, for to tease is a characteristic propensity of man; other animals are either friendly with each other or they fight, but they never tease one another.

Something quite peculiar in their way, in these gardens, are the "Typoramas," as they are called; faithful and colossal representations of celebrated buildings or landscapes, of mountain ranges or city views. These Typoramas, in the form in which we see them in England, offer, in some respects, the most complete representation of such scenes, very far surpassing the dioramas of Gropius. The Typoramas present the various objects almost in their natural dimensions, or appear to do so, and to produce the required effect have no occasion for any artificial light. Every year the subject of the picture is generally changed. Thus, in the two preceding years the people of Liverpool had had an opportunity of admiring Mount Vesuvius and St. Jean d'Acre, and now the city of Rome was brought home to them. A large pond is made use of as a foreground, and is made to represent a sea, a lake, or a river, as may best suit the purposes of the picture, which is thus thrown into the necessary distance from the spectator. The whole is so admirably painted and put together, that one can discover none of that "halfness" and incompleteness which even the brilliancy of illumination is unable to conceal in theatrical decorations. In the evening lights appear gradually in the different windows of this artificial city of Rome, and on its becoming completely dark St. Peter's Church was illuminated, and at last, the *girandola* was fired off from the Castle of St. Angelo. To me, however, the picture, when illuminated, appeared much less deserving of admiration than when seen by daylight.

In the vicinity of Liverpool, at the Earl of Derby's park, there is a very valuable collection of living birds, which I should have had much pleasure in visiting, but I was deterred from doing so on learning that a number of troublesome formalities were necessary before the requisite permission could be obtained.

With the exception of these zoological and botanical gardens, and the sailing and rowing parties on the Mersey, the public amusements of Liverpool, as of all English towns, are extremely limited, though perhaps not so much so as in the manufacturing towns. There are two regular theatres for the cultivated classes, and an amphitheatre for the equestrian, military pantomimes, and other noisy pieces in which the lower order of playgoers delight. I went to see such a piece at the house in question, which is said to be calculated for the accommodation of 4000 spectators. The piece was called " *The Five Stages of Intemperance; or, the Life and Death of a Drunkard.*" The first act represented the interior of the house and family of Mr. Jones, where the birth of a child, the hero of the piece, is celebrated by plentiful libations of tea and coffee, together with singing, dancing, &c. In the second act, the child has grown into a school-boy, who plays truant, and goes with other young vagabonds to a public-house, where he is initiated into the mysteries of drinking and smoking. The third act displays the " parents' troubles." Edward returns home drunk for the first time, but the offence is frequently repeated, and he is evidently a confirmed drunkard. In the fourth act we have "character lost and turned highwayman"— " murders his master." The fifth act has its " dungeon," the criminal's remorse, the " day of execution," an interminably long leave-taking of the murderer from his family, accompanied by the dismal music of two or three fiddles and flutes out of tune, reverberating sadly through the spacious building. Last of all came the " ignominious death of the drunkard." In Schiller's " Maria Stuart," there is heard, or rather the Earl of Leicester is supposed to hear, the sound of the fatal blow. I was curious to see how the execution would here be managed. It was all true to the life. A gallows was erected, and Jack Ketch (the popular name in England for the hangman) duly made his appearance, bound the delinquent's eyes, and suspended him (or rather a figure substituted for him) in the back-ground. The most remarkable to me were the acclamations and evident delight with which the appearance of Jack Ketch was greeted. " Jack Ketch! Hurrah! Jack Ketch!" as if the hangman had been a popular buffoon or jester. The excitement lasted even for some time, and several oranges and orange-

peels were thrown on the stage, which Jack Ketch might take as he
pleased—as insults or as marks of homage. I observed, however,
that he took them simply for what they were, for he picked up one
of the oranges, and with a slight bow in token of gratitude, put the
fruit in his pocket. There followed a second piece, " *The Drunkard
Reclaimed;* or, *Teetotalism Triumphant*," but I had no inclination
to stop and see it, for the first piece had been quite enough, as a specimen of the way in which the cause of temperance is promoted on
the stage of an English popular theatre; and I think I shall not be
much overstepping the limits of truth, if I assert that one in four of the
spectators of this temperance drama, were to all appearance drunk,
and conducted themselves accordingly.

Such scenes afford no very advantageous idea of the moral condition of the lower classes of Liverpool, and the immense number of
imprisonments that yearly take place, are not calculated to weaken
the impression. According to the report of the Rev. T. Carter, chap-
lain of the borough gaol, no less than 5485 persons were confined
in prison in the course of 1841, making one prisoner for every
twenty-four inhabitants, and yet many arrests at station-houses, &c.,
are not here included. A Mr. Walmsley, a few years ago, estimated
the losses sustained annually by the people of Liverpool from direct
theft, at about 230,000*l.* In 1836 a sub-committee was appointed
by the town council, to investigate the truth of this estimate, and
the report of the committee declared, that so far was the statement
from being overcharged, that the losses were in fact still greater.
According to this report, the cost of her thieves to Liverpool is as
follows:—

1000 grown-up thieves, living entirely by depredations on the public, and gaining each, on an average, 40s. a week, amount annually to	£104,000
500 grown-up persons, living partly by labour and partly by theft, and gaining, on an average, 20s. a week by thieving	26,000
1200 juvenile thieves, at 10s. a week	31,200

The thieves who attach themselves to the docks are
enumerated separately, as:—

70 notorious young thieves under fifteen, making weekly 20s. each, and consequently in the year	3,640
50 hawkers and receivers of stolen goods, either stealing themselves, or encouraging others to do so, and making 20s. each	2,600
100 dock wallopers, at 20s. each	5,200
400 men who assist in unloading ships, and steal either from the passengers or in some other way, to the value of 60s. a week each	62,400
Total for one year	£233,040

or 1,631,280 dollars.

However roughly this calculation may have been made, dealing
wholly with averages and round numbers, it is probably not altogether undeserving of belief, seeing it has been made out by men well
acquainted with the affairs of the town. The only crime here taken
cognisance of is theft. Swindling, and other frauds and violations
of confidence, are left unnoticed. Then we have to consider the

many indirect losses and expenses to which so high a rate of criminality must lead;—public and private watchmen, police, prisons, and other measures for the security of property to be maintained; many business transactions remaining unrealised, through apprehensions of fraud and theft; and many individuals deterred from settling in the town, in consequence of its bad name. In this way the indirect loss occasioned by this vast amount of crime, may amount to millions. In the same report it is stated, for instance, that the houses of ill-fame, whose inmates, for the most part, are addicted to theft, cost the town 499,200*l*. In one house of the kind alone, " the robberies brought before the magistrates in twelve months, involved no less a sum than 1000*l*."

The last day I spent in Liverpool was a Sunday, and I took advantage of the day to visit several churches and chapels, or " places of worship," as the English call them. They are very numerous, but none of them are at all remarkable. The rise of Liverpool happened in the eighteenth century, when few churches were built, and none of any importance. The town has inherited nothing from the church-building middle ages, and could, therefore, derive no advantage from the church-restoring age—the nineteenth century. Including all the innumerable sects which exist in England, the Primitive Methodists, the Wesleyan Methodists, the Independent Methodists, and the New Connexion Methodists; the Baptists and the Welsh Baptists; the Roman Catholics, the Anglo-Catholics, and the mere Catholics, together with many others, whose names I confess myself unable to enumerate; there are in Liverpool 157 churches and chapels, a really large number even for so large a town. The Jewish synagogue makes the number 158. The dissenters are in possession of the greater part. In most of these churches and chapels, divine service begins in the morning at half past ten, and in the evening at half past six. The Roman Catholics only have different hours. The constant increase of the Roman Catholic churches is a remarkable phenomenon. There are now about ten of them, and they are chiefly built for the poor Irish, who are to be found in great numbers in Liverpool. Perhaps in no other English town are there so many Welsh as in Liverpool, where there are no less than twenty chapels in which sermons are preached in the Welsh dialect. It is admitted, however, that this number of Welsh chapels is far greater than is required.

I shall refrain from a description of the marvellous kinds of divine service which I witnessed in some of these chapels, for were I to tell the naked truth on this point, I am sure that many of my readers would look upon me as guilty of a very unbecoming burlesque. One need not, however, go to church in Liverpool to hear a sermon, for there are preachers to be found preaching in the public streets, in the squares, and on the quays about the docks. They are to be seen thus engaged, in fair weather and foul, and are mostly themselves of the lower classes. They mount upon a tar-barrel, or a bale of cotton, and preach and pray in a loud voice, and with the greatest perseverance, whether they succeed in collecting a circle of listeners or not. I listened to one Methodist, who had selected a pulpit such as I have described. He announced, in a sonorous voice, that he had once been himself a drunken blaspheming sailor, and his looks certainly bore out his words; but his understanding, he went on to say, had been enlightened, and his eyes opened. " And you, do you now go, and have your eyes opened. Go, and be converted, and you also will see what truth is, even as I, a miserable sinner, have seen it. But who is there that can do this to you? Do you suppose I can? I, a poor wretched sinner! No! Can your parish priest? No, he may be a very good man, but he has none but human force. It is Christ alone who can open your eyes for you. Hold still to him, and he will bring the work about, as he has brought it about with me, sinner that I am. You need do nothing towards it yourselves but stand still. The thing will cost you no trouble, no labour, no pain, no shilling, no penny. Keep yourselves still, and your eyes will be opened, and you will yourselves wonder at the glory and the splendour that will be unfolded to you." Policemen, armed with their staves, hover about the groups that gather around such preachers, because disturbances sometimes take place. Properly speaking, however, the police ought to be instructed to prevent such people from preaching at all. These fellows have such confined and grovelling notions of religion, that they are utterly unconscious of their own unworthiness to pronounce the sacred words and names that are constantly on their lips, and are bawled out by them in the most familiar manner in the public streets.

The most remarkable church in Liverpool is the floating chapel, lying in the middle of the docks. It is a large East Indiaman, of 800 tons, that has been bought by the Bethel Union, and fitted up for a congregation of 600 persons. I found here white, black, and brown Christians assembled in prayer. The congregation consisted chiefly of sailors.

The silent English Sunday is followed by the animated Monday, the greatest drinking day in the week, and the busy Saturday has gone before, the great market day of England. On this day it is, that a stranger should visit the markets, which offer the most interesting scenes of popular bustle and traffic. These market halls, things unknown to us in Germany, because with us the articles disposed of in such places, are usually bought and sold in the open air, are in England also of recent origin. In almost every English town a market hall was shown me, and I was always told at the same time that it had only been recently erected. The market-halls of Liverpool, buildings admirably suited to the purpose they are intended for, were all erected in 1822, 1831, and 1841. The largest is St. John's market. This is a building covering 8200 square yards, and must therefore contain space enough to allow

8000 persons to buy and sell there with tolerable convenience. The light roof is supported by 116 slender iron columns, and like most of the distinguished buildings of the town, has been constructed after the design of a Liverpool architect, Mr. Foster, whose name was continually repeated to me, and whose works, wherever I saw them, appeared excellent o me. In the evening the whole is lighted with gas, and looks really very brilliant, considering the homely nature of the merchandise exposed there for sale.

WALES.

I cannot tell how many flags were hoisted on the following morning at the different piers of Liverpool, to inform the several passengers where to look for the Glasgow boat, the Isle of Man boat, the Dublin boat, the Cork boat, the Pembroke boat, and all the rest of them. I for my part ranged myself under the flag of Bangor, the most frequented place of transit, to those about to visit North Wales. Uninvited assistants, among whom no doubt were some of the thieves of whom I spoke a few pages back, together with beggars, and other importunate solicitors, surrounded us, and took care that our roses on that morning should not be without thorns. Newsmen offered us the news of the same morning. Others had telescopes for those who wished to contemplate the Welsh coast at their ease. Oranges and gingerbread, with other delicacies of the same kind, were hawked about, and altogether the noise and apparent confusion were enough to make a man run away in despair. The steamers, meanwhile, were humming, hissing, and shrieking around us, but with all their noise and well-known vigour, they lay not the less quiet and orderly at their several places, and gradually as the ear and eye became familiarised with it, the noisy bustling scene became a source of amusement and pleasurable excitement.

" The mouth of the Mersey" is armed with light-houses, land marks, beacons, telegraph stations, and private signal poles, as a mouth with teeth. The Rock Lighthouse is the most important, the most solid, and the handsomest of all these erections, so I was not surprised to learn that Mr. Foster had contributed the design. It is built of hard granite from the island of Anglesey. The stones are all dovetailed into one another, and the whole has been united into one solid mass by a cement of volcanic origin. The coloured light thrown out at night upon the ocean, is said to be one of the most brilliant along the whole English coast. When we passed the place the windows were carefully closed, that the powerful reflecting mirrors might not, by concentrating the rays of the sun, act as a burning-glass, and so perhaps give occasion to a fire somewhere or other.

On account of the frequent fogs to which the English coast is liable, peculiar precautionary arrangements have been deemed necessary, that will probably never be thought necessary on the confines of more sunny regions, such as Arabia, Persia, &c. Among these means of precaution, the fog bells deserve to be first mentioned. These bells are fixed upon empty casks or buoys, and as these are tossed to and fro by the waves, the bells toll in single irregular strokes, to warn the seaman of his proximity to rocks and sandbanks, when the fog makes it impossible for him to see them, or even to distinguish the lighthouses. He is thus enabled, when he can no longer *see* his danger, at least to *hear* it. The steamboats have likewise adopted precautionary signals to prevent accidents during a fog. They have their " fog-whistles," for instance, which are connected with the steam-engine, and every now and then, in foggy weather, send forth a few shrill piercing notes over the bosom of the ocean.

We were soon out at sea, but even there on the waste of salt water I saw more smoking chimneys at one glance than I had seen altogether on the Steppes of Southern Russia. The chimneys I allude to were those of the various steamers hastening to and from Liverpool. Each observed its line of way, as strictly as if it had been marked out for her by a regular macadamised road. Our line passed at no great distance from the north coast of Wales. We looked into the mouth of the Dee, a wide, hollow, lifeless space, whence nothing proceeds, now that Chester has become so interesting to the antiquarian. The weather was beautiful as we rounded Orme's Head, a Welsh promontory that stretches far into the sea, while sea birds and rock-pigeons flutter around its chalky summit. We then passed into the Bay of Beaumaris, and dropped anchor in the middle of the Menai Strait. I landed immediately along with another passenger, in whose company I proposed on the following day to ascend Snowdon, the highest of the Welsh mountains, and with whom, meanwhile, I started for Caernarvon, the more immediate place of our destination. We hired a small boat in which we sailed a little way up the strait, and then landed at a place whence a carriage conveyed us along the coast to Caernarvon. On the watery element, where we might so easily have got wet, we remained perfectly dry, but we had scarcely set foot on dry land when we were drenched to the skin, a heavy rain coming on, which never ceased till we and our open carriage had arrived at Caernarvon, where we were well pleased to obtain at length the shelter of a roof, a shelter of which we stood no longer in need when we had it, for as soon as we were housed the rain ceased.

We saw the Menai Strait under very unfavourable circumstances; nevertheless we saw enough to convince us of the interest and agreeable variety afforded by its banks, beautifully wooded acclivities, while the naked mountains rise in stately majesty behind. The Anglesey side is more flat and monotonous; and indeed Anglesey, though on the maps it appears as a part of Wales, is of a

conformation so different from that of the principality, that it
might with fairness be treated as a different country. The Menai
Strait is always animated by the presence of vessels engaged in the
exportation of slates, the staple produce of Wales. These Welsh
slates are of such excellent quality, that they have obtained
the preference throughout England, and every little harbour along
the coast is full of vessels taking in cargoes of slates.

It is to a work of human hands, however, to a work of our own
times, that the Menai Strait owes its wide-spread fame. I allude to
the Menai Bridge, which crosses the narrowest part of the strait,
and unites Anglesey and Caernarvonshire, but which was built chiefly
as an improvement to the main road through North Wales and Anglesey to Holyhead, whence the principal packets start for Ireland.
This narrowest part of the Menai Strait is supposed to have formerly
been an isthmus, for even in the time of the Romans, it is said, the
Roman and British cavalry were able to ride across at low water.
At present the channel is deep enough to allow coasting vessels of
all sizes to pass through, at any period of the tide. This bridge, as
most of my readers are probably aware, is a chain suspension bridge,
but its dimensions are so enormous, that they cannot fail to excite
wonder. It is supported by sixteen chains, each of the length of
1714 feet, and made fast at each end in the solid rock. These chains
are supported at each end by two immense columns, whose bases
rest in the sea. From the surface of the sea, at high water, these
columns rise 156 feet, but to the roadway of the bridge only 103
feet. On the top of each column is a large roller, over which the
chains are passed, to allow of the contraction of the metal in winter,
and its expansion in summer. The length of the roadway of the
bridge is 1000 feet, and it is borne by 796 iron bars made fast to
the chains. Coasting vessels can pass under the bridge with all
their sails set.

Magnificent, however, as all these figures appear on paper, the
proportions of the bridge often produce an impression of disappoint-
ment when seen for the first time. The mountains of Wales, the
vast plains of Anglesey, the long Menai Strait, and the open ocean
on the other side, are all of such vast dimensions, that the wonderful achievement of human science appears lessened by the comparison; but when we come close to the bridge, when we pass over it,
and yet more when we sail under it, an impression is produced
quite in accordance with the greatness of the work, and the genius
which alone could triumph over the difficulties of the undertaking.

It was towards evening that we arrived at Caernarvon, the chief
town of the county, and one of the largest in Wales. Like most
Welsh towns, it contains a mixed population of native Welsh and
English residents, and being surrounded by slate quarries, its chief
commerce is in that article, one apparently insignificant, but which,
like many a branch of British manufacture, acquires immediate importance in our eyes, when we are told whither it is carried for sale.

Ask a Birmingham button maker whither his buttons go, and his immediate answer will probably be,—" All over the world, sir." Ask a similar question of a maker of crockery in the Staffordshire Potteries, and you will receive the same answer; and here in Caernarvon, when I asked where all the slates went to, I was again told that they went " all over the world." They are so excellent, it seems, break into such large pieces, are so elastic, so little apt to crumble, so black, and their colour, at the same time, so durable that there is a demand for them " all over the world," particularly of late years, so much so that slates have become the staple article of produce for North, as iron is for South Wales. A native writer, speaking of the prospects held out by this trade of recent growth, says : " Among the various causes which, in the last few years have effected a great alteration in the condition of North Wales, those most deserving of mention are the slates and slate quarries, and the great and growing demand for the excellent material found in this part of the country. The several quarries give occupation to some thousands of workmen, promoting, at the same time the well being of all classes, and leading to the improvement of roads, and to the establishment of other conveniences for travellers and internal communication. These circumstances have given birth in North Wales to a spirit of activity and speculation, that must lead to important results, and has, indeed, in some measure already had that effect. The means of land and water carriage have been greatly increased, and this remark applies particularly to the increased number of steamboats. New interests starting into life, compete with the old establishments long in possession of public patronage. Good inns and public carriages spring up in the wildest districts and the most remote mountain passes. Commerce has already so far advanced in its work of improvement, that many articles of luxury and comfort, rarely seen here a few years ago, and scarcely known among us, even to the world of fashion, are now to be seen in the greatest abundance.

In all directions, in this part of the country, the mountains may be seen to have been bitten into by the slate quarries. The largest and most famous of them all is that of Llandegais, six miles from Bangor, formerly the property of Lord Penrhyn, but now of Mr. Pennant. The number of workmen employed there (in 1842) exceeded 2000; a gentleman from Liverpool, commercially connected with the quarry, said the number was at least 2500. This quarry has its own seaport, Port Penrhyn, capable of sheltering vessels of 300 and 400 tons, whence the slates are shipped direct for North America, as well as for all parts of Great Britain. This may afford some idea of the importance of the quarry, as well as the fact that the railroads, and inclined planes, constructed for the conveyance of the slates from the quarry to the harbour, cost Lord Penrhyn no less a sum than 170,000*l*. Immense masses of slate are here detached by the aid of powder, or of hammer, wedge, and crowbar, and the rude shapeless mass is then fashioned on the spot into the forms in which it is afterwards intended to be used, into school slates and slates for roofs, into chimney-pieces, gravestones, table slabs, &c.

No other slate quarry is equal in importance to that of Mr. Pennant, yet I was told of several that employed 500 workmen, and of one in which upwards of 1000 were employed. The several quarries alone, of which the produce was shipped from the town of Caernarvon, I was assured, gave occupation to at least 2300 men. Slates form, in fact, the chief article of export from the place, and indeed the only one, with the exception of some copper from the neighbouring copper mines. About the pretty new quay I saw nothing but slates, and the vessels, large and small, that lay in the picturesque harbour, were all going to receive cargoes of countesses, marchionesses, princesses, duchesses, and queens. These are the vain-glorious titles that have been given to the various descriptions of an article in itself of so little intrinsic value. Nor must it be supposed that these are mere fanciful titles applied by an individual; they are the names current in the trade, and in the price currents the several descriptions of slates are regularly ranged according to the table of precedence, as: Imperials, Queens, Princesses, Duchesses, Marchionesses, Ladies, Fat Ladies, and a few others equally whimsical.

Wherever any thing new springs up in England, a number of active hands and inventive heads are immediately in requisition, to improve and extend the sphere of its utility. Such has been the case with the article of slates. This stone, though not to be reckoned among the precious ones, has the advantage of great cheapness, and of being easily worked, and somebody in London has lately invented a process of polishing it, so as to give it the appearance of the finest black marble. Another has succeeded in turning it, and certainly these inventions seem calculated to increase very much the demand for the article, particularly in England, which is any thing but rich in the finer descriptions of stone. As slate can be split into very thin tablets, there is no difficulty in imagining that it may be worked up into neater and more delicate pieces of furniture and ornament than stones of a more brittle kind. I saw in London, at the exhibition of slate furniture, wardrobes, escritoires, tables, &c., of the most elegant form and workmanship. They looked like the finest ebony and black marble. The chief uses, however, to which slates are applied are to covering the roofs of houses, and then as tombstones and chimney-pieces; but it is probable that they will, in time, come to be applied to many other uses.

Caernarvon Castle is the most interesting object which the town has to show to strangers. It is one of the largest and handsomest ruined castles that Wales, rich as she is in ruins, has to boast of. This ruin lay almost opposite the door of our inn, and we accordingly climbed up to it that very evening. The castle, though it is said to have been built within the space of one year, does not look less solid than other castles of the middle ages, and in spite of the six centuries during which the tooth of Time, and the artillery of man have been at work upon it, the castle, with its massy walls and numerous turrets, holds itself still stately and upright, and continues to present a very imposing appearance. It is the castle, famous in British history, that was built by King Edward I., the conqueror of Wales, and in which his wife, Queen Eleonora, was delivered of the first Prince of Wales, afterwards King Edward II. The room is still shown in which this important birth occurred. The king, in presenting the native Welch prince to the proud chiefs of the country, used the Welch words *Eych dyn* (this is the man), which have since been preserved as the motto of each succeeding Prince of Wales. The words are now written *Ich dien*, whence many have supposed them to be of German origin, and to signify, " I serve." There is another version of the story. Over these enigmatical words wave the ostrich feathers which constitute the crest of the Prince of Wales, said to owe its origin to the plume which Edward the Black Prince, at Cressy, plucked from the helmet of King John of Bohemia. In England, not only the Prince of Wales, however, but almost every child, wears ostrich feathers, if not in his crest at least in his hat, and I should like to know, whether this mass of ostrich feathers, with which the heads of little English children are so overladen, may not be in some measure a fashion taken from the prince's plume. In an English caricature the little Prince of Wales may always be known by his nodding feathers.

From the Eagle Tower, to which we ascend by 158 steps, our eyes wandered over the flat plains of Anglesey, beyond which the sun was just sinking into the sea. I remained till the sun had set completely, and till a number of small white owls, the resident inhabitants of the castle, began to flutter about the tower, and then abandoned myself to the pleasure of studying the tones of a language entirely new to me, but which here in North Wales continues to be everywhere spoken in its ancient purity.

People generally suppose that as in a language there are usually from twenty to twenty-four letters, there are only the same number of tones; but these are liable to so many modifications, that it may be taken for granted, there are in every language, at least 100 elementary tones, and if the different languages spoken in the world are attended to, many thousand such tones will be discovered. I gave myself a great deal of trouble yet could not at all succeed in articulating the marvellously rough and difficult sounds of the Welsh tongue, and my English companion seemed to find the thing just as difficult as I did. The *ll*, so liquid and melting from Spanish lips, is remarkably hard and difficult in Welsh. The *l* appeared to me to be followed by a guttural sound from the very bottom of the throat, except at the beginning of a word, where the guttural seemed to precede the *l;* and yet it was not a purely guttural tone, for when I listened very attentively I thought I could distinguish something like the sound of a *t* before the guttural. We also encounter again in the Welsh language the tone which gives foreigners so much trouble in English, and which is represented by *th* in English, and by *dd* in

Welsh. This sound the English certainly did not receive either from the Angles, the Saxons, or the Normans, but have probably retained from the original Celtic language.

South Wales is less mountainous and much more anglicised than the northern half of the principality, where, in the wild secluded valleys the old Celtic Welsh or Kymbrish has been preserved in greater purity, and not the language only, but the manners of the people likewise. Thus in a large town like Caernarvon, half the population speak only Welsh, and in the country round about, few people are to be found who can understand more than a few words of English. I entered several cottages near the town, but could nowhere make myself understood. Even the children who begged on the road had but two words of English—" halfpenny, sir"—which they pronounced so well, we were surprised to find their knowledge extend no further. Even at the places where we changed horses, in this part of Wales and in Anglesey, I always observed that the coachman spoke to the ostlers and other servants of the inn, only in Welsh. I never made a similar observation in Ireland or in the Scottish Highlands, on any main road. Even in our inn at Caernarvon, the servants spoke but a broken kind of English, and never addressed one another except in Welsh. Nothing like this either do I remember to have seen in Ireland or in the Highlands. Yet considering the relative positions of the different parts of the United Kingdom, it is certainly surprising that the Celtic language should have offered so much more energetic a resistance to the English in Wales than either in Scotland or Ireland. In Ireland it is supposed that only one-third of the population are able to speak Irish, and this calculation, many think, is rather over than under the truth. I have in no English work met with any similar estimate respecting Wales, yet I think I am far within the mark, if I reverse the calculation, and assume that, in North Wales at least, not more than one-third of the inhabitants can speak English. I have already mentioned that in Liverpool there were no less than twenty chapels in which the Welsh language was used, and yet Liverpool is not a Welsh town; neither in Cork nor in Dublin would there be found any thing approaching to that number of chapels in which sermons are delivered in the native Irish language. Firm, however, as has been the resistance offered by the Welsh language, it has, of late years, been giving way very rapidly. The kindred dialects of Cumberland, Lancashire, and Cornwall, were a kind of outwork to Welsh, and they vanished altogether, early in the last century. Since then the Welsh language has been constantly attacked in its own fastnesses. English luxury, going hand in hand with industry and commerce, has extended even into the mountains; the roads and other means of internal intercourse have been improved; but it is by the establishment of good schools that the amalgamation with the mother country will be completed. In these schools, now springing up in all parts, the Welsh language, it is true, is everywhere used as a medium of instruction, nevertheless, as the knowledge of English is felt to carry with it many advantages, when the people have been taught to read and write Welsh with facility, and have had their intelligence awakened, the importance of the predominant language will become more and more sensibly felt by them, and greater efforts will constantly be made to acquire it.

My companion with whom I spent the evening at Caernarvon, was of opinion that a close affinity existed between the Welsh and the Tyrolese. He told me he had been in the Tyrol, and had there remarked the admiration with which his servant, a native of Wales, observed everywhere the Tyrolese, their manners, and their costume, and everywhere discovered something that reminded him of home. In some of the valleys of the Tyrol, he said, his Welsh servant was even able to understand the language of the place, and to make himself understood by the people. Upon these facts my companion grounded an opinion, that the Tyrolese and the Welsh must be one and the same people. His opinion seemed to me the more deserving of attention, as he was no scholar, nor at all pre-occupied by learned theories. He understood nothing of German, knew very little of the distribution of the Celtic race, and nothing of the various dialects spoken in the Tyrolese valleys. In these dialects, even among those who speak German, it is a well-known fact that a great many old Celtic words occur. Indeed, a part of the Tyrolese may be looked on as a tribe of German-speaking Celts. These Celtic words, no doubt, caught the ear of the Welsh servant. Much that is Celtic, it is equally true, has been preserved in the manners of the Tyrolese, and I am not surprised that the Welsh servant should be struck by a multitude of things that reminded him of home. The love of music, poetry, and song, is common to the Welsh and the Tyrolese, not merely because they are both mountaineers, but, probably in consequence of their common Celtic origin. In the costume I also was struck by many similarities, such as the round, high, tapering, black beaver hat of the Welsh women, which is seen nowhere else in Great Britain, nor anywhere in Germany, except in the Tyrol. The Welsh women enjoy also in England the same reputation for personal attraction, or rather for the want of it, as the Tyrolese in Germany. In some parts of Wales, too, I am told, the men wear the same kind of short breeches as in the Tyrol, covering merely the thighs, without reaching to the knees. This naturally makes one think of the kilt of a Scottish Highlander, who disdains breeches altogether, seeming to indicate among the Celtic tribes, the most remote from one another, a general distaste for the nether habiliment. When I then thought of the bacon dumplings of the Tyrolese, of their millet porridge, buttermilk, and hard bread, and then turned to Leigh's book on Wales, and read that the Welsh " are very abstemious, bacon, oatmeal porridge, sour milk, potatoes, and a hard, heavy kind of black bread, being their chief food, I

was almost inclined to agree with my companion that there must be
a very close affinity between the two races. " The Tyrolese are
famous in Germany," said I, " for their quickness to quarrel and
take offence." " There we have it again. Precisely the character
of our Welshmen: quarrelsome, violent, a most violent people."—
Temperate as the Welsh are, in general, it seems they are apt to
be guilty of much intemperance at their weddings, fairs, and other
festivities, when explosions and quarrels are by no means uncommon.
Camden, perhaps, may have had some notion of this affinity between
the Welsh and the Tyrolese, when he spoke of the Welsh mountains as the *Alpes Britannicae*, a title which the sublimity of nature
in this part of the world certainly does not warrant. We might
just as reasonably call the Lake of Constance the Bavarian ocean, as
magnify the Welsh hills into Alps.

On the following morning we started for Snowdon, the tallest of
these Welsh Alps, whose summit is about ten miles from Caernarvon. To reach the foot of the mountain we hired a small gig,
and, as the morning was beautiful, we had an agreeable drive to the
inn in the vale and village of Llanberris, which to Snowdon is
what Chamouny is to Mont Blanc. Here we prepared ourselves
for the ascent by a hearty breakfast, and then joined a large party
of English sight-seers, of whom there is always a considerable
influx into Wales at this season of the year, intent on seeing all
the waterfalls and views of the country, not forgetting its valleys
and its 126 ruined castles. These tourists have increased greatly
in numbers since the facilities of internal intercourse have been so
greatly increased. They are mostly people whose time or pecuniary
means do not allow of continental excursions, and who are therefore forced to content themselves with looking on the beauties of
their own country. Be this as it may, I was myself very well satisfied with my companions, agreeable, well-bred people, who entered with the true spirit into the enjoyment of the scenes around
them.

Behind our inn was a slate quarry, to which we first directed our
attention. In this quarry, we were told, upwards of 1000 persons
were employed. There were several smaller quarries in the neighbourhood, and from all of them we heard a constant succession of
explosions of gunpowder, and an almost uninterrupted noise caused
by the slate slabs rolling down the hills. That on which the great
quarry was situated, had already been cut into a succession of terraces to the height of 1000 feet, connected by a flight of steps each
a hundred feet high, and on each the busy work of breaking and
blowing up the stone was going on merrily. On several the blocks
of slate were undergoing their metamorphoses into duchesses and
princesses, and were then sent down, in large masses along the slanting
railroads that wound themselves around the hill. One of their chief
customers, some of the persons employed on the works told me,
was the colony of the Cape of Good Hope, where, to judge from

the great demand that has lately sprung up, almost every house must by this time be roofed with slates.

In the vale of Llanberris are two long narrow lakes, in which, I was informed "real beauties" of fish were to be caught, but the land beauty that was wont to charm these water beauties from their limpid retreat has quitted the scene of her protracted triumphs. She was a woman of great celebrity, and died here in 1801, at the age of 105. Her name was Margaret uch Evan, but she was generally known by the more familiar appellation of Peggy. According to Mr. Pennant, one of the best describers of Wales, Peggy had at least a dozen of sporting dogs on her establishment, and all excellent in their kind. She killed every year a good round number of foxes, plied her oar with a vigorous hand, and was the undisputed lady of the lakes. She played the fiddle moreover, admirably, and was well acquainted with all the old Welsh music. Nor did she neglect the mechanical arts, for she was a good carpenter, and at the age of seventy she was still so good a wrestler, that few young men would venture to try a throw with her. She shod her own horses, made her own shoes, and built and repaired the boats in which she used to convey the copper down the lake from the mines. All the neighbouring bards of the 18th century (she was born in 1696) had tuned their lyres to celebrate her achievements, yet she gave her hand at last to the most effeminate of all her admirers, as if determined, even in matrimony, to maintain the superiority with which she felt nature had invested her.

The heights by which we ascended to the summit of Snowdon were perfectly naked, and without a vestige of wood. At the bottom the valley was covered with fragments of rock, but a little further up was grass, a great relief to the pedestrian. These pastures were everywhere occupied by sheep, grazing in a perfectly wild state, unguarded either by dog or shepherd. The animals, we were told, were accustomed to this way of life, and if taken into England began immediately to pine away. Nay at times when carried away and sold at the other side of the border, they would often run away, and find their way back to their native hills. Formerly goats were more generally kept than sheep, and Wales was as famous for her goats, as the Tyrol for her chamois, and goats are still everywhere to be seen here ; but in proportion as agriculture and horticulture improve and extend, the goat falls into disfavour, and the sheep supersedes him. The sheep is not only more useful, but also much less mischievous, the goat being not only a bad gardener, but also a bad farmer.

A little higher up, we were shown a level meadow, placed at a tolerably high elevation, and called Consultation Hill, or Foylcynhnorion, where the old Welsh chiefs were wont to assemble and deliberate, when at war with the English. The meadow bears a striking resemblance to the Rütli, on which the three Swiss heroes swore their patriotic oath.

The summits of these hills are generally moist, and even after the dry summer of 1842, we still found places that were wet. This humidity and consequent slipperiness of their hills, gave the ancient Welsh many advantages in defending them against their Saxon assailants, who found it difficult to maintain their footing on such unaccustomed ground.

On our way, we passed several copper mines, among which lay many small lakes, the water of which had been dyed green by the metal. The place was surrounded by sheep, but the creatures, they assured us, had too much sagacity ever to taste the poisonous water. There are numbers of these small lakes among the mountains, and some even in very elevated parts. Two of the Snowdon lakes enjoyed at one time considerable fame on the strength of popular belief, that assigned to one of them a floating and erratic island, and to the other a stock of one-eyed fishes.

Like most elevated points,—like Mont Blanc, the Imaus, Davalaghiri, and others, which the people are accustomed to see wrapped in snow, it is to snow that Snowdon (the snow down) stands indebted for its name. The name is Saxon, but the old Cambrian name, Craig Eryri, has, according to Camden, precisely the same signification. It is strange that while so many objects of minor importance should have retained their native denominations, that the whole country (Wales) and the highest mountain in it, should have been named by the conquerors. Wales is a general Germanic term for the Celtic lands ; the old British name is Cambria, or Kymria.

The mountain tapered at last into a complete cone, terminating in a summit, on which there was just room enough to spread out a tent for the protection of some mathematical instruments. The soldiers in charge of this tent, erected with a view to a new survey of the country, had constructed a small path of stones around their canvass mansion, and thus it became easy to enjoy the prospect on every side. The officer of engineers in command of the post had pitched several tents, a little lower down, for the accommodation of himself and his men.

For an extensive prospect Snowdon is quite a unique point in England. There are higher mountains in Scotland, for Snowdon is only 3571 feet high, and Ben Nevis 4370, but these Scotch mountains, though higher, enjoy a much more limited prospect, because they are either hemmed in by other mountains, or are situated at the extremity of Great Britain, so that the prospect from their summits ranges chiefly over the ocean, which affords but little variety. Snowdon, on the contrary, lies right in the centre of the British world, and commands from its summit, views at once of England, Scotland, Ireland, and Wales, and of the intermediate islands of Anglesey and Man. The atmosphere around these English mountains, to be sure, is seldom clear enough to allow one the full enjoyment of the whole horizon. The officer told me that during the two months he had spent on Snowdon, he had not seen

the coast of Ireland more than four times, and yet the summer in
England, as elsewhere, had been a remarkably beautiful one. The
highest point to which the thermometer had risen during the months
of July and August, had been seventy-four degrees of Fahrenheit.
We had on the whole very favourable weather, for we were neither
incommoded by fog nor rain, but large masses of cloud swept by the
summit, affording us only at intervals delightful views of the slate
teeming mountains of Wales, or the Irish Sea, covered with sailing
vessels and steamers, and of the flat and sandy Isles of Anglesey and
Man. Our officer of engineers told us that the breed of eagles on
Snowdon had now been completely extirpated, though many of the
birds were still to be found there only a few years ago. Even the
old Cambrian name of the mountain, Craig Eryri, which, according
to Camden, as I have already said, signifies the same as Snowdon,
is derived by others from another Welsh word, from Craig Eryrod,
or the Hill of the Eagles.

On our return we visited several of the huts of the Welsh mountaineers, of the " Kymrag, Kymrag," as they called themselves,
when, with a shake of the head, they endeavoured to intimate their
ignorance of the English language in which we addressed them.
These huts, which, on account of their wretchedness, are spoken of
by the English with little respect, are nevertheless very superior to
the cabins of the Irish peasantry, or of the Scottish Highlanders,
and reminded me strongly of the Russian houses in the Ukraine,
partly on account of the manner in which they were whitewashed
all over. The Welsh, I was told, had inherited from their forefathers, the ancient Silures, the habit of whitewashing their houses
every year. This gives them at least the appearance of great neatness, sometimes indeed too much so, for in their zeal to make all
things white, they often whitewash wall, roof, window-frames, and
door, and even then extend their favours to hedge, pigsty, and
every other dependency of the little establishment.

In the afternoon, we extended our excursions further into the
interior of Wales. We hired a large open carriage, sufficient for
the accommodation of our whole party, and drove through the celebrated Pass of Llanberris, arriving, towards evening, at Beddgelart,
a delightful little place to the south of Snowdon. The Welsh must
really be a very pious people, to judge from the fact that the names
of more than half their towns and villages are composed with the
syllable *llan*, which signifies *church*. On my map of Caermarthen-
shire, I find sixty-three names of places, and forty-two of them,
consequently two-thirds, are composed with *llan*.

The Pass of Llanberris (the Welsh call it Cwm Glas, or the Blue
Valley) is a very wild piece of mountain scenery, and my London
companions were in a constant state of wonder and delight as they
contemplated it. Nevertheless, there were too many small fragments of rock, and too few openings on a large scale, to allow of

this pass being placed on a level with any of the mighty passes of our Alps. Then the rocks are altogether naked and desolate, and there is no soft scenery to set off the wilder parts, and make us feel the beauties of both by the contrast. The half-wild sheep, of which I have already spoken, were seen scattered over all the surrounding mountains and rocks.

Beddgelart is a pretty little village, surrounded by fresh meadows and fine large trees, and is charmingly situated in the centre of an amphitheatre of hills, at a point where three valleys meet. We found there an inn with all the comforts and accommodations of an English country-house, and as much life and bustle as an exchange. It was fair day, and a multitude of people were collected from the surrounding country; "most violent people," but virtuous withal, if we may judge from the parliamentary criminal returns, from which it appears, with all their quarrels, that murder, theft, and similar crimes, are of less frequent occurrence in Wales than in any other part of the United Kingdom.

In all the twelve counties of Wales, according to the returns alluded to, there were 371 persons convicted of crime in 1841, whereas, during the same year, there were single counties in England—Lancashire and Middlesex for instance—where the convictions were nearly 3000, and even above that number.

The population of Wales that year being 911,321, it follows that of 2400 inhabitants, one was convicted of crime.

In all England, exclusive of Wales, there were in that year, 19,909 convictions, and 14,999,508 inhabitants; consequently, of 750 inhabitants one was a criminal.

The criminality of Wales, therefore, compared with that of England, was in the proportion of 750 to 2400.

If we compare Wales with Lancashire, the most criminal of all the English counties, we find that the said county had in the same year 3137 criminals, and 1,667,024 inhabitants, consequently one criminal to 530 inhabitants, making a degree of criminality four times greater than that of Wales.

Even if we take Westmorland, the least criminal of all the English counties, we find twenty-eight criminals in a population of 56,469, which still shows a greater degree of criminality than all Wales.

South Wales, the more cultivated and anglicised part of the principality, is more fertile in crime than North Wales. The worst county is Glamorganshire, with 193,462 inhabitants, and 136 convictions, or one criminal in 1300 inhabitants; this is a degree of criminality double that of all Wales, but still only half that of all England.

The two counties in Wales most free from crime were Anglesey and Merionethshire, in each of which, during the last eight years, there had been, on an average, six or seven convicted criminals, being one for every 7000 inhabitants.

Most of the above facts are borrowed from the returns of 1841, but these are accompanied by similar returns for the eight preceding years, which present results nearly the same.

We spent a very agreeable evening at Beddgelart. The brightly illuminated little fair, encircled by the black forms of the mountains, appeared to great advantage. There was a negress in a van, who was shown for a halfpenny, and a " royal shooting gallery," where there was abundance of shooting with cross bows, with large heaps of hazel nuts for prizes. These seemed to afford an infinity of diversion. The peasants were mostly of short stature, with broad fresh-coloured cheeks, and the women, if not beautiful, were at least cheerful and pleasing. When, to crown the whole scene, the moons rose in all her majesty over this remote valley, my cockney friends could not control their admiration and enthusiasm, and " beautiful!" " magnificent!" " glorious!" resounded on all sides, amid the mountains of Beddgelart.

Nothing interested me more strongly at our hotel than a harper whom I saw there, who was almost always sitting in the hall, and playing his old native melodies. He was a regular member of the establishment, engaged for the entertainment of the guests. He played in a masterly style, and I was never tired of listening to him. His harp too was a splendid instrument; like all Welsh harps it had three rows of strings, and I could not but admire the dexterity with which the artist passed his fingers in, between the outer to touch the centre strings, which, however, are, in general, but little used. The playing on the harp (in Welsh *Chwareu'r Telyn*) belonged in the olden time to the twenty-four most esteemed games of the ancient Britons, as cited by Williams in his " Observations on Snowdonia." These twenty-four games were divided into several classes. First came the domestic games : *Bardoniaeth*, or poetical composition ; the harp ; the reading of Kymrian books ; Singing to the harp ; *Penmillion*, or the alternate singing of three or four individuals ; heraldry ; and lastly, drawing and painting, which were chiefly devoted to the illustration of heraldry. Then came the *Gurolgampan*, or manly sports, such as lifting weights, riding, running, swimming, jumping, casting the spear, and shooting with the bow.

In Scotland the caverns are still shown, which, on memorable occasions, afforded shelter to Robert Bruce or to other Scottish worthies, and even so in Wales the caverns continue to be pointed out, where Owen Glyndwr, or some other hero with an unpronounceable name, concealed himself on the occasion of some inroad into England. Such a cavern was shown us near Beddgelart. Every spot in Wales, however, seems fertile in legendary lore ; quite as much so as Scotland. The very place at which we were—Beddgelart—owed its name to the legend of Gelart, the faithful dog of Prince Llewelyn, who killed the noble animal in the belief that it had torn his child to pieces; but when the cradle was raised, the infant was found underneath unhurt, and a dead wolf killed by Gelart. Llewelyn, in his

grief erected a monument to his dog, and a priory, that was shortly
afterwards built there, assumed the name of Beddgelart,—the grave
of Gelart.

ANGLESEY.

As it was my intention to proceed to Ireland through Anglesey, I
returned over Caernarvon to Bangor, an episcopal city, and the most
ancient after St. David's, the Welsh Canterbury.

Immediately beyond Bangor, we passed over Menai Bridge, and
had now an opportunity of contemplating this noble monument from
a different point of view. It is a real pleasure to pass over it, for
though the whole floats in the air like a spider's web, when seen from
below, it assumes all the firmness and solidity of a rock on nearer
inspection. It is only when the wind is very high, and then only
towards the centre of the bridge, that any vibration is felt.

Here then, thought I, when we had passed the bridge is the famous
isle of Mona! We left the picturesque mountains of North Wales
behind us, and rolled into what appeared to be a wild yet monotonous country, bleak, bare, and destitute of natural ornament. The
way to Holyhead passes in a diagonal line from one corner of Anglesey to the opposite corner, and certainly, to judge from what I saw
along this road, the celebrated Mona has few of those natural charms
to recommend it, with which fancy has led history to endow it.
Much more accurate is the description of Giraldus : *Tellus arida et
saxosa videtur, deformis aspectu et inamoena.* Its fertility indeed is
justly lauded, but even the decorations of a highly cultivated land are
wanting. Trim hedges like those of England are nowhere to be seen,
and the cottages are without neatness. The whole looks like a land
of transition between England and Ireland. Fine trees and stately
groves, that serve so well to relieve the monotony of a flat country,
are nowhere to be seen. Paulinus Suetonius, who, according to
Tacitus, cut down the druidical forests of Mona, (*exisique luci saevis
superstitionibus sacri*) must have performed his work of destruction
with wonderful effect. There are two or three hills in the island, but
they are of trifling elevation. The two usually pointed out to strangers are Holyhead and Parys mountain, the latter celebrated for its
productive copper mines, but both together are only a few hundred
feet in height. Yet these two hills are constantly pointed out
to a stranger's attention. If you enter the Menai Strait, in the
steamer from Liverpool, the first things the captain points out to his
passengers are Parys mountain and Holyhead; nay, from the summit
of Snowdon, whence you see Anglesey spread out like a map, Parys
mountain and Holyhead were the first objects to which the officer
of engineers called my attention. The island, as I have already observed, is, nevertheless, famed for its fertility ; so much so as to have
obtained among the Welsh the honourable distinction of being denominated " *Mona mam Cymbry*" (Mona the Mother of Cambria).

To the left of Menai Bridge we saw Plas Newydd, the celebrated residence of the Marquis of Anglesey, to whom a large part of the island belongs. This marquis is another of the 300,000*l.* a year men. He lost his leg at Waterloo, and near his mansion, on a rock close to Menai Strait, a column, 100 feet high has been erected in honour of him. These magnificent private monuments are peculiar to England.

Holyhead, the only striking object in a flat landscape, and visible, therefore, from a great distance, could scarcely escape being declared *holy*. It was probably a very ancient seat of Druidical worship. It has in more recent times become known as the most convenient point of embarkation for Ireland, and in proportion as the communication between the two countries has increased, a small fishing village has grown up into a handsome town. On the rocks around, large light-houses have arisen united by elegant suspension-bridges, that have taken the place of the rope bridges formerly in use here. We had little time, however, to examine all this, for, on the arrival of a second stage coach with the mail, the steamer lost no time in quitting the shore. It was a boisterous sea, and the fog bells on the sunken rocks rang out a loud continued peal. Gulls, puffins, and other sea birds, that inhabit the Skerry islands and the rocks round Holyhead, flew screaming to the shore. Our little vessel was soon tossing on the angry waves, now sinking into the trough of the sea, and now lifted on the summit of some billow topping all the rest. It was little, however, that we saw of all this, for night was coming on, and soon the lights of Holyhead and the Skerry Islands glittering like two solitary stars, were the only objects we were able to discern.

[As the account of the journey through Scotland and Ireland which follows here has been already published, we now proceed with the author to Carlisle where his next chapter opens, observing the same order in which Mr. Kohl has himself found it advisable to publish his series of tours.]—Tr.

CARLISLE.

From the beautiful border valleys of Scotland we passed into the beautiful plains of Carlisle. Not that the county of Cumberland is everywhere a plain. On the contrary, to the north, the west, and the south, it is encircled by hills, that make of it a little district separated from the rest of the country. In the centre of the level part of the country are concentrated the waters and the population, in and about the city of Carlisle.

The cathedral of Carlisle belongs to the same class as those of Dublin and Chester. Not only the style of their architecture, but the materials of which they are constructed, are precisely the same; and as they were built nearly about the same time, they are all three in a corresponding state of decay. The soft red stone with which

they were erected, has in all three suffered much from the effects of
the weather, till nearly each separate stone has been rounded off by
the rain.   The window of painted glass, respecting which my
curiosity had been so much excited, seemed to me undeserving of
mention, but the carving of the stalls was a beautiful specimen of
antique workmanship.

To see the cathedral, I repaired early in the morning to the old
sacristan, whom I found at breakfast, with his family, on oatmeal
porridge, which in Cumberland, as in the neighbouring Scotland,
forms the chief diet of the humbler classes, and of children, even
among the wealthy.   It would seem to agree with them, for the
people appeared to me to be a fine vigorous race, bearing a strong
resemblance to their northern neighbours.

Even in their political institutions, these parts of the country
have preserved much to remind them of the wild times of border
warfare.   Certain local taxes, then imposed, continued to be levied,
as was the case till very recently in Saxony (at Leipzig), where
taxes were likewise paid that had originally been imposed in the
times of the robber knights.

In the cathedral, my old sacristan showed me a bell that had
been cracked while ringing somewhat too joyously in honour of the
victory of Waterloo.

The city was very full this morning of country people, male and
female, servants, farmers, and *statesmen*.   The last word is used to
designate landowners, and applied in the same manner as " lairds"
in Scotland, and " squires" in the more southern parts of England.
As this was the 12th of November, the customary day for changing
servants in the market place and along the principal streets, long
rows of men were drawn up.   Those among them who were in
search of service had whisps of straw in their hats, a custom, they
told me, of very remote antiquity.   When the statesman, or farmer,
has hired a servant, the latter receives what is called the arl-shilling,
which he keeps while he remains with his master, and to return
which, is equivalent to a warning to quit.

The beauty of the weather had, no doubt, contributed to draw
great numbers of both sexes to Carlisle, and many, it may easily be
supposed, allowed themselves to be beguiled by the temptations
held out to them by their vicinity to Gretna Green.   " I have no
doubt," said a gentleman to whom I had a letter of introduction,
" but fifteen couple at least will go over to Gretna to-night."

It is generally supposed that the hymeneal priest of Gretna is by
profession a smith, but I could learn nothing at Carlisle of any smith
who had ever held the office.   A tobacconist, a stone-mason, an inn-
keeper, and several others, had succeeded each other, and at present
the high priest is one Simon Laing, whose father, Andrew Laing,
officiated before him.   As in other professions, however, so in this,
there is no lack of competition, and the most fashionable operator re-
sides, not at Gretna, but at the neighbouring village of Springfield.

The most remarkable circumstance is, that this handicraft, which might just as well be followed in any other border village, has for more than sixty years been confined to Gretna and its immediate vicinity.

Perhaps not the least disgraceful part of the story is, that the service of the Anglican church is often read on these occasions. All that is required to constitute a marriage in Scotland, is a declaration by the bride and bridegroom in presence of witnesses, but the marriage-smith is always ready to go through the English forms, if the consciences of his customers require it. Not less than from three hundred to four hundred couples are yearly joined together at Gretna, nearly all of them of the lower classes; but though the marriage thus contracted is legally binding, the greater part do not consider themselves properly married, till they have been " married over again" in an English church. Now and then persons of respectability, and even of high rank, are married at Gretna. Perhaps the most *illustrious* among the inscriptions in the matrimonial records of the place, is the following:—

" Gretna Hall, May 7, 1836. Married here this day, Carlo Ferdinando Borbone, Principe di Capoa, figlio del Francisco Primo, Re del Regno delle due Sicilie, and Penelope Caroline Smyth, daughter of the late G. Smyth, Esq., of Ballynatrag, in the county of Waterford, in Ireland."

FROM CARLISLE TO NEWCASTLE.

A railroad now runs right across the island of Great Britain from Carlisle to Newcastle. There are four such railroads running across the island. That from Glasgow to Edinburgh, that from Liverpool over Leeds to Hull, the Great Western from London to Bristol, and that from Carlisle to Newcastle.

As I saw nothing of Northumberland but the Tyne valley through which I flew along the last named of these railroads, I was disposed to set the county down for one of the most beautiful and delightful countries in the world. I never was upon any railway which afforded so agreeable a trip. Most railroads run half their length through deep ravines, with ditches and walls on either side, and the other half along raised dikes. With the railroad I am now speaking of this is not the case, for it winds like a road amid meadows, corn-fields, gardens, and villages. There is a tunnel, however, not far from Carlisle and the Cowran Cut, 100 feet deep, and 2000 feet in length, one of the largest works of the kind to be seen on any railroad.

Handsome villages, stately groves, teeming fields, busy towns, and here and there a hill or a group of rocks, crowned with the remains of some ancient castle famed in the chronicles of border warfare, passed in quick succession before us. The most remarkable

town along the whole line is Hexham, the most interesting castle
that of Prudhoe. Hexham was already a famous station in the time
of the Romans, and its history, down to the troubles arising from
the Jacobite insurrections, is a stormy and a warlike one; but collieries and railroads have an astonishing effect in pacifying a
country.

Prudhoe Castle is not very far from Newcastle, and, being situated on a bold steep rock, is seen from a considerable distance. Two
huge towers, one completely enveloped in ivy, like a Scottish chief
in his plaid, rise proudly from amid a mass of crumbling ruins.
This castle also dates its history from the times of the Romans, who
occupied a fortified station here. At a later period it became the
seat of the Norman family of Umfranville, and subsequently it fell
into the hands of the more famous Percys, who still own it.

NEWCASTLE AND THE COLLIERIES.

Newcastle, already a frontier station in the time of the Romans,
and situated at the eastern extremity of their celebrated Wall, lies
nine miles from the mouth of the Tyne, in a beautiful, level, fertile
country, whose chief wealth, however, is buried below the surface
of the earth.

The museum of the town contains, as might be supposed, a rich
collection of Roman antiquities, found in the vicinity or along the
line of the wall. These consist chiefly of the gravestones of Roman
officers, surgeons, and civil servants, stationed at this northern
extremity of the empire. I had seen similar antiquities at Carlisle
in the Athenæum, but the Newcastle collection is far more complete. Similar collections of funereal monuments raised in honour
of the Roman frontier officers, are to be seen at Mehadia and Ka-
ransebes, in the Austrian military frontier, and at several other
points along the Danube border; as also at Carlsruhe, Mannheim,
and other cities along the Rhine. What makes the Newcastle
museum most interesting, however, is a complete collection of all
the geological formations of the coal mines, including some beautiful specimens of the gigantic ferns discovered buried in the earth.
These trees are more than five feet in circumference, and the specimens at the museum are eight feet in height. Most of these trees,
I am told, are still found standing in a perpendicular position, just
as they are supposed to have grown.

Of the buildings of Newcastle, none surprised me more than the
Newsroom, which bears about the same relative importance to similar institutions in Germany, that a double *Times* does to a Leipzig or Frankfort paper. The room in question is a noble hall of a
semicircular form, and its large and lofty dimensions are calculated
to awaken the idea rather of a temple than of a reading-room.
Under the same roof are two banks, the post-office, club-rooms, the

stamp-office, &c., and the whole building bears the name of the Royal Arcade. It was erected by Mr. Grainger, a very celebrated builder at Newcastle, who unfortunately, like many builders of houses, has ruined himself by his building. He has built whole streets, in many of which, on account of their distance from the central parts of the town, it is impossible to let either a house or a shop.

In the evening (it was a Saturday), the bustle in the streets was quite astonishing. The side pavements were crowded with pedestrians, idle and busy, most of whom, however, seemed intent on making purchases, and a few on begging. I was struck by the circumstance, that it was generally the father and not the mother that carried a child on the arm.

I was startled by the sight of several well-dressed beggars, standing mute and motionless by the side of the pavement, with their hats stretched forward. One, a young man evidently capable of hard work, stood with his eyes so completely fixed, that I supposed him to be blind, and asked if he were so. " No, sir," was his reply, " I am not blind, but I am sorry to say I am out of employment. I accept thankfully what is given me, but I should be ashamed to be troublesome in my appeal." The streets were brightly illuminated with gas, and large and handsome buildings rose on every side. I could almost have asked the beggars, whether they were not ashamed to beg in such a place. There was nothing but the coal black mud of the street, and the dense smoky atmosphere that harmonised in any way with the wretchedness of the poor mendicant.

Newcastle stands on a widely spread bed of coal, reaching southward to Durham, and to the north as far as Blythe. Eastward it extends under the sea, it is scarcely known how far. Newcastle is not the only town in England that stands on an extensive field of coal. Glasgow, Manchester, Leeds, Sheffield, Birmingham, Wolverhampton and others, are similarly situated. Newcastle has, however, the advantage that its coals are raised at the mouth of a navigable river, and can thus be easily conveyed to a distant market, while the inland districts must find a way of using up their coals at home. England at present consumes annually 20,000,000 of tons of coal, of which more than 5,000,000 are raised in the neighbourhood of Newcastle, and shipped from the Tyne, and from a few ports in the vicinity, such as Sunderland, Blythe, &c. Newcastle alone ships 3,000,000 of tons, which if each ship was large enough to carry 500 tons, would make 6000 cargoes of coals shipped from Newcastle every year.

Coals are sent from this place to all parts of the world. London is the chief customer, taking off no less than one-seventh of the whole quantity raised. France, Germany, Russia, the Baltic and the Mediterranean, are also among the places to which the staple commodity of Newcastle finds its way; nay even at Odessa, on the Black

Sea, I remember to have seen large depôts of Newcastle coals. Across the Atlantic they go to Brazil and the West Indies: the question indeed is, whither do they not go?

From thirty-five to forty colliers sail from Newcastle weekly for London, and whole fleets of these vessels may be seen in the Thames. Indeed, in most of the large English harbours, a fleet of colliers is as constant an apparition, as a fleet of rafts of wood in one of our German ports.

The sailors that man these colliers are highly esteemed in England as seamen, and enjoy in time of war, the privilege of exemption from impressment. One would have thought that such excellent seamen were just the men government would be most anxious to impress, but perhaps the object is to foster so good a maritime school, whence a number of men are sure to find their way into the navy.

Intending, on the following day to travel across the southern division of the Newcastle field of coal, I chose the northern division for this day's examination. Lying entirely in Northumberland, it is also called the Northumbrian field, while the southern, for a similar reason is called the Durham field. The southern is more than twice as large as the northern field, the former comprising 590 English square miles, and the latter only 240. Under this surface lie many strata of coal of varying thickness. As many as twenty-three strata have been counted in some places, some, however, of the thickness only of a few inches, and much too thin, consequently, to yield a profit if worked. The average thickness of the coal strata in regular work, is from ten to fifteen feet. It has been calculated that there are still lying in these fields 9,000,000,000 tons of coal, enough, supposing the annual consumption of Great Britain to amount to 20,000,000 of tons, to supply the country with fuel for 450 years to come. Buckland estimates the coal-fields of South Wales as much more extensive, and capable alone, of supplying the present annual demand for the next 2000 years.

Nature could not have provided any country with a more convenient kind of fuel than she has furnished England with. Turf is to be obtained only from large marshes, injurious to the climate, and consequently to the health of the people, and a constant obstruction to the extension of agriculture. Where wood is burned, a vast extent of country must be occupied by forests, and withdrawn altogether from the labours of the husbandman. Coals, on the contrary, a powerfully condensed species of fuel, lie below the surface, exercise no evil influence on the climate, and leave the soil above for human food to be raised upon it. It would seem as if nature had acted with a view to the economical, industrious, and calculating nation, destined to dwell on British ground. By means of her coal mines, Great Britain is able to maintain double the population that she could without them. Indeed, the limits of the densely peopled manufacturing districts, are almost everywhere defined by

the extent to which the several coal-fields go.   Coals are to England,
what animal warmth is to the human body; they are the *nervus
rerum*, not only of British manufacturers, but of British commerce,
and of British agriculture.

A coal mine, in this part of the country is called a " coal pit,"
and the pit, with the buildings and other dependencies belonging to
it, is called a " colliery."   Along the Tyne, the whole country is
covered with such collieries, lying like old smoky castles, among the
green meadows and teaming corn fields.   The owner of a mine is
not in general the owner of the soil over his mine, and as the underground labours frequently lead to a subsiding of the surface, the
landlords and minelords often come into collision, the latter having
sometimes heavy damages to pay for injuries done to buildings, &c.

The general appearance of the country is very remarkable.   Two
classes of men are seen mingled together—the miners and the hus-
bandmen—whose pursuits, manners, customs, and way of thinking,
vary as much as it is possible to imagine.   Close to the handsome
farm-houses and the neat labourers' cottages, lie the black dismal
openings to the pits.   Here you see the seat of some wealthy land-
lord or capitalist, there a rural village peopled by agriculturists, and
a little further on, in a straight line, a regular uniform row of colliers' cottages.   These dwellings are generally built for the colliers by
the owners of the works, and are all fashioned after nearly the same
architectural model.   The houses mostly stand in a long row, all
under one roof, partitioned off so as to give to each family as much
space as is considered sufficient.   I entered several of these houses
at a venture, and found them all neat and tidy, and not deficient
even in ornament.   It happened to be a Sunday, so, no doubt, I
saw every thing in its best array, but, if there prevailed much disorder on ordinary days, I could not fail to have discovered traces of
it.   In many of these houses there were carpets on the floor, the
grate and fire-irons were bright, and the steps in front of the house-
door were everywhere neatly strewn with yellow sand.

As it was Sunday, I was unable to descend into any of the pits,
or to see the people engaged in their customary occupations; but the
Sunday appearance of such a population is also a sight well worth
seeing, and I had, moreover, the advantage of talking leisurely with
a number of the men, which I could not have done on another day.
The men appeared to quite as much advantage as their dwellings.
They were as well clad as men of moderate wishes could desire to
be, and when I saw a number of the young men together, they at
first appeared to me, to be a party of sailors in holiday attire just
come ashore.   The friend who accompanied me, and was himself
an owner of coal-mines, told me, indeed, that there was much simi-
larity between the characters of the colliers and seamen, both classes
being distinguished among the labouring population of England,
for their cleanliness and love of dress.   Like the manufacturing
labourers, however, the colliers are a riotous and discontented race,

and any unpopular measure on the part of their employers soon leads to a " strike," which passes with all the rapidity of a bad example from one work to another, and soon becomes general.

The colliers are not more famed in England for their insubordination than for the hardness of their work, which equals in severity any labour assigned to slaves in other countries. I had, therefore, expected to see a wretched, sickly race, and was surprised to find the very reverse. I visited a church and a Sunday school, and there, as everywhere else where I saw the people grouped together, they appeared to me to be cheerful and healthy, always neatly, and often luxuriously dressed. Their wages are probably higher than those paid to any other description of miners in Europe. They live rent free, have nothing to pay for fuel or light, have small kitchen gardens attached to their houses, and the lowest wages paid them are two shillings a day, for which they remain at work in the pit for at least eight hours. There are of course many persons engaged on higher terms. Thus a common coal hewer can earn as much as five shillings a day. The dangers to which they are constantly exposed are partly the cause of the high wages paid them, but five shillings a day for so simple an occupation as that of hewing coals, must be considered good pay, even in England. The average earnings of the common labourers in the collieries about Newcastle, are from three to four shillings daily. Yet strange to say, they are by no means a contented race, are continually combining against their employers, and hang together much as was formerly the case with the clans of Scotland. This I attribute partly to the fact that most of the workmen are extremely young. Half of them are under twenty and of the remainder few are much beyond thirty. Such young men are naturally inconsiderate of the consequences to which their rashness may lead. Then, as they not only work together in the same mine, but may likewise be said to live under the same roof when above ground, they naturally acquire a family or clannish spirit. Agricultural labourers, on the other hand, neither work together nor live together, and the operatives in the manufacturing towns, though they assemble together at the hours of labour are afterwards scattered about the different suburbs. The employers say, and no doubt with much truth, that high wages are no protection against discontent, and that the more they concede the more is demanded of them. Besides the habits of the English are much more expensive than those of the continental labourer, and the collier, like the sailor, being engaged in a perilous and disagreeable pursuit, is the more anxious to indemnify himself in his hours of recreation.

In the collieries about Newcastle, about 16,000 pitmen, or underground labourers, are employed, and as Newcastle furnishes about one fifth of all the coals obtained from the various mines of England, it may be assumed that about 80,000 labourers are employed under ground in the several coalworks of the country. These men are under the direction of what are called " over-men" and " under-viewers," and the whole subterranean proceedings are placed under the guidance of the " viewer," who is sometimes also called the " agent" or " engineer." The particular office of the over-men and under-viewers, is to give the necessary orders to the men, and to look to the proper ventilation of the several seams. Another part of their duty is to superintend the placing or taking away of the props by which the roof of the mine has to be supported. When a new seam of coal is worked, large square masses are left here and there to support the roof, but when the seam has been exhausted, it is naturally thought desirable to turn these temporary columns also to account. Before this can be done, props of a different kind must be substituted, and this is a delicate operation, to be performed only under the superintendence of the overmen. These props also are generally taken away when a stratum is about to be quite abandoned, when the roof falls in, occasioning those alterations on the surface of the ground to which allusion has already been made. I was shown a place where I was told a seam, six feet in height had been allowed to fall in, but on the surface the ground had subsided only two feet. Several other places were pointed out to me, where the ground had evidently sunk, and one church, the wall of which had received a large rent, in consequence of the sinking in of a mine below.

The deepest coal pit of which I heard was said to be 280 fathoms in depth; but far as these works descend into the mysterious bowels of our planet, and rich as they are in noxious gases and other marvellous and unexplained phenomena, nevertheless, the imagination of these English pitmen has invented none of those pretty traditions about under earth goblins, mountain spirits, and divining rods with which our German miners are so abundantly provided. These mines un-tenanted by demon or spirit, are illustrative of the sound, intelligent, but unimaginative character of the English people.

In general, the coals obtained from the top or bottom strata are considered inferior to the " main coal," as it is called, and which is taken from the intermediate seams. The most usual classification, however, is made according to size, into " round coals," " small coals," " beans," &c. The coal-dust is allowed to accumulate about the pit mouth, where it often ignites of itself, or is burnt by the workmen when the ground is wanted. We came to one colliery, where we found a mass of coals burning, and, on inquiry, I was told, that no less than 300 chaldrons, or a million and a half of pounds, of coals were then on fire. Of subterranean conflagrations in coal-mines I could learn nothing.

Some of the coal-mines are estimated at the value of 100,000l., and some even as high as 300,000l. These are mostly owned by sharing companies, yet many of them are the property of private in-dividuals, and some of the large landowners, as the Marquis of Lon-donderry, and several others, are also owners of coal-mines. The capital sunk in these mines must be enormous, seeing that the re-

venues derived from them are said to amount to 10,000,000*l.* sterling
annually.

The works on the surface, intended to facilitate the conveyance of
the coal to Newcastle, Sunderland, and one or two smaller harbours,
are also highly interesting. Roads, most of them railroads, cross the
country in all directions, many of the larger works having railroads
for their exclusive use. The common roads, as well as the bridle
and footpaths, are all made with the rubbish from the mines, and are
said to be the firmest and driest paths in the world. Imagine these
black roads winding through the verdant fields; the long trains of
waggons, heavily laden with their black treasures, rolling lightly
over the railroads; the burning mounds of coal scattered over the
plain; the black pit mouths, and here and there a simple unadorned
Methodist chapel or school house, and you have a tolerable idea of
the country which the English delight to call their " Black Indies,"
and from which they have perhaps derived quite as much direct
profit as from both the other Indies taken together.

The men employed above ground are, of course, less numerous
than the pitmen; still they amount to one-half the number of these,
and all are alike included under the general term of " colliers," by
which not only the workmen are designated, but likewise the
vessels in which coals are shipped, and even the wholesale merchants who deal in the article. The trade is so important a one,
and so peculiar in its character, that it is separated from almost
every other branch. So much so, that in London the colliers have
their own exchange, exclusively devoted to the buying and selling
of the produce of the Black Indies.

The banks of the Tyne being in many places high and steep,
are very inconvenient for loading vessels, and the works executed
with a view to obviate the difficulty, are themselves well deserving
of examination. Here and there a sloping tunnel has been made,
down which the trains of coal waggons descend to the water side.
In some places may be seen what are called " slopes," a kind of
Russian mountain, down which the coals rattle into the very holds
of the vessels. These slopes, however, are apt to break the large
coals, and to avoid this, machines called " frame-works with coun-
terbalance" have been erected, which place the full coal waggon
itself upon the deck of the vessel to be loaded. The railroads that
come from the works up the country, extend not only to the edge
of the high shore, but are even continued a little way into the air
over a strong scaffolding of beams and iron bars. Thus the waggons can be brought immediately over the vessel lying at anchor
in the river below; and by a powerful machinery they are then
deposited on the deck, and after delivering up their contents, are
quietly lifted up again through the air.

How large must be the number of vessels often collected here at
one and the same time, may be estimated from the fact that 4000

vessels, laden with coals, sail yearly from Newcastle. It may be doubted whether there exist another branch of trade giving occupation to the same amount of shipping.

It is generally asserted at Newcastle that the great coal merchants realise on the whole much larger profits than the owners of the mines, who are frequently liable to unexpected expenses, and often form exaggergated expectations respecting their underground treasures. The merchants have a much less hazardous business, and there are many wealthy men in the town to whom the doggrel rhyme,

" At the Westgate came Thompson in,
    With a happing, a halfpenny, and a lamb's skin,"

would be just as applicable as to the gentleman in whose particular honour it appears to have been composed.

Many foreign merchants have likewise been drawn to Newcastle by the coal trade, and among them several Germans and Frenchmen, and as the foreign coal trade is at present rapidly on the increase, foreign mercantile establishments are likely to become still more numerous. One German merchant told me that he knew of eight or ten German houses at Newcastle, and that there were at least fifty young Germans there in counting-houses. The German houses have the greater part of the coal trade with the Hanse Towns, Prussia, Denmark, and Russia, in their own hands. The foreign coal trade is at present in such a prosperous condition, that even the export duty lately imposed, has, I am assured, had no visible effect.

I spent the evening in an agreeable party composed chiefly of Scotch and Northumbrians. The conversation ran very much on the peculiarities to be observed on the two sides of the Tweed, and it afforded me considerable amusement to trace, in the friendly jests and repartees that passed between the borderers, a faint remnant of the sanguinary and warlike state of things that formerly prevailed here. I made the remark that the Northumbrians appeared to me to be half Scotch, instancing among other things that they said *hame* for *home*, that they called the gipsies "fawgang," and that like the borderers on the northern side of the Tweed, the Northumbrians always wore clogs and the plaid. My Northumbrian friends, however, protested zealously against the idea of their having any thing Scotch about them. They were genuine Englishmen, they said, and more genuine perhaps than those that dwelt further south; for in Northumberland it was that the Angles settled in the greatest numbers, and thence it was that they extended their influence over the rest of England. The Scotch, on the other hand, had always been the chief enemies of the Northumbrians, and Newcastle, generally, the first object of every border inroad. The Newcastle people, in consequence, had known the borderers beyond the Tweed only as *rievers* (robbers), or as " moss-troopers," on account of their always pouring down from the mossy hills into the valleys in front of the town.   The Highland drovers too, were formerly never allowed by the magistrates to enter Newcastle except on market days, and even then they were obliged to confine themselves within certain limits, they being at all times suspected of treachery and violent designs.

My Scotch friends admitted all about the frequent robberies of their ancestors; but then the Scotch, they said, were freebooters only in a barbarous age, when strife and violence passed for virtues, whereas the Northumbrians of Newcastle made their commercial dealings subservient to their plundering designs, levying contributions upon their friends in a time of profound peace, not by open violence, but by cunning stratagem.

I diligently led the conversation back to the subject of the colliers, and learned many interesting facts respecting them.   They have even dishes and cakes of their own; and among these I was particularly told of their " singing hinnies," a kind of cake that owes its epithet " singing," to the peculiar hissing noise it makes when put into the pan, and to the custom of serving it hissing hot upon the table.   These singing hinnies are great favourites.   They are very buttery, and must never be absent on a holiday from the table of a genuine pitman.

The strikes and riots of the colliers, to which I have already made allusion, are of such frequent occurrence, that they have come to be designated by a provincial expression, " coalyshangie," the etymology of which I did not succeed in ascertaining.

Of the different manufactories of Newcastle, I had time, on the following morning, to visit only one, namely, a rope-walk.   I might, no doubt, have seen a similar establishment, in many of the English towns through which I had passed, but somehow or other I had never seen any thing of the kind.   The place was "a mile and a bittock" from Newcastle, as my Northumbrian informant told me; nevertheless, I contrived to run out and see a good deal of it before the Durham train started.

Not only the marine of England, but many of her manufactories likewise, require hempen ropes of all possible forms and dimensions, from the thinnest packthread to huge cables of more than eighteen inches in diameter.   Sometimes the ropes must be round, at others square, and sometimes even flat.   I saw one rope, three miles long, that was intended for the Edinburgh railroad, and similar ropes for other railroads.   In these great English ropewalks, it need hardly be said that every thing is not made out of the hand and the apron, as I have seen in our German ropewalks; machinery and contrivances of a peculiar kind have, on the contrary, been found requisite.   I took a particular interest in observing the preparation of the large flat and cornered ropes, of which a great many are used in different kinds of machinery, and likewise in many of the collieries.   Their form is given to these ropes by immense pressure, after they have been well softened in warm water.

Of nearly equal interest was the machine by which round ropes of the requisite length and thickness are prepared. This machine is a combination of large and small iron wheels and spindles. At first a number of small spindles are supplied with Russian hemp, which they spin into thin threads. These threads are taken up by a second division of spindles, that spin the separate threads together. This operation is repeated several times, till the threads grow into ropes, and till at last the huge cable is seen to twist itself into existence, around the last iron spindle, a fellow of enormous dimensions.

I mentioned just now a rope three miles in length, intended for the Edinburgh railroad. This hempen colossus weighed fifteen tons; about enough to form the cargo of one of the Newcastle coal barges, called "keels." The hemp used in these works is almost all Russian, and so is the tar, which is obtained chiefly from Archangel. These afford agreeable reminiscences to England of her discovery of that part of Russia in the 16th century, for well may the first arrival of the English in Archangel be classed with the important maritime discoveries of that age. In return for all this hemp and tar, England now sends to Russia the ingenious rope-machines of which I have been speaking, for I was told that several of them had been sent thither only a short time previously.

St. Nicholas Church at Newcastle has a beautiful steeple, of a remarkably light architecture, resting on four elegant arches, which in their turn are supported by four columns. I regretted much that I was not able to mount this steeple, which appeared to particular advantage amid the smoke of the town. Newcastle has also a number of large glass manufactories, in which, as a German, I could not but feel a strong interest; the more so, as they told me that it was to Germans the town was indebted for the introduction of this branch of industry. I am sorry to say, I could find no time to visit any of these works, nor any of the sword-makers of Shotlaybridge, likewise originally Germans.

One whole evening I spent in examining a wonderful collection of shells, arranged in the most beautiful order, and, in point of completeness, I was assured, unique in its kind. Here I had leisure to examine the houses of snails, from the largest dimensions down to those perceivable only by the aid of the microscope.

FROM NEWCASTLE TO DURHAM.

The country lying to the south of the "coaly Tyne," is intersected by railroads even more than that lying to the north of that river. Here are railroads to Shields, to Sunderland, to Stanhope, and to many other places. Durham may indeed be said to be of all counties in England the one in which there have been constructed the greatest number of railroads of small extent. This gives to the country an aspect remarkably new and surprising in the eyes of a continentalist. In all directions he sees small trains in motion, small locomotives with two or three passenger carriages, for, as the intercourse is between places at no very great distance from each other, the trains can probably run frequently, but on that very account, perhaps, are obliged to content themselves with a small number of passengers at a time. If, however, the passenger trains are small, the trains of coal waggons are all the longer, and to one who could take a bird's eye view of the country, it would seem to swarm like an ant-hill, with locomotives, hurrying trains, and long lines of coal waggons. The most delightful part of the story is, that despite this busy movement, the country looks everywhere so beautiful, so verdant, so hilly, so undulating, so charmingly wooded, that it has none of the prosaic business-like appearance of Holland, but, on the contrary, wears quite a face of romance, quite an Arcadian air. It suggests the idea of a lovely girl, with a mind all poetry and eyes all fire, occupied by the domestic avocations of the kitchen, or the unimaginative duties of a shop.

Notwithstanding this abundance of small railroads, the great one, between Newcastle and Durham, and which eventually is to connect those towns with London, was not yet complete, and I could avail myself of its services only for a part of the journey. The hilly, or, at least, the uneven character of this part of the country, has led to the construction of some of the most distinguished specimens of English civil engineering. Among these the Victoria and Sunderland bridges are particularly deserving of admiration. The latter crosses the Wear near Sunderland, at a height of 100 feet over the level of the river. The former crosses a tributary of the Wear; is 130 feet high, 820 feet long, and is supported on four arches, of which two have a span of 100 feet each, one of 160, and the fourth of 144 feet. Let the reader picture these proportions to himself in the air, let him, in his imagination, fill up the outline with stone and iron, and he will have an idea of the magnificence of the work.

The coal trains are of astonishing length. In some I counted as many as fifty waggons. Each waggon contains two tons and a half of coals, and the whole weight of the loaded waggon is four tons. A train of this kind, therefore, must weigh 200 tons, and with this astonishing load behind them, equal to the cargo of a small vessel, the steam engines start at a rapid pace.

Upon these, as upon most of the railroads of England, the rails were originally laid upon large blocks of granite, partly with a view to greater durability, and partly, perhaps, owing to the scarcity and high price of wood in this country. Experience, however, has shown that carriages running over railroads resting on stone, are liable to more violent concussions, and wear out much more quickly. For this reason, in the construction of new railroads, wood is now everywhere preferred to stone, and even on the old lines, as oppor-

tunity permits, the stone is taken away and wood substituted. The
blocks of wood are not laid crosswise but lengthwise, which gives
great elasticity to the rails, but, at the same time, is attended by
some disadvantages.

At almost every station, some interesting novelty presented itself.
Either a bridge similar to those I have spoken of, or a coal-pit with
some important improvements in the machinery, or a new " self-
acting inclined plane" on a large scale, or some beautiful view into
the rich and animated landscape. Could we have looked *into* the
earth, the view might have been of equal interest, for the soil here
is undermined by countless subterranean passages, and humanity is
moving, creeping, and running about, quite as busily below as
above.

DURHAM.

Durham contains little to interest a stranger, but its Acropolis,
with its old castle and its celebrated cathedral; but the latter is an
object of such eminent, such extraordinary interest, that it is quite
enough to occupy all the thoughts of a traveller, and to awaken all
his enthusiasm. The cathedral of Durham, whether contemplated
from without, or examined within, is one of the most distinguished
and remarkable pieces of architecture to be seen in the world, and
is probably the most beautiful and perfect church, in its own particular style, the Norman, as the English call it, not only in England, but in all Europe. It was built by the Normans, shortly
after the conquest, towards the close of the eleventh century, at a
time when people were poor in money, but rich in other materials
of power. It would scarcely be possible, in these days, to raise the
money which the erection of such a building would require; yet,
upon the whole, people must have paid in proportion quite as much
then as now for such work, and there are three times as many arms
and hands to be had now as then. To say the truth, this church
was the work of a dead man, namely of St. Cuthbert, whose mira-
culous bones drew together great multitudes of people.

> " From the four corners of the earth they come,
> To kiss this shrine, this mortal, breaking saint."

It was resolved, therefore, to erect to the saint a church worthy of
his glory, nor were the means for such an undertaking found wanting.

St. Cuthbert may be looked on as the great, the prominent saint
of northern England. He lived, as bishop, on a small island, since
then called Holy Island, off the coast of Northumberland, whence
he afterwards withdrew to lead the life of a hermit on a still smaller,
one of the Fern islands, whose picturesque rocks are tenanted by a
multitude of wild seafowl, that, even to the present day, by the
common people, are called St. Cuthbert's geese.

It was only till the period of the reformation that Durham cathe-

dral continued to stand in its full glory.   That event stripped it of
many of its altars, and, in the course of time many Protestant deans,
one of whom was married to a sister of Calvin, removed from the
interior of the church a multitude of things that savoured to them
too strongly of popery.   The Scots, in the time of Cromwell, chopped
up the beautiful carved stalls, to boil their porridge and brose, and
in modern times a great deal of mischief has been done in the way
of repairs, for to renovate the floor it was thought necessary to remove a number of monuments, and even to lay sacrilegious hands
upon a part of the building itself.   It is only within the last ten
years, a period during which a salutary attention has been paid to
many cathedrals, that repairs really tasteful and suitable have been
undertaken, and that the glorious structure has been restored to a
condition in which it has again become an object of just admiration
to every traveller.

On first entering the church, a stranger might imagine himself in
an Egyptian temple, for he beholds a forest of massy and colossal columns that support the nave and transepts.   These huge columns
consist of immense blocks of stone, and are sixty feet high.   The
roof is of a more modern date, and is built, not in the Norman, but
in the Gothic style, for it presents the pointed arch.   All the other
arches about the building, however, are Norman or round; for what
the English call the Norman style, because they received it from the
Normans, is the same that we call the Byzantine.   The huge columns
I have been speaking of, which are about twenty ells in circumference; the numerous round arches, by which the different parts are
united; the vast dimensions of the whole building—the church is
420 feet long and 80 broad, with no incumbrance within to prevent
the eye from taking in its whole extent at a glance;—all these things
together act powerfully upon the imagination, and carry it back, as
by magic, to a time of which few traces now remain in this rail-
roading and coal-breaking district.

The proportions of height, breadth, and length, harmonise admirably, and the noble pile, looked at as a whole, makes a kindly impression upon the mind.   It is strange that those who were able to
arrange the whole so beautifully and correctly, should have manifested so barbarous a taste as is shown in the detailed ornaments of
the columns.   They are neither plain nor fluted, like Greek columns,
nor do they present the rich and fanciful decoration of the Gothic
split columns, but from top to bottom they are engrained with the
most fantastic lines, and that in such a manner, that on no two of
the columns do the patterns resemble each other.   On one, the lines
descend perpendicularly, round another they wind like the tendrils
of a vine, on a third they are horizontal and zigzag, and on a fourth
they are spiral lines that intersect each other, and cut up the whole
surface into lozenges or diamonds.   Nor is this engraining by any
means well executed.   The lines are very irregular, crooked, and
badly drawn.   It is as if artists had constructed the cathedral, and

Vandals had undertaken to decorate it. Yet barbarous as it is, I must own this grotesque decoration of the columns did not fall disagreeably upon my eyes at the first glance; so there may be something in it that harmonises with the style of the whole, and my eye may have felt the harmony which my judgment rejected.

On measuring the columns I found that they varied in thickness. I found one that was twenty-two ells in circumference, while another was only eighteen. These variations are apt to occur in most of the buildings of the Norman and Gothic styles. Some arches were also more narrow and less elevated than others. A modern architect would scarcely be guilty of similar violations of correctness and proportion, and yet our modern architects, taken collectively, seem utterly incapable of inventing a style of architecture so great and sublime as was the Gothic. The ancient architects looked only to the effect of the whole, and were satisfied if the details harmonised so far that the eye of the observer could discover nothing discordant in them. Thus the thinnest of the columns I have been speaking of, are thick enough to do the work required of them, nor is the difference in dimension such as could be detected otherwise than by careful measurement.

The whole building bears the stamp of the stout old Normans, among whose faults littleness was certainly not one; but many of the objects still existing in the church, as, for instance, the beautiful marble font—are magnificent, even taken singly, and it is only to be regretted that so many other treasures of art should have been destroyed or removed by the misguided zeal of the Protestants. Several deans are said to have unreservedly declared, that they would allow no trace of any monument to St. Cuthbert to remain in the cathedral, and have acted in the spirit of such a declaration. Poor Cuthbert! His spiritual successors in the see of Durham have been worse enemies to him than the women, of whom he stood so greatly in awe, because the daughter of a Pictish king once falsely accused him of making love to her. It was enacted, after his death, that no woman should approach his coffin beyond a certain line, and that line is still pointed out.

The cloisters, the several courts about the church, the churchyard, the deanery, and various other dependent buildings of great antiquity, are all so quaint and full of interest, that I can only regret my inability to make my book a sort of magic lantern, that would convey to my readers an exact picture of what I saw. It is quite unaccountable to me, however, that no splendidly illustrated work, on the subject of this interesting cathedral, should yet have been published, and the absence of such a work is sufficient to show, that, even in England, much still remains to be done. As we leave behind us no buildings of our own likely to outlive these noble structures of a bygone time, we ought, at least, to take care to leave to our posterity correct representations of what our ancestors bequeathed to us.

We crossed to the other side of the river, whence the view of the hill on which stand the castle and cathedral, was truly beautiful. The bold lofty Norman pile turned its most richly decorated side towards us. The steep hill, whose foot is washed by the clear waters of the Wear, is beautifully wooded on all sides. The river as it passes from the town, winds between banks bordered by lofty old oaks, and seems to be hurrying away to lose itself in a romantic wilderness. The whole landscape is not alone so beautiful, but it looks as if it had been so purposely grouped for the pencil of an artist, that I am surprised that pictures of celebrity, multiplied by innumerable engravings of this magnificent view, should not long ere this have been given to the world. The evening sun was sinking in the horizon behind me, as I contemplated the glorious scene; the bright rays were brilliantly reflected from the windows of the cathedral, and wantoned playfully on the yellow glittering leaves of the oaks; could I but have faithfully transferred at once to canvass, the magnificent picture that my eyes were so thirstily imbibing, I feel assured that that canvass would have carried off the first prize at any exhibition in the world.

I must not forget to say, that the old episcopal castle contributed not a little to the richness of this picture. The Bishops of Durham exercised formerly many of the rights of sovereignty in the north of England, where, in addition to their spiritual mission, the duty devolved upon them of protecting the country against the incursions of the Scots. They occupied, accordingly, a position something like that of the Bishops of Salzburg, whose duty it was to look to the safekeeping of the eastern borders of the empire. The castle testifies to the former greatness of the Bishops of Durham, and their successors continue to enjoy some of the advantages of that greatness, in the shape of an enormous revenue.

At present the greater part of the castle has been given up to the use of the university established here about ten years ago, and endowed with a portion of the revenues of the wealthy dean and chapter, in whose hands the government of the university has been placed, the bishop himself being one of the visitors. I thought it strange that the only regular professorships should be those of divinity, mathematics, Greek, and Latin. The teachers of jurisprudence, history, and of the several physical sciences, bear only the title of readers. A large flag was flying over the main building of the castle, as a signal that it was term time, that is to say, that the lectures were going on. During the vacation, this flag is taken down.

FROM DURHAM TO YORK.

It was with some difficulty I tore myself away, that same evening, from so delightful a place as Durham. I traversed the southern part of the county in a stage coach, to arrive at Darlington in time for

the last train to York. The country continued everywhere of a
" coaly" character, and as night soon set in, we saw heaps of small
coals burning on all sides of us. The language and the manners of
the people of Durham continued to show the influence of Scottish
vicinity. The farmers still plough with the Scottish plough, the
Scottish mountain race of sheep, the " Cheviots," are everywhere to
be seen, the mountains in the interior are covered with moors and
bogs like those of Scotland, and in every town a little Scotch colony
is sure to have established itself.

The principal landowner in the county of Durham is the bishop,
whose beautiful country seat was pointed out to me as we passed it.

Darlington is a manufacturing town that already contains nearly
12,000 inhabitants. New houses, we were told, were daily springing
up, and were filled with tenants as fast as they were finished. The
Quakers have immense influence here, and are said to be the soul of
every great undertaking. They also have a good deal that is
" clannish" about them. They assist one another, and cling together
like the members of a clan. It is they who are said to have built the
North of England railway, upon which we now rolled along from
Darlington to York.

YORK.

This is neither a large tumultuous mercantile city, nor a busy
restless manufacturing town, but a quiet old place, deliciously rich
in ruins, antiquities, and fine antique churches and chapels. The
equipages of the great roll not through its streets, heavily laden
waggons encumber not its pavement, nor do mighty machines and
huge towering chimneys offend the eye and ear. Every thing has a
quiet, pleasing, and becoming air. Yet with all its antiquity and
quietness, there is nothing about the place to indicate poverty or
decay. The streets are clear and handsome. Even the ruins are
adorned with ivy, that looks as if a gardener's hand had tended it.
New houses too are seen here and there among the old ones, and if
the city contain no cotton lords, no dukes and marquises, and no
wealthy settlers from the East Indies or the Black Indies, I observed
at least that there were fewer beggars, than in London, Manchester,
Glasgow, or Newcastle. The people, like the city itself, seemed all
to have a decent and orderly look. The streets, though not so wide
and regular as those of the more modern parts of London and Edin-
burg, are also not so narrow and close as in the more ancient parts of
those two cities. They are moderately broad, and sometimes
moderately crooked, and wind gracefully amid the houses and chapels.
With the commercial and manufacturing towns of England, York
has, in outward appearance, so little in common, that it scarcely seems
as if it could belong to the same country. Yet York may be said
to belong to a class of cities existing in England; antique, yet manifesting no signs of decay, with a stationary population, not advanc-

ing in a rapid career of commercial prosperity, but full of quietness
and interest.   Such cities are Durham, Oxford, Cambridge, Salisbury, Winchester, Chester, and a few others.   York, however, is
the queen of them all.

The cathedral of York does not occupy so advantageous a position
as that of Durham.   On three sides it is surrounded by small houses,
which on one side advance almost up to the walls of the building.
On the northern side alone has space enough been gained, to allow
of a complete enjoyment of the venerable pile.

In all the ancient Gothic churches of England, two characteristic
circumstances have struck me.   Firstly, that they have all been
finished, whereas on the continent, most of the colossal old Gothic
structures still continue incomplete; secondly, considering their extraordinary length, they have all too small a relative height; many
of them are quite as long as the Gothic cathedrals of Belgium and
France, or those on the Rhine and the Danube, but almost all of
these are of a superior altitude.   Among the twenty-four distinguished Gothic cathedrals that England possesses, there are no less
than five that are more than 500 feet in length, and fifteen that exceed 400; yet most of them are only sixty or eighty feet high, and
only two rise to a height of 101 feet.   The steeples, too, seldom exceed 200 or 300 feet, only two, Ely and Salisbury, boasting of a
greater height.

Among all the Gothic churches that I know of, the cathedral of
York bears most resemblance to that of Westminster; the former exceeds the latter in length both of nave and transept, but the latter
has a greater elevation, though only by a few feet.   These two
cathedrals, moreover, in common with that of Strasburg, have had
the term " minster," from *monasterium*, applied to them.

Like the temple of Ephesus, so the noble cathedral of York has
had its fanatical and lunatic destroyers, whose sacrilegious designs,
however, were less successfully carried out, than those of the Asiatic
incendiary.   The Herostratus of York was a sailor of the name of
Martin, a man filled with an insane hatred of the church and clergy,
and who fancied he had seen two visions urging him to the destruction of the splendid edifice.   His motives, however, were probably
not quite free from the love of notoriety that fired the Ephesian, for
Martin, before he kindled the fire, cut off a piece of velvet from the
archbishop's throne, aud some gold tassels from the pulpit, to serve,
according to his own account, as proofs that the work of destruction
was his own.   This fire consumed a vast quantity of beautiful
carvings in wood, and it cost 100,000*l.* to repair the damage.   The
second fire, in 1840, attributed to the imprudence of one of the
workmen, was less destructive, the damage done requiring only
30,000*l.* to repair it.   The facility with which these 130,000*l.* were
raised in England by subscription, naturally makes one think of our
great national work, the restoration and completion of the cathedral
of Cologne, for which, notwithstanding the mighty enthusiasm said

to have been awakened among us, we have not yet been able to collect as much as has been already expended on the repairs of York Minster. Yet a much larger sum will be required at Cologne, and the work is one of far greater importance. Perhaps of all the Gothic buildings in Europe, York Minster is the one on which, within the present century, the most money has been expended. For Notre Dame in Paris the Chamber of Deputies voted lately a million of francs, or about one third of what the repairs at York have cost.

In fine specimens of painting on glass, the English cathedrals are decidedly deficient. The art seems not to have flourished in England, in the same degree as architecture. York Minster has many painted windows, it is true, but in real value they are insignificant, compared to the magnificent, the marvellous representations on the windows of some of our German churches; for instance, on those of the cathedral of Cologne. The subjects on the windows of the minster consist chiefly of heraldic decorations; but independently of this triviality of matter, the colours are dull, and the figures without animation. They showed me here a piece of stained glass, which they told me had come from Rouen, and certainly it appeared to great advantage among the others.

If the English, however, have attained to no great eminence in the art of painting on glass, they have been all the more successful in that of carving in wood. Their cathedrals are generally full of admirable specimens. From the account given of the quantity of woodwork burnt here in 1829, the carvings must have been extremely numerous. The half-calcined remnants were bought by a turner, who has decorated his shop with them, and has been working them up ever since into boxes, knobs for walking-sticks, and into other articles, to be preserved as relics. Wherever it is possible, he endeavours, as a proof that the article is genuine, to leave some trace visible of the agency of the fire.

One of the most wonderful things in the whole church is the organ screen, one of the richest, most luxurious specimens of chiselling in stone that the world has to show. It contains such an extraordinary number of towers, turrets, columns, and other devices winding and twisting about, that it looks a veritable forest of stone figures. There are crosses, and flowers, and creeping plants, and that in such vast numbers, that one shrinks from the idea that all this endless work has arisen under the slow and toilsome strokes of the chisel. Amid other figures, the screen contains the kings of England, from William the Conqueror to Henry VI.

Among the monuments in the cathedral are some noble specimens of art; but it may be added, as a general remark, that the inscriptions on English tombs are of a tedious length, and seem intended for funeral orations rather than for epitaphs. This is a strange fault in a people generally so fond of brevity and conciseness. On one of the tombs at York, it was that of a Viscountess Lora ———, I read the following, in letters of gold on white marble: " For her

character and other particulars, see the ' Gentleman's Magazine' for
May, 1812, from which the following is an extract: ' A firm desire
to act rightly, and hereditary personal graces, both of form and face,
completed her picture, &c.' " I believe that in no country less rich
in periodical literature, would it have suggested itself to any one to
quote a magazine on a tombstone.

I descended into what may be called the subterranean works of
the cathedral, where there are to be seem some crypts, vaults, and
arches, supposed to have belonged to the church that stood upon the
ground prior to the existence of the present structure. Some of
these are of recent discovery, and their full extent has not probably
been yet ascertained. The losses sustained by fire have made people
so cautious here, that we were not allowed the use of candles on descending into the vaults, so that I was obliged to content myself
with touching many things that I would fain have seen. I was
also shown a Roman altar, supposed to have belonged to a Roman
temple that formerly occupied the same site.

Another wonder in stone is the Chapter-house, in which the
members of the chapter were wont to hold their meetings. It is a
regular octagon, sixty feet high, and sixty feet in diameter. The
fashion of the windows, the admirable proportions preserved throughout, the exquisite chiselling of the window-frames, the neatly turned
arches, and the delicate columns, contribute all to make such an impression on the beholder, that when he examines them, he may
almost fancy he is investigating the regular and harmonious structure of a flower. A similar chapter-house, upon which, in general,
a vast deal of ornament has been expended, will be found attached
to almost every English cathedral; but, for the most part, it is a
deformity, harmonising neither with the general plan of the building, nor with the holy purpose to which it is dedicated.

Till in the year 1799, the cathedral of Durham was thought to
have the handsomest chapter-house in England. It had been built
about the end of the twelfth century, at a time when the Norman
style was at its zenith. The windows were profusely ornamented,
and so was the roof, under which, splendidly decorated in the old
Norman fashion, stood a number of stone chairs, in which the
bishops and dignitaries of the diocese had been wont to place themselves for 600 years. This beautiful building has ceased to exist.
The reverend gentlemen, it seems, thought the room cold and uncomfortable, and very inconveniently arranged for the transaction
of the affairs of the deanery. One of them was accordingly charged
to do whatever was necessary to make the house comfortable. The
clerical architect set to work accordingly, and began by sending
some men upon the roof, to take away the keystones, upon which
the whole building had been balanced for six centuries. It cost
some trouble to get these stones away, but perseverance overcomes
many difficulties, and so it did on this occasion. The stones were
at last removed, and the whole roof fell, a heap of ruins, upon the

floor beneath, converting the antique chairs and the tombs of the bishops likewise into ruins. It was an economical and expeditious way of taking off the roof; and having gone so far, the chapter thought they might go further still; the whole building was broken up, and with the materials a very comfortable chapter room was constructed.

Many of the smaller churches of York possess monuments and architectural beauties of no small interest, but they are hardly worth naming after the cathedral. The old Abbey of St. Mary's, however, deserves a passing mention, as being already in ruins, it will soon be lost entirely to the admiration and wonder of the stranger. It lies upon the banks of the river Ouse, outside the gates of the city. The whole neighbourhood has now been turned into a beautiful garden, which is the habitual promenade of the gay world of York, and in the midst of which the York Museum has been erected. The broken columns, aisles, and arches of St. Mary's, overgrown with luxuriant ivy, form the most picturesque and interesting part of the garden. It is not the slow canker of time, nor the stormy havoc of war, which has caused the massive and gigantic buildings of St. Mary's to dwindle away into these few insignificant remains. The wanton destructiveness of a peaceable civic community has been as effectual a foe to them, as the fiercest invader or the longest succession of ages could have been. At various times, different corporations and companies have obtained permission to use the stones of St. Mary's Abbey, for the erection of new churches or prisons; and thus, by degrees, the greater part of the buildings have been carried away. Only forty years ago, the stones of St. Mary's were actually burnt for lime at a limekiln in the neighbourhood.

The museum is an elegant building lying between the ruins of St. Mary's, and those of an ancient Roman edifice. Both these ruins have been presented by the English government and the corporation of York, to the society which has erected this museum. Its lower rooms are consequently now filled with the spoils of its two ancient neighbours.

The Roman antiquities of such a city as York, which was the first town in Great Britain when the latter was a Roman province,— the birth-place of Constantine the Great, and the residence of the Emperors Hadrian, Severus, Caracalla, and Constantius—would naturally be expected to be very curious and interesting. They do not, however, as yet at all answer these expectations; but, as it is only since 1822 that the work of collecting them has been going on, much may yet remain to be discovered and investigated. Among the Roman gravestones, I saw one in which a father lamented the loss of his little daughter, lost to him in this remote province. " *Simpliciæ Florentinæ Animae innocentissimæ. Felicius Simplex pater fuit.*" In the coffin, under this gravestone, was found a female skeleton about ten years of age.

The most complete department of the museum at York is that of geology, for whose classification and arrangement the city is in-debted to the well-known geologist, Professor Philipps.

York is the only city in England, besides London, whose chief magistrate is dignified with the title of *Lord* Mayor. The county of York embraces so large an extent of territory and such numerous diversities of population, that its government is that of a kingdom in miniature. It is divided into three provinces, the North, East, and West Ridings, each governed by its own lord-lieutenant; and the city of York, with its lord-mayor and corporation, is as com-pletely cut off from all connection with the county government, as that of London itself. The lord-mayor of York has his Mansion-house, and the city its Guildhall. The latter is one of the most interesting old buildings in England. It is built on the banks of the Ouse, and its projecting windows and buttresses stretch out so far, that it almost seems to stand in the middle of the river. The arms of York, five golden lions with a red St. George's cross upon a silver shield, are represented on many parts of this building. Wil-liam the Conqueror gave the city these five golden lions for a crest, in commemoration of the five brave magistrates, who defended York against him, and were only compelled to capitulate by the pressure of famine. The energetic old mottos of different mayors of York, such as " Essayez !" " Credo !" " Nil desperandum !" " Sans Dieu rien," &c., decorate the windows and walls of the principal hall.

The old walls of York form an irregular quadrangle of very pecu-liar structure, to which I have never seen any thing at all similar, except at Chester. They have lately been repaired and restored in their original style. England is, I think, the only country, some of whose cities have, of late years, restored their antique fortifi-cations to their original state, out of mere antiquarian taste. In Germany, a modern city possessing old fortifications, like those of York, would no doubt have demolished the outworks, rounded off the walls in an elegant manner, and laid them out with trees, flower-beds, benches, and little summer-houses. At York the only path along the walls, is a narrow stone trottoir, upon which two persons can scarcely walk abreast. This is very inconvenient, but it is picturesque and interesting. Sometimes this trottoir winds in between large masses of houses, sometimes it runs out into more open ground, and permits many a delightful glimpse of the open country beyond, and of the rich landscape round the city. Some-times the walls are interrupted by old gates and towers, sometimes they are broken by the course of a railway, so that the passenger has to descend a stone flight of steps, cross the railway and ascend another flight of steps before he can continue his walk.

Upon the peninsula formed by the junction of the Ouse and the Foss, stands the old castle, which still contains the courts of justice and the prisons. The county gaol,—for the principal towns in all the English counties contain county goals distinct from the city goals,—is of course one of the largest in England, on account of the great size of the county in York. I took an opportunity of seeing the whole of this excellent prison. The average number of criminals it contains is 150, but on account of the late disturbances in the manufacturing districts, it contained 380, when I was there.

I was told that during the winter months, from December to March, so many crimes were committed, that at the spring assizes there were usually twice as many criminals tried as at those of autumn. This may be partly owing to the facilities for crime afforded by the long nights of winter, and partly by the circumstance that there are always many more people out of employment in winter than in summer. The manufacturing districts of the county, contribute many more criminals to the county gaol than the agricultural and cattle-grazing disticts.

Many of the English prisons contain very interesting studies for the phrenologist and physiognomist, in the shape of skulls and casts of different notorious criminals. I saw at York the skull of a celebrated highwayman, called Dick Turpin, and of another criminal, named Daniel Clarke. I also saw for the first time the much dreaded *cat-o'-nine-tails*, used in the English navy and in the prisons; its appearance is, however, perhaps less terrific than its name. It consists of a short, thick stick, to the end of which are attached nine knotted thongs of leather. It is no doubt a painful and terrible instrument, but it does not belong to the same barbarous class with the Russian knout, the Chinese bamboo, or the Turkish karbatsche.

At York I became acquainted with many highly respectable Quakers resident there, some of whom introduced me to their celebrated Quaker asylum for the insane, which is tenderly and appropriately denominated " the Retreat." It is certainly one of the most perfect and admirable institutions in the world. As the Quakers have no poor among them, but belong invariably to the educated middle classes of society, an order, refinement, and comfort, is possible among them, which would be perhaps unattainable in the institutions of other sects. Small as is the body of Quakers, society is in many ways deeply indebted to it. The Retreat at Dublin was the first asylum for the deranged in all Ireland, and the Retreat at York has led the way in the march of improvement, and has served as an invaluable model in the reform of other English madhouses. It lies outside the town, surrounded by its beautiful gardens. Its internal arrangements are everywhere characterised by the most admirable order and refinement. The whole system of treatment pursued, is one of invariable mildness and benevolence, founded on the principle of kindness, as the only rational mode of influencing the insane. Gardening and agricultural employments have been chosen as the usual occupation of the male patients, on account of the beneficial and tranquillising influence universally found to be exercised upon the insane by these pursuits. This discovery has only been made in England during the last four years; but its practical application has immediately and extensively followed the discovery. At present such employments form more or less the occupation of the patients, in all the madhouses of Europe.

The diet observed in the Retreat is that common among all the middle classes of England; and this more nourishing and agreeable regimen is found far more wholesome for the patients than the meagre and scanty allowance customary in most madhouses.

The statistical tables of the Quaker Retreats have a peculiar value, on account of the well-known conscientious accuracy of statement observed by the Quakers, and also on account of the close connection maintained among them, which enables them to illustrate their statistics by many interesting and valuable personal details. I shall, therefore, note down here a few of the results afforded by a comparison of the tables for forty-four years.

Most Quakers are either merchants or manufacturers, and few, comparatively, devote themselves to agriculture; but among the patients a far greater number in proportion are agriculturists. There were twenty per cènt. more women in the Retreat than men. I believe, however, that there are many more female than male Quakers, and that the number of male lunatics will generally be found, all over the world, to exceed that of females. The female patients seem to be always more curable than the male; for in these forty-four years, fifty-one out of every hundred female patients were cured, and only forty-two out of every hundred males. A similar result is afforded by the statistics of all other lunatic asylums with which I am acquainted. A greater number of the patients had gone mad in the third centenary of their lives, that is between the twentieth and thirtieth years, than at any other period. Sixty-six of every hundred patients received were unmarried people; and of the married patients, twenty out of every hundred had never had children. Out of 415 patients, no less than 142 had had parents, or grand-parents, who were either actually mad, or had shown a strong tendency to insanity.

The following are a few interesting particulars, well worthy of the attention of those interested in the subject. A woman inclined to insanity, had four children, three of whom she suckled herself. These all three died in the Retreat. A fourth child, which she did not herself suckle, was never insane. Three insane patients were the children of parents closely related to each other. All the other five children of this pair were weak in body and intellect, while the parents themselves were healthy and intelligent. Two female patients were specified as having gone mad through the use of opium. I do not believe that in Germany there are any persons who are addicted to the habitual use of opium. But in England, I have been told, that there are villages, among whose inhabitants the use of opium threatens to become as common as that of tobacco.

Among seven patients whose insanity was attributable to unhappy marriages, three were Quakeresses, who had married non Quakers.

The Quakers are very much attached to one another, and among the 135 patients whose disease was of moral origin, eighteen had become insane through intense grief for the loss of near relations. This class of patients contained three times as many women as men. There were no less than twice as many female as male patients among those whose madness was produced by disappointed affection. Fifteen per cent. of the patients were inclined to suicide, or suffered as the English say, from " suicidal melancholy." Idiotcy seems an uncommon form of mental disease in England.

A comparison of the statistical tables of thirty-four of the principal madhouses in Great Britain and Ireland, of which none are older than 1751, and of which by far the greater number were erected during the last thirty years, shows that, upon an average, forty per cent. of the patients received are cured. This fact is surely a just ground for exultation, on the noble contributions which our age has made, towards the progress of the human race. These thirty-four institutions have restored to the daylight of reason, and to the possibility of a clear and noble existence, no less than 24,000 poor benighted human souls ! How glorious and how encouraging to benevolent exertion are these results !

I spent my evenings at York with my Quaker friends. Among these excellent people I always find myself at home. The liberal and cordial hospitality which they extend to every stranger does not injure the order, contentment, and privacy, of their happy family circles. Once admitted to intimacy with any of the Quakers, the thread of intercourse is never afterwards broken ; for the fraternity is distributed over the whole Anglo-Saxon world, and the traveller is sent from one " friend" to another, lengthening at every place the chain of his Quaker acquaintances.

My Quaker friends had been recently travelling on the Rhine, and expressed themselves much pleased with the civility they everywhere experienced, and with the entire immunity they there enjoyed from the insults and mockeries which their peculiar costume often excited in England and Scotland. The Quakers, as is well known, pay no tithes, and regularly allow their goods to be seized and sold in consequence. My Quaker friend at York, told me that it was computed that no less than 10,000l. worth of Quaker property was annually seized and sold on this account in England.

The wife of my friend had not been born a Quakeress, but entered the community afterwards, out of love for her husband, whose parents would not hear of his marriage with any but a Quakeress. This motive was, of course, kept secret, for the Quakers do not profess to receive into their society, any but those whose conversion is matter of pure conviction.

The next day I continued my journey towards Leeds. The city
of York lies close to the point of junction of the three Ridings of
Yorkshire. The East Riding, stretching to the sea and including
the great seaports of Hull and Scarborough, is the chief commercial;
the North Riding, lying between the great coal-plains of Durham and Leeds, the chief agricultural; and the West Riding,
including the great manufacturing towns, the principal manufacturing district.

The manufacturing districts have increased immensely in population, of late years, while the agricultural population has not only
remained stationary, but has even somewhat diminished. This is
partly because the growth of the great manufacturing cities absorbs
daily more and more of the rural population, and partly because the
great landlords have of late years been making perpetual efforts
towards diminishing the number of small farms, and putting all the
land into the hands of great farmers. This tendency has certainly
manifested itself much, of late, throughout the British Islands, although in some places, particularly in Ireland, many energetic efforts
have been made against it; and its certain effect is to drive the
population more and more into large and crowded cities.

Opposite to me to-day sat a Quaker, who has made his name well-
known in England, by the invention of a kind of fancy biscuit,
very popular there, in which he carries on such an extensive business, that he sells five or six tons of them every week, and his agents
and commercial travellers cost him nearly 300l. a year. His present
journey, however, had nothing to do with fancy biscuits. It related to some charity-schools which he had established in different
parts of the kingdom, and with whose progress he wished to make
himself personally acquainted. This is another example of the manner in which the Quakers often unite the most successful spirit of
enterprise in worldly avocations, with the most enlarged and fervent
zeal in works of benevolence and philanthropy.

After a short journey, of I know not how many minutes, I found
myself at Leeds.

LEEDS.

Leeds, like its brethren, Sheffield, Manchester, and the other
great manufacturing cities of England, can boast of no interesting
antiquities, no historical associations, no classical appellation like
that of " Eboracum," the Roman name for York. But it has many
peculiar and interesting features to boast of, perhaps quite as valuable as any of these.

Leeds is the central point of the English woollen manufacture.

There are, indeed, woollen manufactories in Gloucester, Somerset, and Wiltshire, but they are unimportant in comparison with those of Bradford, Wakefield, Huddersfield, Halifax, and above all, Leeds. Three-fourths of the woollen-cloth produced in England is manufactured in the West Riding of Yorkshire.

I visited the Cloth-hall of Leeds, which consists of a plain quadrangular house, containing long spacious galleries, in which the cloth-makers display their wares for sale. The house is damp and foggy, but this pleases the cloth-makers, because it is softening and beneficial to their wares. The galleries are divided, on both sides into little cells, called " stands," about twenty-two inches wide, in which the sellers are stationed, with a path down the middle, through which the buyer walks. Each stand is the property of a manufacturer, who has bought it and who may sell it when he pleases.

The regulations of the Cloth-hall are rather curious; there are only two market-days, Saturday and Tuesday, and even on these days, the time for transacting business is rigorously limited to precisely eighty minutes. The meaning of this is to save time, by promoting the rapid and energetic despatch of business. It is found that in this short time, as much, nay, perhaps more business is done, than in the former longer periods; for no time is now wasted in hesitation or delay, but both buyer and seller say at once what they mean, and lose neither words nor minutes over their bargains. I would fain put this whole paragraph in italics, for the benefit of my German countrymen, who might borrow a useful hint from the busy Cloth-hall of Leeds. The enormous mass of business transacted there during the year, requires, in consequence of these regulations, only about 135 hours.

The sellers in these cloth-halls are principally the smaller manufacturers, living in the neighbouring villages, who here sell their wares to the great "cloth-dressers," by whom it is finished-off, packed, and exported. There is some cloth which never comes into the cloth-halls at all, but is privately sold by the weavers to the great dealers.

It is rather strange, that with all which the improvement of machinery has done to promote the " factory-system," there should still exist, as is the case, so many little weaving-establishments, entirely independant of the great manufacturers.

During the last forty years, the number of the former has even increased, although not in the same proportion with that of the great factories. Perhaps the fact is, that many branches of the business can never be so well carried on in the factories as in the houses of the weavers. In bad times their number generally increases, probably because the great manufacturers are soonest and most powerfully affected by disastrous conjunctures, and their labourers thrown out of employment, often set up for themselves in a small way of business.

During the late bad years, from 1838 to 1841, it is computed that the amount of wages paid was on an average, 2707*l.* sterling *less* every week, than during the period from 1833 to 1835. The number of oxen, pigs, and sheep, consumed every week in Leeds during 1835, was 2450; in the year 1841, it was only 1800! Yet a Leeds manufacturer told me that wages had fallen much less at Leeds than at Manchester, and that the inhabitants of Leeds had also remained much more quiet. The swarms of insurgent workmen came all from Manchester.

At Leeds I went over some of the great factories, in which the wool is carried through its various processes. One of these manufactories is considered to be among the most perfect of its kind in England. The whole arrangements of the establishment, the elegance, solidity, and size of the machines, surpassed any thing I had seen before. I was shown two spinning-jennies, of which each spun with 520 bobbins. Two workmen were thus enabled to superintend 1040 bobbins. I could scarcely believe this; but giving myself the trouble to count them, I found the number exact. The son of the manufacturer, who accompanied me, assured me that in one week a thread 40,000 miles long could be spun in their manufactory. At this rate they could " put a girdle round about the earth," if not in " forty minutes," yet in little more than three days.

It is certainly a remarkable fact, that mankind should have gone on spinning, and weaving, in the same imperfect manner, for many hundreds of years, without any perceptible improvement, and that this lethargy should have been followed, during the last century, by so brilliant and unexampled a series of innovations. The thousands of years which elapsed between the days of old Homer's spinning princesses, and the latter part of the eighteenth century, did not do one-quarter as much for the improvement and acceleration of this manufacture, as the last sixty or seventy years have done. Nay, so great has been the difference, that, according to present appearance, *over*-improvement and *over*-production has now become the crying evil. Strange, that after a torpor of centuries, profound as that of the Seven famed Sleepers, the spirit of mechanical invention, starting from its long slumber, should suddenly put on its most formidable seven-league-boots, and fairly *out-run itself!*

When, after the senses and understanding have been for some time astonished, and bewildered, by the examination of these bustling noisy giants, with all their spinning, carding, twisting, weaving, brushing, cutting, dressing, and finishing apparatus, and the heart has swelled with pride, at the thought of these brilliant conquests of human intellect over the subject world of matter, and of the increased impetus which all improvement naturally gives to the spirit of progress in the world—when after this, I say, the spectator turns for a moment to contemplate the fate of those helpless and unhappy thousands, whom every improvement in the world of machinery, seems only to grind down still lower into the abyss of wretchedness and degradation, how painful and tormenting is the doubt which then forces itself upon him, whether after all, this brilliant array of power and ingenuity, be not rather a curse than a blessing to the human race, and whether the same change which seems almost to have elevated machines into intelligent beings, has not in reality degraded intelligent being into machines.

Leeds, like all the great manufacturing cities in England, is a dirty, smoky, disagreeable town. Though its streets are laid out on a regular plan, there are very few neat rows of houses to be seen, because the factories take up a great deal of room, and do not submit to any regular arrangement. The streets are not all paved, and no provision has yet been made for the regular carrying off of mud and rain-water. The River Aire, which runs through the town in different canals, is everywhere thick and dirty, in consequence of the various contributions made to its waters, from all the different manufactories. The attention of parliament has lately been drawn to this state of the city, and many provisions for its improvement have been made. Among other regulations it has been enacted that all the factories should provide themselves, before the 1st of January, 1843, with chimneys for perfect combustion, by which Leeds will be spared the infliction of much of their noxious smoke.

Though the woollen fabric is the principal employment of Leeds and its vicinity, many other sorts of factories are there to be found. Leeds contains chemical works of various kinds, leather, mustard, and brush manufactories, and glass works, and potteries of different kinds, many of which I visited, and in all of which I saw or heard something that was both new and interesting to me.

The manufacturing cities of England are none of them very attractive or pleasing in appearance, but Leeds is, perhaps, the ugliest and least attractive town in all England. In Birmingham, Manchester, and other such cities, among the mass of chimneys and factories, are scattered, here and there, splendid newsrooms, or clubs, and interesting exchanges, banks, railway-stations, or Wellington and Nelson monuments. Leeds has none of these. I was, therefore, not sorry when, after seeing what interested me in the manufactories of Leeds, the time came for me to seat myself once more in one of those cheerful and comfortable flying-houses, in which I scarcely ever failed to enjoy, besides their own comforts, the society of some communicative and interesting fellow-traveller; for stiff and reserved as the English are said to be to each other, I have always found them, in their own country, friendly, hospitable, and sociable towards the traveller and the stranger.

Who can fail to admire the ease and simplicity with which the, elsewhere complex and troublesome, business of travelling is carried on in England! The traveller appoints what time he will for setting off, for almost every hour furnishes an opportunity; he is secure of finding room, for the size of the equipage varies according to its customers. On the way he talks, reads, or writes, just as he pleases, for the conveyance is convenient, and brilliantly lighted, and the motion smooth and easy. And, above all, he knows the exact minute when he shall arrive, for the English trains are the most punctual in the world, and are seldom one minute longer in reaching their destination than the time set down for them in Bradshaw's "Monthly Railway Guide."

FROM LEEDS TO MANCHESTER.

I booked myself only as far as Wakefield, because I had a visit to make at a country-house not far from that place.

My only associations with the name of Wakefield being those of Goldsmith's far-famed and delightful "Vicar," I had expected to find a quiet, pretty little village, or, at least, an old-fashioned, picturesque, little country town, and I even pictured to myself the pleasure of finding among the inhabitants some aged gossip who still retained recollections of the good old pastor, and his two beautiful daughters. I was, therefore, not a little surprised when, on leaving the station, a great lumbering omnibus, full of passengers, carried me through the busy, gaslit streets of a large thriving manufacturing town, with a population of nearly 30,000. Wakefield is, however, a well-built, pleasant-looking place, and is not so exclusively devoted to manufactures as Leeds. It has a pretty old church, called the church of All Saints, whose chimes ring out a different melody every day in the week. There are also many interesting old houses here, decorated with quaint devices, in black wood, and built with projecting stories one above another. At the end of a bridge, on the eastern side of the town, still stands the old chapel, erected over the spot where the young Earl of Rutland fell by the hand of the revengeful Clifford, in that battle of Wakefield, well known to every reader of Shakespeare. This chapel is built of stone and decorated with various quaint figures and devices; but it is at present used as a turnpike house.

From the Yorkshire country-seat, in the neighbourhood of Wakefield, at which I had the pleasure of spending a few days, I made many little excursions to the different farm-houses in the neighbourhood. I know not whether the Yorkshire farm-houses enjoy any particular reputation in England; Mac Culloch calls them " rather indifferent," but those which I saw astonished me by their extreme neatness, order, and cleanliness. Yet these were not the houses of the gentlemen farmers, but of the simple farming peasants. The excellence of the cattle and their accommodations, the luxuriant growth and admirable cultivation of the fruits and flowers in the gardens—the order and shining brightness of the kitchens—the resplendent cleanliness of the dairies—all these things excited my admiration not a little. The rooms, passages, and staircases are often covered with carpets, which seem only just to have come from the manufactory; and in the rooms, I do not mean the sitting rooms and company rooms, but in the bed rooms, reigns an exquisite order and neatness, which, if it were not so praiseworthy in itself, I should call almost painful in its precision. We have nothing of the kind in Germany. We have, indeed, large, orderly, well-kept farm-houses, such as those in Southern Bavaria, Austria, Westphalia, the valleys of the Prussian rivers, and those of the Elbe and Weser; but they are not like those of England. In the first place, every thing is more rude and boorish with us, and there is, at the same time, something much more poetical and picturesque. An English farm-house would offer but few materials to the painter, there is too much precision and regularity, and every thing appears to be laid out on the model of the best books on agriculture.

I admired the stone trottoirs for foot passengers, which line all the roads and lanes in this part of the country. They are called causeways, and consist of large stones, laid close beside each other. All the cottages and farm-houses in this part of the country are built of large stones, and not of tiles as in Staffordshire.

As I was returning to the railway-station at Wakefield, a heavy shower of rain obliged me to seek shelter in a cottage by the way side. The old woman who inhabited it, told me that she had lived there for eighty years, and so quiet and stationary had been her life, that she had scarcely ever gone more than two miles away from her cottage. Poor old soul! What events had passed unnoticed around her, during those eighty years, among the most remarkable in British history! Her principal friend, she said, was the clergyman, who sometimes visited her when he made his rounds, " to look after the souls." "I was a hard labouring woman," said she, " and so I think that God in the sky-heaven, will reserve me a place in his kingdom."

I am told that there are in Yorkshire as in Westmoreland, Saxon families among the gentry, who date their grandeur back far beyond the conquest, and are far prouder than the less anciently descended nobility of the country.

The Yorkshire people boast that its population is not, like that of most counties in England, split into two hostile and conflicting parties, but that in this county, every one has his own individual opinions, and there are many who never trouble themselves about political parties at all. These neutral men are indeed quite numerous enough in England, to form a third party by themselves, and they are so vehement in their neutrality, so hotly opposed to all existing parties; there is, in short, so much party spirit in their impartiality, that they furnish only another illustration of the natural tendency of all Englishmen to party spirit.

In the interior of the country, as well as in the neighbourhood of Leeds, Newcastle, &c., we were met by crowds of poor beggars from the manufacturing districts. There was, of course, a good deal of rabble among them, but many families were respectable-looking and decently dressed. They go from house to house, offering their little wares; cutlery or cotton, or other manufactures. They all repeat the same dismal story: " We are out of employment, sir, and have no bread for our children; and now we are wandering about, selling our little wares for the support of our families." There is often an earnestness, a fixed despair in their manly countenances, which leaves the spectator no room for doubt as to the truth of their statements. Their respectable appearance, their polite manners, and their gratitude for the smallest purchase, are all witnesses in their favour. I never saw any beggars whose appearance was so ominous, and so well calculated to inspire terror, as well as pity, as these workpeople in the English manufacturing cities, whose respectability, industry, and order, are all so many proofs that it is from some deeply-rooted evil in the social system, and not from their own fault, that they suffer. They often express the reluctance with which they follow their mendicant calling; and the single word " out of employment," is often their only petition. I wish I could have lightened with gold the heavy weight which oppressed my heart, whenever I heard these words used.

I drove to Manchester in company with a German resident in that city. The number of Germans living in Manchester amounts, I believe, to somewhere about 1000. There are in Manchester great numbers of foreign houses of business, which supply their own countrymen with the produce of this great manufacturing metropolis. Manchester and London are the only cities in England, where oriental mercantile houses are to be found. Among the Germans in Manchester, there are many fur traders; and I was told that the greater part of the fur business, all those branches indeed which deal in Russian, Polish, German, or Asiatic furs, are in the hands of Germans.

My German fellow-traveller told me, that we were driving through a beautiful district, full of rich landscapes and fertile valleys. I believed this readily, from the little which I saw of it by the light of the moon. The meadows, faintly lighted by her weak rays, looked often very rich and beautiful. Sometimes we beheld, in the picturesque valleys, spots glittering with a great cluster of lights; these were the wealthy and populous towns of Huddersfield, Halifax, Rochdale, Oldham, &c.; many of them containing 50,000 inhabitants. What numbers of rejoicing and sorrowing souls were hidden within those obscure towns, whose names are hardly known out of their own county! Lancashire contains nearly a dozen of these obscure great towns, and is the most populous county in England with the exception of Middlesex, containing three-fifths as many inhabitants as the whole kingdom of Scotland.

MANCHESTER.

I know no town in Great Britain, except London, which makes so deep an impression upon the stranger as Manchester. London is alone of its kind, and so is Manchester. Never since the world began, was there a town like it, in its outward appearance, its wonderful activity, its mercantile and manufacturing prosperity, and in its remarkable moral and political phenomena. But before attempting to give any idea of its more general features and character, which to a reader unacquainted with Manchester, would be very difficult, I shall endeavour to describe some of its particular parts, which I had an opportunity of investigating; regretting only that that which I saw, was so little in comparison with the mass of interesting novelties it contained. When entering for the first time a town like that of Manchester, the stranger, overwhelmed by the new and interesting spectacle presented to him, scarcely dares to look this giant full in the face at once, and prefers becoming gradually accquainted with some of the details before venturing to make a general survey of the whole.

Opposite to the splendid hotel where I lodged,—the Albion Hotel,—stood one of the most interesting buildings in the place: I mean the great Manchester Hospital, an institution offering a fund of most interesting, medical, statistical, and miscellaneous information. It is to be regretted that this building lies in the very heart of the town, as this circumstance deprives the patients of the very desirable advantages of spacious gardens and country air. Manchester, however, is an open airy town; and the founders of this institution could never have guessed, in 1752, that the growth of Manchester would be so rapid, as so soon to place the hospital, then outside it, within the very heart of the town.

Six physicians and six surgeons are appointed for this hospital, which affords relief annually to about 20,000 patients. Of these, however, only about one-tenth enter the house itself; the rest being out-door patients. The receipts of the house amount annually to about 9000*l*. sterling. In the year 1841, owing to the bad times, from which all private and public institutions suffered more or less, the list of subscribers to the Manchester Hospital lost 153 names, which diminished the funds of the institution by 508*l*.

The physician of this hospital told me that nervous diseases were remarkably frequent in the manufacturing districts. I believe there is no hospital where there are so many cases of St. Vitus's dance as at Manchester. Scarcely a day passes without its receiving some persons afflicted with this disease. Acute diseases seem more common in the agricultural, and chronic in the manufacturing districts. The most remarkable part of the statistics, however, is that relating to accidents, the number of which is here enormous. No less than 4000 serious accidents are treated here every year. The quantity of complicated and dangerous machinery used in the manufactories of Manchester, is probably the chief cause of this. Since so great a proportion of serious accidents probably occurs in no hospital of Europe, and since this forms a characteristic feature in the condition of the inhabitants, a few details concerning it will probably be not uninteresting to some of my readers.

Among the patients of the hospital during the last year, the cases of—

Simple or complicated fractures (of arms, legs, ribs, &c.) were........... 454
Dislocation of the Limbs... 533
Wounds from cuts... 71
Wounds from stabs... 46
Lacerations 714
Contusions 959
Burns 120
Scalds 135
Fractures of the Skull.. 9

besides other less numerous or serious accidents. Of all these, only one-fourth are attributed to machinery; the rest are owing to other causes.

What can occasion this great number of other accidents I do not know. I was told that the carts which convey goods from one part of the city to another, drive very fast; this is true, but the streets are wide and open. The many railroads near Manchester no doubt contribute their shares. The boxing matches and drunken quarrels, so frequent among the lower classes, must also be remembered. Still all this is hardly sufficient to account for the statement.

The statistical tables of the hospital show that one in every eighty-seven of the inhabitants is seriously injured or wounded every year. Or if an average duration of thirty-five years be allowed for the life of every inhabitant, two serious wounds are suffered during life by every five inhabitants.

The distribution of medicines to the out-patients of the Manchester Hospital is a very curious sight. They, or their children sent by them, receive the medicines in a particular part of the building appropriated to the purpose, and arranged something like the bureaus of the money takers at a French theatre. The passages are arranged so that only one person can stand before the bureau at the time. The store of medicines and physic bottles which were shown us in the cellars was really enormous. Homœopathy can have made very little progress among the English, to judge of the enormous quantities in which they dispense their medicines. The library of the hospital contained a great many devotional works, but very few books of voyages and travels, popular science, or fiction. The superfluity of religious works appeared to me as great as that of medicines.

If the prisons of a country are always interesting subjects of investigation to the traveller desirous of making himself acquainted with the character and condition of the people, this is peculiarly the case in England, where the superintendants of the prisons are always so liberal in affording him opportunities and assistance. The New Bailey of Manchester, which was built by the celebrated Howard, at the end of the last century, is one of the most extensive, important, and interesting prisons in the country. It contains on an average, at all times, about 718 prisoners. The prisoners, however, are continually changing, and very few remain here long. After a short time some are set free, others transported, and others sent to the county gaol of Lancashire, to await the expiration of their sentence.

There are other smaller prisons in Manchester, and in the year 1841, the number of prisoners received in all the prisons of Manchester put together, amounted to 13,345. A comparison of this sum with that of former years, and with the increase of population, will show a great increase of crime of late:

In the year 1825 the population amounted to 200,000, and the prisoners were 1679
"   1831   "   "   "   "   266,000   "   "   "   2423
"   1835   "   "   "   "   300,000   "   "   "   8203
"   1841   "   "   "   "   354,000   "   "   "   13,345

Thus while the population has scarcely doubled since 1825, the number of criminals has increased seven-fold. No doubt the increased severity of police discipline may have something to do with this surprising fact. Nor must it be forgotten that crime always increases with an increased population, in rather greater proportion than the population itself; because a large population not merely contains more criminals, but offers more temptations and opportunities for crime than a small one. But making all possible allowances of this kind, an enormous increase of crime still remains to be accounted for. I attribute this partly to the demoralising influence of the occupations of the workpeople in the great factories, and partly to the distress occasioned by the late bad times.

The deplorable state of ignorance among the manufacturing population is sufficiently proved by the statistics of the prisons. Of the 13,345 prisoners of the year 1841, there were 6971 who could neither read nor write at all; 5162 who could read and write a little; 992 who could read and write well, and only 220 who had received any further instruction. Of these the women were the most ignorant. Only one in twenty-six of the female prisoners could read and write well; while one in every nine of the male prisoners was so far educated.

Although the men, therefore, are three times as well educated as the women, the tables of population show that criminality is three times as frequent among the former. In the year 1841, there were 185,000 women and 170,000 men in Manchester, that is 15,000 more women than men. Yet the number of female criminals was only 3420, while that of the males was 9925. Of course this is no argument against the beneficial effects of reading and writing; the prevalence of drunkenness among the male population, as well as numerous other concurring circumstances, may well account for the difference.

The number of juvenile criminals in England is always a subject of surprise and horror to the stranger. In the New Bailey of Manchester I found great numbers of boys and girls under seventeen. The number of juvenile criminals is probably greater in Manchester than in any other town of Great Britain, because the juvenile popu-

lation itself is larger. More than half the entire population of Manchester is under twenty-three years of age.

In the year 1841 were convicted and sentenced to transportation
in Manchester alone, 177 children under seventeen years of age.
Eighty-seven boys and fifteen girls were sentenced to seven years
transportation, fifty-five boys and five girls to ten years, and twenty-
six boys to fifteen years.

When I was in the New Bailey, almost all the solitary cells were
filled with boys who had committed fresh offences since entering the
prison, and were, consequently, condemned to solitary confinement;
a punishment, for many reasons, probably the most pernicious in the
world for growing children. One of the boys was already a third
time in prison. The guilt of these children rests of course ultimately
upon the neglect and immorality of their parents. One of the boys,
formerly an industrious and well-behaved lad, had become a thief out
of sheer desperation and want, because his drunken father deprived
him by force of his week's wages every Saturday night, and then left
him to suffer the most bitter privation for want of it. An interesting
investigation, lately made at Manchester, places the responsibility of
the parents in the clearest light. Out of 100 poor children who had
committed crimes, there were,

Children of dishonest and profligate parents	60
„　　　profligate but not dishonest parents	30
„　　　respectable and industrious parents	10
	100

Nine-tenths of the children, therefore, had been early contaminated
by vicious example and education; and of the remaining tenth, the
greater part probably owed their corruption to early contact with bad
neighbours and children. " Confirmed bad habits" is the universal
complaint of those connected with the English prisons, when they
speak of the youthful criminals. Such was also the burden of the
lament of the good old schoolmaster at the New Bailey. This excellent old man showed me a journal, which he had for some time been
in the habit of keeping, concerning his depraved young scholars.
He also showed me a letter which a mother had entrusted to him, to
be sent to her son, who had been transported to one of the penal
colonies. The following is a passage from this letter. " How it
grieves me, my dear son, that you had such a stormy passage to Australia. I thought something must have happened to you, as you did
not write to me. My little shop does not go on a bit better; on the
contrary, it is worse this year than the last, and every thing grows
worse here every year. I feel very comfortable with James, for we
have family prayers together twice a day, every morning and every
evening. God be with you, my dear son. Your affectionate mother,
&c." The traveller should never omit to notice these little things,
which often throw much light on the manner in which the obscurest

corners of the country are affected by periods of public prosperity or adversity.

Another frequent subject of surprise to the visitor of English prisons, is the number of times which the criminals have been convicted and punished. Among the 6380 prisoners tried at Manchester in 1841, more than a third had been convicted before, and many had been in prison three or four times. One woman was convicted for the *twenty-third* time; and in London, at the Old Bailey, I saw a woman who had been in prison more than *a hundred times.* It would seem that there is a regular prison population, who are all their lives employed in committing offences and being punished for them. This certainly argues some defectiveness in the system of punishment. Perhaps the superiority of the diet and lodging in the prisons, to that in the habitations of the poor, offers some temptations to those who have experienced it.

Perhaps the English laws do not increase the punishment of an offence in proportion to its repetition. It is certain that with us, a woman who had committed the same offence twenty-three or a hundred times, would have been long ago restrained by imprisonment for life.

The following is the weekly provision of a full-grown prisoner, in the Manchester New Bailey.

	s.	d.
Seven loaves of twenty ounces each, costing	1	1
Thirty-one ounces of flour	0	4
Five pounds of potatoes	0	1
One pint of pease	0	1
Three ounces and a half of salt	0	0
One pound of beef	0	4
One quart of beer	0	0
	1	11

The lodgings of the prisoners are always clean, spacious, and airy; as for the prison discipline, I believe it is milder in England than with us. The chapel attached to the prison is of course Episcopalian, and the prisoners are all obliged to attend service there. As a great many of them are Irish Catholics, I asked whether they did not sometimes make objections to do so; but I was told that such an instance had never occurred. The employments used here are the same as those used in most English prisons, namely, shoe-making, mat-making, the twisting of cocoa-nut thread, and finally the far-famed *treadmill.*

The treadmills are the worst and most detested employments used in the English prisons, particularly those arranged upon the new, *solitary system.* In the old treadmills, six or eight persons worked close together, and even if they were not allowed to speak with one another, they had at all events the consolation of seeing each other's faces, and working in company. According to the solitary system, each labourer is separated from the rest by thick wooden walls, and must continue his dreary, Tantalus-like occupation, in silence and solitude.

I know of no kind of labour which seems so miserable as this useless, monotonous, and lonely treading. In summer time, those who are kept at it, tread for twenty hours together, making 12,400 steps; in winter they tread for seven hours and a half, making 10,500 steps; all being steps upwards in both cases. Every step is about eight inches long; so that their day's treading takes them nearly as many steps as to mount half way up Mont Blanc. Yet they never get a step the forwarder, and always remain at exactly the same place where they were before. It is inconceivable to me, why an industrious nation like the English, has not contrived to turn all this treading to account, and to connect the treadmills with useful machinery of various kinds.

While I was in the prison, the governor received a visit from the so-called " contractor for removing the convicts," and I now learned that, in England, it is not the government which undertakes the conveyance of criminals, but that this is in the hands of private speculators. The contractor gave the governor a receipt, in which he certified having received " the bodies of twenty-five convicts," in order to put them on board the hulks at Chatham. I now learnt that those sentenced to transportation for a short period, are only removed to some harbour, such as Chatham or Woolwich, where they are confined in old ships fitted out as prisons, and called " hulks." When criminals are to be removed to these hulks, from any prison in the interior of the country, the governor of that prison gives public notice that he has so many prisoners to transport to such a place, and that the conveyance will be entrusted to whoever will undertake it at the lowest price. The contractor must of course give security, that he will deliver the right number at the right time and the right place, undamaged and in good condition; but otherwise he may do what he pleases with them. The commander of the hulks gives the contractor a certificate of the safe and full delivery of the convicts, which he must again hand over to the governor of the prison whence he received them. Formerly the contractors used large vans for this purpose, but of late they generally hire the horse-boxes of the railway trains, which are fitted up with benches for the purpose. Two-hundred and fifty criminals are annually transported in this way from the New Bailey of Manchester.

The criminal tables of Lancaster and Manchester show that crimes of all kinds are much more prevalent in the manufacturing, than in the agriculturing and cattle-grazing districts, and even than in the populous metropolitan district itself.

Lancashire contained, in 1841, 1,667,000 inhabitants, and 3137 convicted criminals. Middlesex (containing the greater part of London) contained 1,577,000 inhabitants, and 2709 convicted criminals. Thus in Lancaster there was one criminal to every 530 inhabitants, and in Middlesex one to every 590. The heaviest crimes are still more frequent proportionably, in Lancashire, than the lighter ones. Of sixty-six persons accused of murder in England in 1841,

MANCHESTER. **113**

eleven were from Lancashire, eight from York, and six from Middlesex. Of 218 tried for manslaughter, one-fifth were from Manchester, and only one-tenth from Middlesex. From Lancashire came 108 burglars, and from Middlesex only 44. In considering these facts, however, it must not be forgotten that the police is far more vigilant and efficient in London than in Manchester.

The number of houseless beggars, of destitute vagabonds, and of poor workmen without employment who fill the great towns of England, and whose number increases every year, has attracted the attention of the benevolent among the English of late years, and has led to the establishment of night-asylums at various places, whose object it is, to afford some sort of nightly shelter, gratis, to those unable to pay for it at public houses of entertainment. The Night-Asylum of Manchester has been opened for about four years. I visited it late in the evening, for it is only at that time that it can be seen in operation. In the entrance-hall was a sort of tribune, at which sat a few citizens of Manchester, who were acting as secretaries or directors of the society, by whom the asylum was established. The poor wanderers came before this tribune, one by one, and after answering a number of questions concerning their ages, names, employments, &c., they were dismissed, into the great sleeping-room. No one is allowed to come to the asylum more than two nights running. Each, on being admitted, receives a piece of bread and a small allowance of coffee, which he heats at the fire burning in the middle of the sleeping-room.

During the year 1840, 17,700 persons were sheltered here; during 1841, 24,400; and by the middle of November, 23,490 during 1842. The present average number of applicants is ninety, every night. When I visited the asylum, the night's number of ninety was complete, and I saw the greater part of them seated on long benches round the fire, at which they were warming their coffee. Most of them were smoking, for this is allowed here, because tobacco-smoke is considered a good remedy against infectious disorders. Many of them were Irish, and these I readily recognised, by the potatoes which they had laid among the ashes before the fire, and which they occasionally turned to see if they were done. I saw one black negro face among the white ones lit up by the friendly blaze, and I was told that a short time ago there were seven negroes here at once. Sometimes a poor brown Hindoo, or Malay, knocks at the asylum door, and in one of these great rooms, Africans, Asiatics, and Europeans often creep together for shelter, from the chilling blasts of an English winter's night.

I was particularly struck by the perfect silence pervading the assembly, which was carefully guarded by a few vigilant overseers who walked about among them, everywhere maintaining order and stillness. No one was allowed to speak above a whisper. I was told that this strict silence was absolutely necessary to prevent quarrels and disturbances. It seems that the English silent system is maintained in other places than the prisons. Such a system would be looked upon in some countries, in France for instance, as the very height of tyranny.

This silence is sometimes broken by one of the town missionaries, who come to these places to preach sermons and distribute tracts to the poor destitute wanderers. These town-missionaries are the servants of a remarkable association at Manchester, called the Town-mission. There are, in all the great towns of England, a vast number of persons who do not belong to any religious denomination whatever, and do not practise any kind of religious worship. Among 50,409 persons, examined eight years ago on this subject in Manchester, there were found 4481 persons who held no kind of Christian or unchristian belief. The number of such uncared-for outcasts of the churches is far greater in London. Astounded by the discovery of this state of things in Manchester, a number of benevolent men founded this Town-mission in 1837. This association has sixty agents or missionaries in its employ, belonging to all the different religious denominations, who visit the most secret haunts of misery in all parts of the town, instructing the poor, and endeavouring to awaken religious sentiments in their minds. Each has a particular district assigned him, as the sphere of his activity, in which he holds religious meetings, distributes tracts and bibles, and visits the prisons and the dwellings of the poor. We have no such associations among us; and, it must also be said, have no need of such.

I was much interested by the appearance and answers of poor wanderers, who prayed for admittance into the Night Asylum. I recognised most of them as Irish by their dialect. The greater number of the petitioners were artizans and mechanics. One among these particularly excited my interest. He was an Englishman, and, as his letters of recommendation stated, " an industrious, hardworking man." Driven by the necessities of the times, he had left England with his little savings the year before, and had gone over to Belgium, in the hope that English labour would be wanted and valued there. He could get no work, however, and had gone both to France and Germany, everywhere seeking work, but the opinion at present entertained of English labourers on the continent was, he said, so bad that he could nowhere obtain any. As he had gradually consumed his little savings, he was at last reduced to beggary, and was driven over the frontiers as a vagabond. He had then returned to England, and had wandered on from town to town, seeking work and finding none. Having now arrived at Manchester, he had come to the Night Asylum, in hopes of being permitted to rest his weary head there for a few hours. This man's face alone was a sufficient proof that he was suffering, not from his own fault, but from the misfortunes of the times. The gentlemen present told me, that the pressure of the times was now felt in regions which it had never reached before, and that they could easily trace, by means of the different applicants to this institution, the manner in which the waves of the national misfortune reach further and further at every rise of the tide, and make havoc in the obscurest corners of society.

The course of adversity in Manchester has probably been some-what as follows: first, the merchants were affected by the stagnation of trade, and they again influenced the manufacturers, by no longer requiring their wares. Thus, factory after factory was stopped, and its owners became bankrupts. This stopping of the factories turned numbers of labourers out of employment. All the smaller trades-people and shopkeepers now suffered from the failure of their cus-tom; and the masons, carpenters, and bricklayers, could get no work, because no new houses were built, and those already building were stopped. Next, the butchers, bakers, and grocers, began to go down in the world, on account of the decrease in their custom, and they again affected the farmers and gardeners in the neighbourhood of the towns. The decrease in the price of provisions of late is not merely owing to the alteration in the corn laws, but in great part to the decrease of the demand for them. The remark I made in speak-ing of Leeds, that the inhabitants now eat only two-thirds as much meat as they did in 1836, would probably apply equally well to Manchester.

In the accounts kept at the asylum, concerning the applicants, it was noted down, which could read and write, and which could not. Out of thirty which I counted at random, there were twenty who could neither read nor write. The gentlemen also assured me, that among those who were recorded as possessed of the art of writ-ing, a great many could only write their own names, sometimes they were only equal to their initials. In a report concerning the mar-riages solemnised in Lancashire and Cheshire in the year 1840, it is stated that of the 17,565 pairs, 6798 men, and 11,505 women, that is more than half of the whole number, were unable to sign even their initials, and could only make their marks! Yet Lan-cashire is by no means the worst of the English counties in this respect. There are shires in which sixty in every hundred are un-able to write. I could not help wondering at this state of things in England, when I remembered that the wild Tartars of the Crimea are almost all able to read and write.

Out of the 24,000 persons received at the asylum in 1841, 16,900 were poor mechanics or labourers seeking work; and only a small proportion were vagabonds and beggars. I learnt, that in connexion with this night asylum, there is, at Manchester, a place called a soup-kitchen, at which platefuls of soup are distributed at very tri-fling cost. I was not able to see this institution, as it was just under-going some alterations, but I looked over the accounts of the distri-bution, and found that Thursday was invariably the day of the week on which most soup was applied for. From Sunday to Thursday,

the quantity required regularly increases, and after that day decreases
again. What the reason of this may be, I do not know.

The same night I visited one of the Manchester police-offices, to
which the kindness of a friend procured me admission. It was half
underground, and was reached by a descending flight of steps. It
consisted of rooms, in which the police commissioners sat as judges,
although it was twelve o'clock at night, and behind were several
lock-ups, as the temporary prisons of the police-offices are called.
At Manchester, there are, in winter 300, and in summer 250 policemen in constant employment. All persons guilty of offences in the
streets are seized by the policemen, and taken to the police-offices,
when they are either dismissed with a warning, or put in the lock-
up.   On entering, the police-commissioners allowed us to walk
round the rooms, and our eyes immediately alighted on a dirty,
noisy fellow, seemingly both mad and drunk, whose face was stream-
ing with blood, and who was held down by force on a wooden stool,
by two policemen, while a third was shearing his hair in order to
examine his wounds.   Such scenes are sure to meet the eye of the
visitor to any London police-office, from the Mansion House in
London down to the subterranean lock-up in Manchester. Behind
the bars of the lock-up sat several drunken fellows, who were
swearing and quarrelling in a frightful manner, so that the noise
rang all through the subterranean vaults. In the same cell with
these wretches, were shut up a couple of little boys. As I approached
the bars, a wild-looking girl started forward, thrust her arm through,
and pinched me in the leg; she then raised a savage laugh, which
was echoed by all her companions.

As we returned to the outer room, two little boys were brought
into it, who had been taken up on suspicion of theft. The chief
suspicion rested upon the handsomest and liveliest of the two, a
short but powerful-looking, bright-eyed urchin of fourteen; it turned
out that, young as he was, he had already been in prison four times,
and had been repeatedly taken up by the police. The other, a
dull heavy lad, had been only taken up because he had been found
in company with the other little vagabond; he was dismissed after
a severe admonition from the magistrate, never again to let himself
be found in such bad company. His father, who had come in with
him, took him home. The little criminal of fourteen looked so
fearless and good-humoured, that I could not help thinking he
would have made an excellent sailor in the British navy. Perhaps,
had his childhood been better attended to, the native boldness and
dauntless spirit of enterprise, which in his case, led him only into
crime and degradation, might have rendered him a useful and perhaps distinguished member of that body. The boy had no parents,
and he had been dismissed by one master after another, until he
had become a regular member of the idle and depraved street-popu-
lation of Manchester.

In a work concerning Manchester, by a certain Mr. Love, which contains much useful statistical information, I found that in the year 1841, no less than 2730 lost children had been found by the police, and restored to their parents. This number sounds incredible, but I have seen other works in which it was exceeded. In the same year, 1841, there existed in Manchester 160 houses for the reception of stolen goods; 103 houses for the resort of thieves; 109 lodging-houses, where the sexes sleep indiscriminately together; 91 mendicant lodging-houses; 1267 beer-houses and public-houses. Of these 1267 public-houses, 462 were charged before the magistrates with being disorderly houses. Mr. Love, in his work on Manchester, mentions a new kind of attraction, recently adopted by some of the public-houses to draw costumers. A great organ is put up in some spacious room, which on Sunday evenings is played by some musician hired for the purpose, and often accompanied by the voices of good singers. In order to lay at rest the pious scruples of those whom it is desired to attract, little else but psalmody and church music is played. This generally attracts a full audience. " If you pass the door of one of these houses on Sunday evening, you hear only the sacred music of the solemn instrument. But if you enter, you see a number of both sexes, well-dressed work-people, and gaily-attired girls, sitting about in various groups. Before each group stand jugs of porter and ale, at which men, women, and children, are drinking together. Some half drunk, and others quite drunk, are attempting to join the pious melody. In this way the host, while pretending to edify by religious music, is really only encouraging drunkenness, and filling his pockets, while sowing the seeds of future crime. Dreadful are the scenes that often take place here. How many respectable and decent people, who visit such places for the first time, only to pass an innocent and cheerful evening, are gradually corrupted by a taste for, and a habit of, bad company, which eventually leads to crime and degradation, and ruins them both for time and eternity !"

There are English writers who maintain that Manchester is not more criminal or immoral than other large towns. They assert that, although, like all large cities, it possesses a large criminal population, this population is not proportionably greater than that of other places. Other writers, on the contrary, are intent on blackening the character of Manchester to the utmost. It is well known how plausibly party writers know how to support their statements, by all the weapons of logic, rhetoric, and statistics; so that each side, looked at by itself, would seem to possess indisputably the truth, although, when compared, the opposite statements are found flatly contradictory. I shall not meddle in the strife, but simply give a few of the statements of one who never wrote at all; namely, a notorious convicted criminal, who favoured the commissioners for the constabulary force, with a full account of his adventures and experience.

"Take it all in all, Manchester is a very bad town for a thief. For if you say, in any other part of England, that you are come from Manchester, you are set down for a thief at once. It is something the same with London, Birmingham, and Liverpool; but they say that Manchester and Birmingham contain more thieves than London and Liverpool put together. The thieves of Manchester and Liverpool are considered the most experienced. They are mostly of Irish parentage, and are the cunningest of all."

The number of uneducated and neglected children, who grow up in vice and ignorance, in the streets of Manchester, made me very anxious to investigate the state of the schools of this town.

Including day schools, evening schools, infant schools, dame schools, common boy and girl schools, grammar schools, charity schools, and superior private boarding schools, Manchester contains in all nearly 1000 schools, and about 60,000 scholars. I myself visited only three schools in Manchester; the Royal Lancastrian School, the Blue Coat Hospital, and the Grammar School.

The Royal Lancastrian School of Manchester is probably the largest and most interesting yet established on the Lancastrian system. It was founded in the year 1809, and since then has afforded instruction to no less than 24,000 poor children. This school contains on an average, at every time of the year, about 1000 children, who are all assembled in one large, airy, and well-arranged hall. On the day of my visit it contained no less than 720 boys, and 320 girls. Formerly the instruction was quite gratuitous; but of late years the income of the school has been so scanty, that it has been found necessary to charge a penny a week for each child. The head master told me that this tax had rather increased than decreased the number of scholars. "There are many parents," said he, "who can well spare this small sum, and who do not like the notion of their children attending charity schools. These now send their children to us; and even the poor often prefer paying something for their children's schooling, and are more punctual in sending them when they do so. We are always full, and, generally speaking, there are 100 or 150 applicants waiting for admission. Our working classes are by no means blind to the advantages of education, and are generally anxious that their children should possess more learning than they do themselves. If our poor population has remained behind that of other places in cultivation, the fault is not their own, but of adverse circumstances, which of late years have hindered the establishment and progress of schools." Perhaps the fault rests with the English government—which has hitherto troubled itself little about education—and with the wealthy inhabitants of Manchester. Does it not appear almost incredible, that in a town like Manchester, many of whose citizens are worth ten, twenty, or even thirty thousand a year, a great school like this has a regular income of only 36l. a year, and with difficulty augments this, by the weekly tax of a penny a head, to the paltry sum of 250l. a year, which is all it has, wherewith to remunerate teachers and pay its other expenses? One cannot help thinking, when considering such anomalies, of the learned old Fellows of the Universities, who receive amazing salaries, no mortal creature can tell for what! If a few dozen of these fellowships were to be abolished, and their receipts applied to the education of the people, what an extensive benefit would be conferred upon the working class! and what would the world suffer by the loss?

The great hall of the Lancastrian school is decorated in a rather peculiar way. At one end is painted up the Bible, with the British arms resting upon it, and round the walls, figures in large letters the much lauded saying of George III.: " May every poor child in my dominions be enabled to read the Bible!" This royal wish has remained as empty and fruitless as that other equally famous saying of Henri Quatre's, that he wished every poor man in his kingdom might have a fowl boiling in his pot. The outward arrangements of the school are thoroughly excellent, and the appearance of the children, although, as the director told me, they mostly came from the poorest and meanest districts of Manchester, was remarkably satisfactory. They all looked healthy, lively, clean, and decently dressed.

All the children are instructed at the same time in the same room, by the same teacher, who selects from among the children themselves, his under-teachers and inspectors. For such of my readers as are unacquainted with the Lancastrian system, a short account of it, as pursued at this school, may not be without interest. The benches stand in two long rows, one for the girls and one for the boys; between the benches a considerable space is left. Each bench is occupied by a certain number of scholars, and is placed under the superintendence of a monitor. There are 108 of these monitors in the school. Several benches are placed under the direction of an " inspecting monitor," who sits at a little raised desk, with his face to the benches. Of these there are sixty. Several such classes are governed by one upper monitor, called a " captain." These captains walk up and down before their classes, keeping a vigilant eye on all that goes on, and noting down on their little tablets, remarks on the conduct of monitors and scholars. There are twenty-eight captains in the school. Finally come the four captain-generals, of whom there is one always walking round the school, to keep order, and watch the conduct of captains and monitors.

Of course the captains and monitors are never all on duty at once, but relieve guard; for it is requisite that they should at the same time be receiving their own education. The teacher himself instructs only the captains and captain-generals; each in turn, as he is relieved from his inspecting post. Some of the captains are always busy, instructing those of the inspecting monitors who are off duty; and these again instruct the lower monitors in the same way. These last, mostly little fellows of eight or ten years of age, have each their ten or twelve scholars under them.

The lowest classes, who are still learning their letters, are called alphabet classes; those who are learning to spell, a-b-ab-classes; and those who can read words, reading classes. Every month a general examination of teachers is held, and a general promotion of advanced scholars from one class into another. The benches and classes are all numbered, so that the inspecting captain can easily note down his remarks on any offender without inquiring after his name. I met a little captain only twelve years of age, who had just noted down on his tablet: "Monitor N. 3 a-playing." The entrance of the scholars, their seating themselves, their standing up for morning prayers, their marching out for recreation, and their final breaking up, all are conducted with more than military, with machine-like regularity.

The teacher himself gives his orders from a high tribune, towards which the faces of all scholars are turned. There are also little telegraphs put up between the benches, by means of which telegraphic signals are conveyed to the monitors and captains. General orders to the whole school are preceded by the sharp ringing of a loud bell. The regularity and order with which every thing is carried on affords the same sort of pleasure to the spectator, that is afforded by the spectacle of a great machine at work.

The instruction is confined to reading, writing, and arithmetic. Few of the children remain longer than fifteen months at the school, being generally taken away by their parents as soon as an employment can be found for them. I was sorry to observe, when I looked at the stranger's book of the school, that this institution had not attracted so much public attention of late as it used to do. During the whole of last year it received only thirty visitors, while in former years it could boast of hundreds, and of highly distinguished and illustrious names.

The Blue Coat Hospital is a well-endowed old school, which educates eighty poor boys at once. In Manchester it is generally called "the College." The scholars, in their long dark robes, their lofty old church, their great halls, their ancient and wealthy library, all have a certain monastic appearance and character. The costume of the scholars, their long blue tunic, yellow under clothes and blue stockings, has remained precisely the same as when the school was first established, by the "worthy Humphrey Chetham," in the middle of the seventeenth century.

The scholars are the children of poor but respectable parents, and must all be brought up to some particular handicraft. When we consider what a noble renown the old worthy has earned for himself by this foundation, what benefits he has conferred, and still will confer, upon future generations, and what blessings have glorified his memory for two hundred years, we cannot help wondering how the wealthy can ever resist the temptation of thus building up for themselves an immortal monument in the gratitude and reverence of posterity. Many might do so at little or no sacrifice. If among every

hundred or every thousand inhabitants of Manchester, who attained
great wealth, only one were to think and act like old Humphrey
Chetham, the whole land would be crowded with similar beneficent
institutions. But these people seem all to carry in their hearts the
precept which old Chetham only bore on his coat of arms: " Quod
tuum, tene !"

The Grammar School is another old establishment, which dates as
far back as 1520. It formerly confined its instruction to the classics,
but an English school has recently been added to it. In going over
this school I was astonished at the quantity of inscriptions and engravings which covered the walls, benches, tables, and desks. Canals, railroads, and rivers, with barges, ships, and locomotives upon
them, seemed the favourite subjects. The same hieroglyphics often
ran along several places, each continuing the work of his neighbour.

The cotton manufacture of Manchester must, of course, be the first
subject to attract the stranger's interest. Cotton—this gigantic Her-
cules, of whose power the world did not dream a hundred years ago,
but which now unites and severs empires, and forms the support, the
occupation, and the chief interest of millions of human beings; cotton is the grand central force which holds together this youthful
giant—Manchester.

I remember once upon a time, in my younger days, a friend made
me blush to confess my ignorance of the situation of the town of
Burg, near Berlin, by exclaiming, " What? Not know where Burg
is, a town of 12,000 inhabitants? Oh! for shame !" But in England,
one gets hardened in ignorance, more especially in Lancashire, where
a man would never have done blushing, if he were to do so every
time he discovered a town of 10,000 inhabitants, of which he had
previously known nothing. Within a circle drawn round Manchester at little more than a dozen English miles from its Exchange,
there would be found, among others, the following great towns, all
of which have more than 12,000 inhabitants. Ashton-on-the-Lyne,
35,000; Great Bolton, 28,000; Little Bolton, 12,800; Dean,
22,900; Bury, 15,000; Dunkinfield, 15,600; Ecles, 28,000; Leigh,
20,000; Macclesfield, 23,000; Middleton, 14,000; Oldham, 32,000;
Oldham, with Prestwich, 67,000; Preston, 36,000; Pilkington,
11,000; Rochdale, 58,000; Saddleworth, 16,000; Stockport, 66,000;
Warrington, 19,000; Wigan, 44,000. Most of these towns are so
many Manchesters in miniature, and they are all exclusively occupied
and maintained by the cotton manufacture.

The factory which I visited, that of Messrs. Orell, commonly
called Orell's Mill, was recommended to me as one of the finest in
Manchester, and as one in which all the newest improvements in
machinery had been adopted. Down to the present day the machinery used in the cotton making has continued to improve with
astonishing rapidity and regularity. At present the sorting and
putting in of the raw cotton, and the catching up of broken threads,
are the only operations, in the whole manufacture, which are carried

on by human hands. The cleaning, combing, twisting, rolling, and all the other innumerable operations required, are all performed by machinery. Even the feeding with fuel of the steam-engines employed is taken out of the hands of human labourers, and is accomplished by machines called self-feeders. One of these, which I saw at Orell's Mill, supplied an enormous steam-engine of 240 horse-power with all the coals it required.

Orell's Mill is a very complete factory; the cotton is brought to it raw from America or Egypt, and it is here cleaned, spun, and woven. It employs no less than 1300 looms. These are all placed in one great weaving room, in which 650 girls are constantly at work. The humming, beating, and whirring of all these looms filled the room with a noise like the roaring of the sea. The power-loom is said, not only to work ten times as fast as the hand-loom, but a great deal better; the woof is more smooth and even, because the stroke of the machine is more regular than that of the human hand. Orell's Mill has its own particular steam-worked water-engine, which commands the whole nine stories of the building, and is capable of drenching it with an enormous quantity of water in a few minutes. The work-people determined to let the engine play, in order to show us its power. Scarcely, however, had the water entered the pump than numbers of heads were thrust from the windows, shouting and gesticulating. We had the steam-engine stopped, and on going in found to our consternation that in a few seconds half a floor had been deluged with water. The plugs of the pipes running through the buildings had been left open, and had thus occasioned this flood among the cotton.

This factory is one of the best built of any; yet I found the air intolerably close and suffocating in some parts. I was also sorry to observe the terrible narrowness of the passes between the dangerous machines and their restless and gigantic arms and wheels; in these passes the floor was also extremely smooth and slippery.

According to the regulations of the Factory Act all manufacturers must allow their labourers two holidays, Christmas Day and Good Friday, every year, and eight half-holidays besides. Children under nine years of age are now not allowed to work in the factories at all; children under thirteen are not to work more than nine hours a day; but all over thirteen work twelve hours a day. The distribution of these twelve hours is of course left to the employer. In Orell's Mill that distribution was as follows: At six o'clock in the morning work begins, and continues till eight, when half-an-hour's interval is allowed for breakfast. At half-past eight work begins again, and goes on till twelve, when an hour's interval is allowed for dinner. From one till four forms the third working period, followed by another interval of half-an-hour. At half-past four they begin and continue till eight, when at last machines and labourers leave off for the night.

Every manufacturing district has its own factory-inspector, to whom, in cases of abuse of power, or other grievances, all parties may apply for arbitration. The name and address of this factory-inspector is pasted up in large letters in the hall of the factory.

If England were not so rich in wonders of the same kind, the stranger might fancy the appearance of Stockport unique in the world. The houses of Stockport rise up the deep sides of a valley, watered by the river on which the town stands. Over the whole gulf, right over town and river, from height to height, stretches a gigantic viaduct, across which passes the railway to London. The twenty-two arches of this viaduct are a hundred feet high. Even in England this is a striking and magnificent work.

I was curious to see the calico-printing process which completes the preparation of the printed cottons. For that purpose I visited one of the principal printing-works. The printing process is now almost entirely carried on with copper-plates, upon which the pattern is engraved. Nevertheless I found in one part of the building a few of the old " block printers," who were cutting wooden blocks, and printing with them after the old fashion. Their old occupation is going more and more out of demand, and all the block-printers will very soon have perished of hunger and neglect. Of late years these printing-works, like so many other houses in Manchester, work only half-time, employing only half their labourers. In some parts of the building, I found groups of poor, unoccupied labourers sitting warming themselves by the fire-places, sunk in a sort of melancholy stupor. " It is heartbreaking, sir, to see these men," said the overseer who accompanied me. " Men who would so gladly work, but whom, if we would keep ourselves out of the *Gazette*, we are obliged to deprive of employment. As we allow them to warm themselves at our fires in this cold weather, they come here and sit idle and sad in the places where formerly they worked so busily, looking enviously at those work-people whom we are still able to employ. They have a better roof over their heads here than in their own miserable dwellings."

I was pleased with the humanity of the manufacturers in still allowing these poor people shelter and warmth, although compelled to deprive them of work and wages. When in London, looking over caricatures of the distress of the manufacturing districts, or when on the continent, listening to descriptions of the ignorance, brutality, and lawlessness of the English manufacturing population, the feeling of compassion is blunted, and the most terrible facts are often heard with comparative indifference. I have even met with people in France and Germany, who seemed to feel a sort of malicious exultation in hearing and recounting the humiliations of proud England. But to see the poor sufferers themselves bowed down by want and misery, condemned to idleness and starvation, while willing and able to work, and to hear them tell their melancholy stories, is one of the most heartrending things imaginable.

" Who are you then?" said I to an old man, sitting by the fire.

" Oh, sir! men out of employment."

" What is your business?"

" I am a block-printer, sir, but in this stand-still of every thing, I have had no employment for some months."

" Cannot you find other employment? Can you do nothing else?"

" No, sir, I have been brought up for block-printing, and I have been a block-printer all my lifetime. I understand nothing else. Besides, the whole country is at a stand-still now. In my time I had a cow, and a little garden, which my wife attended to. My wife died last summer, and all the other things are gone away, by the badness of the times."

" Do not despair, the times may mend."

" Oh, no hope, sir! Starving is our lot! No hope, sir! no hope!" muttered the old man in a trembling voice, sighing deeply, and turning his eyes back to the blazing coals.

While I was still standing by these people, one of the overseers came in, and called to one of the poor fellows, with the welcome words: " Tom, I have got a job for you!" The rest looked in silent envy at the happy Tom.—Had it not been for the melancholy impression of this scene, the many interesting operations and processes which we saw at the printing-works would have afforded us much pleasure. One of the most interesting divisions, was the pattern-room, in which were 3000 copper cylinders, covered with engraved patterns. Each of these cylinders had cost, for metal and engraving, from 10l. to 20l. I was told that a pattern seldom stands longer than a twelvemonth, and that even those which are most successful, never last more than two years. The designers and engravers of these patterns are of course well paid, since a great deal both of chemical knowledge, skill, and imagination is required to make a good pattern-designer. There are many Frenchmen always employed in this branch of the manufacture, who are said to have more taste than the English designers.

There are in Manchester, four " India-rubber-web, or water-proof-clothing-establishments," which are exclusively occupied in preparing this Indian gum for all its various useful purposes. One of these establishments, that of Messrs. Birley and Company, uses no less than 250,000 pounds of the gum a year, and 100,000 gallons of spirits for melting it. As the clothes manufactured of this material require to be sewn with India-rubber thread, in order to be water-proof in the seams, and as this is not understood by ordinary tailors, a great sewing establishment is connected with the manufactory. One of the newest applications of India-rubber, is that of superseding bottle-corks, by a preparation of wool and India-rubber, which forms a tight elastic substance, very much like the wood of the cork-tree. This invention at first excited much alarm among the cork-cutters, but certain practical difficulties have hitherto prevented its general application.

In the cotton factory belonging to Messrs. Birley and Company,

5000 gallons of oil, and fifty hundred-weight of tallow, are annually used for the greasing of the steam-engines. On such a gigantic scale are even the most trifling operations carried on in Manchester.

The simple instruments with which our forefathers prepared their looms and spinning-wheels, were a chisel, a hammer, a saw, a file, a plane, and pincers. And even now, it is with chisels, hammers, saws, files, planes, and pincers, that the wonderful machinery employed in the cotton factories is made. But these primitive instruments have been so altered, varied, and magnified, of late years, so wonderfully changed in proportions, numbers, and dimensions, that it is now scarcely possible to recognise them. There is no town in the world where the spectator may have an opportunity of seeing so many splendid machines, and machine-making processes, as at Manchester. I had here the pleasure of visiting one of the greatest machine-making establishments in the world; namely, the so-called Atlas-works of Messrs. Sharp and Roberts. These gentlemen have two manufactories, one for general machine-making, the other for the manufacture of locomotive engines, and of those enormous tools used in the making of machines. I visited first the latter establishment, at which, as I was informed, forty-nine locomotives had been built during the last year. This number at first struck me as rather inconsiderable, but I was told it was the largest number ever yet manufactured there in one year. It was expected, however, that the number for the current year would amount to eighty.

Mr. Sharp died a short time ago, and his funeral was attended by all his mechanics and work-people, 800 in number. As not one of these workmen had weekly wages less than twenty-five shillings, and many earned four or five pounds, a week, the amount of capital necessary to carry on such a business must be enormous.

From the locomotive department we were conducted to the " mule and loom department," in which the spinning and weaving machines are manufactured, with all their latest improvements; and thence to the tool department, which is the most interesting to the uninitiated spectator. Here may be seen saws, planes, hammers, and chisels, of astonishing variety and gigantic proportions; machines whose delicacy and precision of working is, in spite of their power and dimensions, equal to that of the watchmaker's minutest tools. Here are " barcutting machines," which are incessantly employed in chopping and splitting huge beams of iron, as if they were wax; and " planing machines," which pass swiftly and easily over huge iron surfaces, smoothing them down as if they were but velvet, although the resistance to the plane is often equal to that of twenty hundred-weight.

All the machines, engines, and tools, which are to be cut or cast in iron in these great establishments, have to be previously exactly modelled in wood, in order that any practical defects may be discovered and remedied. These wooden models are called patterns, and are made of hard firm woods, such as mahogany; when accepted, these models are painted, and placed in a great room called the pattern room, which is, of course, a very interesting department of the manufactory.

There are some people who find nothing but subjects of vexation and grumbling in visits to these great manufactories, on account of the dust, dirt, stunning noises, unpleasant smells, and close air, with which they are annoyed at such places. But whoever can turn his attention away from these petty grievances, and fix it on the many interesting, astonishing, and, I might almost say, sublime results of human skill, invention, and industry, which are here presented to his senses and thoughts, will acknowledge, that there is an enjoyment in such scenes, seldom surpassed in any place, an enjoyment belonging exclusively to this most wonderful country, of a truly wonderful age.

The English workmen in the Manchester manufactories generally answered, when I requested them to show me any thing : " Yes, certainly, sir, we will show you all, and tell you which is which." I had already seen " which was which," in all the principal manufactories of Manchester, and was now only anxious to enter those great warehouses, wherein the productions of all these wonderful machines are collected in tempting profusion and order, to charm the money out of the pockets of all nations in both hemispheres.

There are, in Manchester, upwards of 1000 immense manufactories. The great mercantile firms which mediate between the manufacturers and the public, are in number 360, among which are many German, Spanish, Greek, French, and other foreign houses. These merchants have all great warehouses or magazines, where their goods are stored up. Of late years, these warehouses have increased so much in number, that they form long streets, containing no dwelling-houses at all. Of these the chief is Mosley Street.

I visited the warehouse of Messrs. Potter, in this street; it is a great building six stories high, the upper floors of which are occupied by the lighter, and the lower by the heavier goods. As the great quantities of cotton and woollen goods perpetually traversing Manchester, between the different spinning, weaving, bleaching, dyeing, printing, and exporting establishments, could not be conveyed by the ordinary means, without great loss of time and trouble, a kind of conveyance called vans have been lately introduced, consisting of enormous, square, watertight boxes, placed on springs and wheels, which are capable of conveying immense masses of goods, in a comparatively small compass and short space of time. At the great warehouses, such as that of Messrs. Potter, machines called " steam hoists," are used, for raising the goods into the vans ; these little steam-engines stand on the ground-floor, and raise great bales of goods with extraordinary ease and celerity. Besides this steam-engine, no less than fifty workmen were constantly employed in the warehouse, in packing and unpacking the bales.

Every country has its particular partialities in the goods it purchases; or, as the Belfast merchants say, "every market has its whim." The speculating merchant must always be well acquainted with these, no less than with the real wants and customs of each nation. From the Manchester, warehouses great quantities of black cloth are annually sent to Italy, in order to clothe the innumerable priests of that country; but this black cloth must always be of a particular coal-black, without the slightest tinge of brown or blue. Goods must also be packed differently for different nations; thus, at Messrs. Potters', I saw bales of cotton intended for China, packed in the Chinese manner and decorated with bright, tasteful, little pictures, representing Chinese customs, ceremonies, costumes, &c. Nor must the manner of transport used in the interior of the countries for which they are intended be forgotten in the packing of the goods. Wares to be carried on the backs of elephants, camels, or lamas, must be differently packed from those to be conveyed by waggons, canals, or railways.

As the wares contained in the great bales, some of which weigh more than fifteen hundred-weight are often of a very miscellaneous kind, little pattern-books are sent off with each bale, containing not only the quantity, quality, price, &c., of the different goods, but a neat little specimen of each. Thus the foreign merchant on receiving his bale of goods, need not take the trouble of unpacking it, but need only turn over the instructive and entertaining pages of the elegant little pattern-book, to settle and direct the further destination of what it contains. Duplicate copies of all these little pattern-books are kept at the warehouse, with names and dates in full, and these are, after a time, bound up in great folio volumes, with all their specimens complete. These volumes, all ranged in order on their shelves, form a considerable library in many warehouses.

The following instances will show the importance of which these pattern-books may sometimes be to the merchant. A South American merchant had ordered a quantity of cotton goods of a particular pattern, from a house in Manchester, and they were sent him as directed. After some years this merchant wrote back, that the wares he had received had been of a bad quality. All his customers had complained of the cotton, for after a short time innumerable little holes had appeared all over it, and it had thus become useless. This the merchant attributed to some fault in its preparation at Manchester, and he now demanded recompense from his Manchester correspondent, for the great damage he had thus sustained in his business. The Manchester merchant turned back to his pattern-book for that date and found the patterns therein quite whole and uninjured. He now presented these before the proper tribunal, and also procured testimonies from several persons in England who had used the cotton in question, showing that no traces of similar decay had been observed. A number of experiments were now made upon the cotton, and it was at last discovered, that the pattern, although durable enough in the cold, damp climate of England, could not stand the intense heat of Brazil, because a certain little green blossom

occurring very frequently in the pattern, had been dyed with a preparation capable of being chemically affected and injured by intense
heat, and had thus occasioned the little holes complained of. As,
however, this discovery had never been made before, and the cotton had been sent as it was ordered, the Manchester house was ex-
onerated from all blame. In the following case the result was
different. An Asiatic merchant wrote that the woollen cloth he
had received, was covered with little brown specks, which materially
injured its appearance and value. The patterns were examined,
and no similar spots were found. Experiment, however, soon proved
that the cloth when sent off, must have still contained a considerable
quantity of animal fat, from which the manufacturers had not sufficiently purified it. The tremendous pressure to which the cloth
was subjected in its bales, had squeezed out this fat in the shape of
brown spots on the surface. The manufacturer bore the blame, and
had to pay the loss of both merchants.

The pattern-books form an astonishing series of witnesses to the
vanity, refinement, and caprice of the world, in the nature of its
whims, as to this one article of cotton. Perpetually is the fashion of
every market changing, as to colour, pattern, quality, and packing.

The enormous quantity of goods piled up in the warehouses of
Manchester—the close vicinity in which the number of its railways
places it, to the woollen factories of Leeds, the shawl and handker-
chief makers of Macclesfield, the silk weavers of Coventry, the
merino dealers of Bradford, the light cotton wares of Preston, and
the heavy cotton goods of Halifax, &c., &c.,—the energy and rapidity of its steam-giant, the universal servant of all work, which, like
Lord Chatham, "tramples on impossibilities,"—all the extraordinary
means and appliances which stand at the command of its manufacturers and merchants, combined with the industry, talent, and energy
of these merchants and manufacturers themselves—all these things contribute to render Manchester beyond dispute the manufacturing capital of the world. Among the most interesting places in such a town,
must of course be the Exchange, the parliament of the cotton lords,
as it is sometimes called. The Manchester Exchange is one of the
handsomest and most spacious in England. Tuesday is the principal
business day at this place, and one o'clock the chief business hour,
or the time of " high change," as it is called at Manchester. On
the evening before the morning on which I visited this Exchange,
the important news from Asia had arrived, bringing simultaneous
tidings of the peace with China and the termination of the Indian
war. The effect of this intelligence, I was told, had been immense,
and the rejoicings of the merchants and manufacturers unbounded.
Agreements, contracts, and purchases of extraordinary number and
importance, had been transacted only a few hours after the receipt
of this news, upon the strength of it. I expected to find nothing
but jubilee, exultation, and merry faces, on the Exchange. What
was my surprise, however, to see nothing of the kind ! The mer-

chants looked as grave, busy, and sober as ever; the whispering might, perhaps, have been a little more earnest—although he must have had a very fine ear who could discover this—the movements of the merchants, from one group to the other, might have been a little more animated than usual; but that was all. English exultation is very quiet and sober, yet it is, perhaps, more heartfelt and intense than it would be if it found vent in garlands, songs, dances, and trumpet-shouts, as in an old Greek triumph.

A " Newsroom" is connected with the Exchange of Manchester, as with all English exchanges. At this room are received on an average, 140 periodicals, English and foreign, *every day*. On Saturday, when the weekly papers are published, 186 is the usual number.

Periodical literature is that which flourishes most at Manchester. In this city are published five or six of those colossal English morning papers, of which the simple German reader, wonderingly asks himself, how any body *can* read them from beginning to end over his after-dinner pipe! Every number of the *Manchester Guardian* alone, contains thirty-six thick close-printed columns, each of which contains the matter of ten good-sized octavo pages; so that each number contains as much as a thick octavo volume ! Newspapers, however, are the only branch of literature which is much encouraged at Manchester.

When I was in Manchester, most of the scientific, artistic, and literary institutions of the town, (in which it was never wealthy,) were in a very decaying state. The Zoological Society was selling its wild beasts by auction; the owners of the Royal Theatre had just been declared bankrupt; the Athenæum was fast falling into ruins; the Lancastrian School was losing support. In a place where the utilitarian spirit of trade is so dominant, as in Manchester, such institutions are sure to be the first victims of any general depression in the commercial and manufacturing world.

Manchester, like most of the other great English towns, contains a Royal Institution for the encouragement of artists, at which is held every year an exhibition of old and new paintings. When I visited it, the exhibition contained 500 pictures, mostly by English artists. Few of these represented great historical scenes, and there were scarcely any Biblical pictures. Remembering the prominent part which Biblical scenes play in all similar exhibitions on the continent, and being well aware of how much the Bible is read and studied in England, this fact rather surprised me. The greater number of the pictures represented landscapes, and most of these were scenes on the Rhine and Italy, or other parts of the fashionable continental tour. There were also plenty of " portraits of dogs," " farmers' boys," " dead game," " horses in a stable," and other such favourite subjects with English painters.

Manchester contains two of the so-called " Mechanics' Institutions," which have of late years become common all over England.

These institutions, designed for the benefit and improvement of the working-classes, generally contain a library, a museum of some kind, a lecture-room, at which popular lectures of different sorts are delivered, and a school for the children of the shareholders. The largest of the two Mechanics' Institutions, at Manchester, contained, in 1841, 1092 shareholders.

As the other institution is smaller than this one, the number of shareholders cannot in all amount to 3000; a rather scanty support for such institutions, in a town like Manchester. Perhaps the most interesting and peculiar part of these institutions are the classes for mutual instruction, which meet to discuss various subjects together, and to read aloud, and criticise, lectures and essays composed by the different members.

The Museum of Natural History, established at Manchester a few years ago, already occupies one of the first places among the museums of Great Britain, and I was not a little surprised at finding such a splendid and interesting collection, among the chimneys and machines of the great manufacturing metropolis. Its most wealthy department is that of ornithology, in which it may fairly challenge comparison with the finest museums in the world. The famous English ornithologist, Waterton, with whom I had the pleasure of becoming acquainted in England, maintains that the stuffed birds, in most European ornithological collections, are mere caricatures of nature, owing to the villanous style in which the stuffing has been performed. He himself has a real passion for this art of stuffing, which he has carried to an extraordinary perfection; he often occupies half a year in contriving and performing the stuffing of a single bird. His own collection, at Waterton Hall, is a real masterpiece in its way, and this of Manchester approaches nearer to it in perfection than any thing I have elsewhere seen.

I was displeased to find in this, so-called, Museum of Natural History, so many antiquarian relics, and ethnographical and historical remains, which, however interesting in themselves, had no business whatever here. This fault, however, is not peculiar to the Museum of Manchester; it is more or less the defect of all the collections of Europe. This barbarous custom of spoiling different kinds of collections, by mixing them up together, without order or classification, has survived from those bygone times, in which scientific collections for definite purposes, were unknown, and when all kinds of " curiosities" were esteemed equal and similar in value and importance. It is a piece of barbarism in science, thoroughly unworthy of this enlightened nineteenth century.

The celebrated Arabian charger, Vizier, presented by the Sultan Mohammed to the Emperor Napoleon, is preserved, stuffed, at this museum. One of the most remarkable objects in the museum, is an English mummy, that of a Mrs. Beswick, who gave orders in her testament that her body should not be buried, but should be embalmed, stuffed, and preserved by a certain Dr. White, to whom, in reward, she bequeathed an annual income of 500*l.* On his death the doctor bequeathed the body of the eccentric testatrix to this Museum of Manchester, where it now takes its place beside a Peruvian and Egyptian mummy.

GENERAL APPEARANCE AND CHARACTERISTICS OF MANCHESTER.

It cannot be said that Manchester is either an ugly or a beautiful town, for it is both at once. Some quarters are dirty, mean, ugly, and miserable-looking to an extreme; others are interesting, peculiar, and beautiful in the highest degree. Come with me, then, dear reader, and let us take a short walk together through these various scenes. We set out from the broad, stately, and imposing Market-street, which runs from the river Irwell, right through the heart of the town, and continuing under the name of Piccadilly, loses itself in the opposite suburbs, under the third *alias* of the London-road. This street is always busy, noisy, and interesting, and contains numbers of splendid shops. In the evening, its thousands of gaslights glittering from the shops and street-lamps, make it almost painfully dazzling to eyes not yet accustomed to these nightly illuminations of the great English cities. In this street the beggars of Manchester love to congregate, importuning the wealthy and idle as they pass. There in the side gutters stand the poor broken-down manufacturing labourers, moaning out their usual lamentation—" Out of employment." Between the idle rich and the idle poor the industrious middle classes push their eager way—busy manufacturers, inspectors, overseers, clerks, and merchants. Here at the corner of the street stands perhaps some poor Hindoo beggar, dressed in dirty white muslin, his dark face surmounted by a white turban, holding the story of his misfortunes, written on a slip of paper, in his hand. One of these Hindoo beggars, whom I saw in the streets of Manchester, seemed to me the very picture of utter desolation. To all that I said to him he could only answer the single word: " Livapoo! Livapoo!" meaning probably that he had come from Liverpool. I bought one of the papers he held in his hand, hoping to find that it contained some account of himself or his birth-place, but I found that it was only a religious tract.

Among these busy and idle crowds, numbers of hackney-coaches and cabs pursue their way, and in still greater numbers, the carts, waggons, and vans, of the merchants and manufacturers, of all sorts and sizes, hurry along. On the side pavement poor girls, laden like these vans, with as much cotton and calico as they can carry, drag themselves from one place to another. These are probably the work-people of the smaller manufacturers, who, unable to purchase vans, load their work-people in this unmerciful manner.

Let us now turn into one of the by-streets which, diverge from Market-street into Mosley-street, or Cooper-street, for instance. Here stand the great warehouses, five or six stories high, all large and imposing, some of them stately and elegant. At night these warehouses are all brilliantly lighted from top to bottom. On the ground floor are the counting-houses, where the merchants and clerks are busy all day long. This class is, I believe, in no town so industrious as in Manchester; nowhere, at least, do I remember to have seen so many wealthy people exclusively and passionately devoted to business. There are people here, possessing annual incomes of many thousands, who work like horses all the year round, stinting themselves in sleep and mealtimes, and grudging every moment given to amusement or society. Those who wonder at this fact should recollect that what passes for pleasure with the idle and dissipated would be intolerably wearying to these " men of business," who are as much in their element in the life they lead, as fish in water, and would be like fish *out* of water if they were removed to the lighter atmosphere of pleasure. Business is their habit, their delight, their very existence; and a place without business would be to them empty and joyless in the extreme. The hopes and fears, the gains and losses, the failures and successes, attending their occupations, afford them an excitement as absorbing, and, after a time, as necessary, as the warrior feels in his battles, or the gamester over his faro-table.

It is at six o'clock in the morning that these streets are busiest and fullest. This is the hour when the great factories begin their work, and, on every side, the pavement is covered with labourers, old and young, men, women, and children, hastening to their daily employments, and clattering over the pavements with their wooden shoes.

From the streets of the warehouses, whose monotonous lines are here and there broken by some splendid museum, music-hall or town-hall, with its columns, arches, and colonnades, or by the Corinthian portico of some blind-asylum, hospital, or deaf and dumb-institute, or else by the simple façade of some plain Methodist, Baptist, or Unitarian chapel, we pass on to the banks of the rivers which run through the city. These are three, the Wedlock, the Irk, and the Irwell. Here the scene varies. The rivers are intersected by an immense number of large and small bridges, in every form and direction. Standing upon one of these bridges, let us look around us a little. What an extraordinary spectacle! There stand rows and groups of huge manufactories, each consisting of numerous buildings which are sometimes bound together by one surrounding wall. Sometimes these walls are fortified and guarded like fortresses, by vigilant sentinels, who allow none to pass but such as have a right to enter. See how eagerly these manufactories suck up, through pumps and buckets, the river water, which dirty as it is, is invaluable to them, and which they pour back into the river, in black, brown, and yellow currents, after it has served their purposes. The river pours on its thick muddy current through the streets of the city to satisfy other thirsty manufactories further on. The blue heavens above are hidden from us by the thick smoke of the huge factory chimneys which weave a close impenetrable veil of brown fog between the city and the sky. For half a century these bridges have not basked in the warm glory of sunshine; only the cold faces of the moon and stars are permitted to look upon them, for at night the factories rest, and the clouds disperse.

Leaving the bridges of the Wedlock, let us proceed to those of the Irk and the Irwell, and admire the magnitude and splendour which characterises every thing we see. Between the great factories which each employ 500 or 1000 work-people, are scattered those of the smaller mill-owners, which often consist merely of the owner's dwelling-house, somewhat enlarged and extended. The great establishments are built in various ways; some piled up story on story; others on the straight line system, in long successive rows; others like huge greenhouses, all on one floor, lighted from the top. From these huge and oddly shaped buildings rise immense chimneys of all heights and diameters, many as tall as the steeples of St. Paul's and St. Stephen's, and sometimes architecturally ornamented with stone garlands, bas-reliefs, and pedestals. As in former times, the huts of the vassals surrounded the castles of their lords; so now, in the neighbourhood of the great manufactories, are seen the dwelling-places of the work-people, mean-looking little buildings, huddled together in rows and clusters. Sometimes the work-people of each manufactory form a little community by themselves, living together in its neighbourhood in a little town of their own; but in general they occupy particular quarters of the town, which contain nothing but long unbroken rows of small low dirty houses, each exactly like the other. These quarters are the most melancholy and disagreeable parts of the town, squalid, filthy, and miserable, to a deplorable degree. Here stand the abominable beer-houses, dram-shops, and gin palaces, which are never without customers. Here the streets are filled with ragged women and naked children. Whole rows of houses stand empty, while the remainder are overcrowded; for in some places the inmates have been expelled by the owners for non-payment of rent, while in others they have voluntarily given up their dwellings in order to live cheaper, by sharing that of another family.

The late disturbances in the manufactories have increased that very misery and poverty which they were designed to remedy. During one week, at that disturbed time, no less than 30,000l. were taken out of the different savings-banks of the town, in small sums, by the rash and deluded workmen, who hoped that they could live upon their savings, until their masters should be forced to yield. Thus they wasted the little sums put by, for sickness and old age, until all was consumed, and they were starved out by their masters, who of course could maintain this dreadful struggle longer than the poor needy insurgents, and they were soon forced by hunger and want to take what terms they could get.

In these miserable dwellings, often in close damp cellars beneath them, are found the poorest of all the inhabitants of Manchester—the hand-loom weavers. It is astonishing how any of these can continue to earn a penny, in the unequal competition with the immense machinery and capital employed in the great factories. Yet it is an indisputable fact, that there still exist, in Manchester alone, no less than 3192 hand-weavers. These work from morning till night, in close places, with scanty nourishment and clothing, and suffering grievously from privation and want. The earnings of the poor hand-weavers are probably, by this time, reduced to their minimum, and they will soon be forced to quit the field. I went through a number of their cellars, and I found many in which the loom was already at rest. Before one such, sat in unwilling idleness, the very image of silent despair, a poor half-starved weaver, who had not a penny to buy cotton, and who told me that he had been in vain seeking employment for eight days. On his table was a small plate of cold watery potatoes, saved from the scanty sustenance of the preceding day, to satisfy the hunger of the next.

In these poor quarters of Manchester are found the so-called *Fent-shops*, where are bought up all the odd ends of calico and cotton, which are thrown aside at the great factories, and sold again to the small weavers. Through these poorer quarters pass many broad, splendid streets, which lead out through the suburbs to Victoria Park, and other more fashionable vicinities, where splendid villas and gardens congregate as closely as chimneys on the river banks, and shops in the Market-street. Thither drive, ride, and walk, at the close of the day, the wealthy merchants and manufacturers of Manchester, to rest from their mental and bodily fatigues, and enjoy in the bosoms of their families a few hours of ease and refreshment, amidst the splendid acquisitions of their laborious hours. The villas and country-houses lie sometimes in long terraces and roads, and sometimes in beautiful detached situations.

It is a strange thing that all over the world, in America and in Europe, there should exist such a very unfavourable opinion of English labourers, and that their undeniable skill and industry, in their particular vocations, should be unable to remove the universal impression of their immorality, lawlessness, ignorance, and brutality. Even where it is found necessary to employ them, this is always done reluctantly and fearfully. I was in Austria shortly after the English labourers had been dismissed from the railroads making there, because their turbulence, brutality, and drunkenness occasioned all kinds of riots and accidents. I went to Saxony, and found, that there too, all the English labourers had been turned away, because their conduct was found quite insufferable. I went to Frankfort, and met a papier maché manufacturer, who told me, with rueful shakings of the head, that he was indeed compelled to employ English labourers in some parts of his business, because they understood their business so well, and were so remarkably skilful in it, but that he longed to get rid of them, because they were the most troublesome, ignorant, and unmanageable of his work-people. I went to Belgium, and read an interesting report of an English Poor Law Commission, in which the evidence of a great manufacturer of Philadelphia, concerning English labourers, was given at full length. This gentleman testified that one-fifth of the work-people, in the American factories, were foreigners, most of them Englishmen, whom, however, the manufacturers employed very unwillingly, on account of their being so "dissipated and discontented." They were, besides, universally disliked, because they were so given to drunkenness. The American labourers are always found better educated, more intelligent, and less given to sensual indulgences. No strikes or combinations of workmen are ever known among the American labourers, as among the English, who are always combining to force higher wages from their masters. The superiority of the American labourers is chiefly attributed to their superiority of education. The American masters are always very particular in having the children of their labourers sent regularly to school.

I came to England, and read further reports on the subject, all equally confirmatory of these statements. A Swiss manufacturer of Zurich, testified that he employed, in his factory, from six to eight hundred work-people, of all nations, Swiss, Saxons, Bavarians, French, Danes, Norwegians, Poles, Hungarians, Prussians, Dutch, Scotch, and English, and that these last were "the most disorderly, debauched, unruly, and least respectable and trustworthy of any nation whatsoever whom we have employed." This gentleman further stated that, in saying this, he spoke the feelings of all the continental manufacturers with whom he was acquainted, more particularly that of the English manufacturers, settled in different parts of Europe. It seemed, he continued, that the ill-educated English workmen, when released from the iron discipline and cold severity with which their masters treated them in England, and when received with that urbanity and cordiality of kindness, which all well-behaved labourers on the continent expect and receive from their masters, lost all balance and self-possession, and became quite unmanageable. He found also that English labourers of the highest class, as to skill and pecuniary remuneration, generally lived worse and indulged themselves in lower ways than those of a far inferior rank of other nations. The townspeople of Zurich dread the English workmen as inmates, on account of their unruly and disorderly behaviour. The English workman of the first class will often spend half his nights in the wine-shop, will let his children grow up in all kinds of ignorance and brutality, and will live in the midst of dirt and disorder; while a German or Swiss labourer, of the very same class, reads, studies nature, cultivates music, has a clean and tidy household, and gives his children an excellent education. This report, while it affords a startling testimony to the ignorance and brutality of the uneducated English, is also a proof, let it never be forgotten, of the admirable candour and generosity of the nation. In no other European country would such a statement have been patiently heard, much less printed and published. This gentleman returned shortly afterwards to Zurich, with an English lady whom he had married in England. The work-people of his establishment hastened to welcome them, to present their master with a little congratulatory address, and his wife with various interesting little specimens of national industry, as nuptial presents; all, except the English labourers, who remained sullen spectators of the general rejoicing, and gave no signs whatever of cordiality and satisfaction!

Thus unanimous is the voice of the world concerning the English manufacturing labourers. A great part of the blame should rest no doubt with the English master-manufacturers, who, with a few rare and admirable exceptions, take no pains whatever to improve the character and open the minds of their work-people. The severity of discipline in the English factories, the cold, harsh manner in which the work-people are addressed by their superiors, the rigid silence enforced among them, and the unfeeling manner with which they are dismissed to steal or starve, at every fluctuation in the fortunes of their masters, all these things cannot but have a hardening and deadening effect on their characters. No less evil in its effects must be the total absence of all intercourse between these despised classes, and their employers, and the mutual indifference of both ranks to the prosperity or adversity of the other. It is commonly said in England that there is less personal intercourse between the master cotton-spinner and his workmen, than between the Duke of Wellington and the meanest cottager on his estate.

No doubt much strictness and regularity of discipline, much stern subordination of classes, is necessary to the maintenance of order in these gigantic establishments, and to the due security of the manufacturer's interests. But surely, surely, all that is necessary or desirable in this way, is not incompatible with a little more benevolence and cordiality of social intercourse, a little more humane and Christian regard for the temporal happiness and eternal welfare of those employed, than is commonly found in England! Might not this iron severity during hours of labour, be sweetened by a little more friendliness and affability at other times?

English manufacturers are generally astonished to hear, that even in Austria, the education of the children of manufacturing labourers is carefully attended to, each master manufacturer being compelled to erect a school near his factory, and allow the children of his work-people some hours every day for education. The English think that the business of a factory is to produce good cotton and bring in plenty of money, not to teach naughty boys their A B C.

The question of education, as regards the manufacturing population, is becoming every day more urgent and more difficult, owing to the increasing amount of juvenile labour employed in the factories. In the factory there is no father to teach and to punish, no mother to love and to reward, no grown-up brother and sister to instruct by example, no companion to animate by emulation and friendship. The most that can be hoped for is a just overseer, orderly fellow-labourers, and punctual wages on Saturday night. All else is wanting; I say *all*, and that includes very much. The dull, ceaseless mechanical occupation, continued all day long, affords no scope for invention or thought, no lessons of experience, no awakening and animating influences. How endless in amount and variety is the incidental information and instruction, conveyed to the son or daughter in the miscellaneous occupations of homes or even those of the shop and the warehouse, compared to that utter void of such things in the long monotonous rooms of the factory, with their noisy machines and silent busy crowds. For the women also, how evil in its influence must be the factory-system! What can those girls who pass their youthful years in this ceaseless mechanical labour, learn of the household and maternal duties, on which the happiness of the present generation, and the character of the future one, so largely depends?

There are many English writers who are ready to defend the factory system from all that can be charged upon it, and to represent all that is said against it, as the result of mere prejudice. They maintain that the children of the manufacturing population would be still worse brought up in the little households of the labourers than in the great factories, which are conducted by men of education and experience, and which are generally cleaner and better ventilated than the dwellings of the poor. The very nature of the factory system, say they, necessitates a certain order, regularity, and industry, which must have a good physical and moral influence on the children. And it cannot be denied that the moral education of the children is likely to be better cared-for in the worst factories than in the worst families. The parents may be profligate, drunken, and criminal, and the factory-system may do much to remove the children from their depraving example and influence. In the factories they can hardly learn many bad habits, the severity of discipline and ceaselessness of labour prevents *that*; and on the other hand, they acquire habits of punctuality and industry which cannot but be useful and beneficial. The factory-system, while it develops no moral germs *within* the soul, does at least, in some measure, preserve it from contamination from *without*. Even the severity and harshness to which the children are subjected in the factories, is, no doubt, often far exceeded by the tyranny and despotism of rude and brutal parents, in those recesses of private households which no legislative restrictions can reach, and where the searching eye of public opinion never penetrates.

Yet all that can be said in favour of the factory-system only amounts to this, that in the factories children are not exposed to all the evils which attend their condition in the very worst private families. Never, however, can they obtain in the very best factories any thing of the moral and mental discipline, of the awakening and ennobling influences, which even a very ordinary family education will afford them. The philanthropist cannot but regret the progress of any system, whatever be its other advantages, which tends to undermine that noblest of all institutions—the family. Since, however, the material advantages of the factory-system are so great, and its consequent growth and development so certain, every prospect of an improvement and mitigation of its evils cannot but be hailed by all benevolent minds with eagerness and satisfaction.

The English government has as yet done lamentably little for the education of the manufacturing population. What has been effected has been so chiefly through the agency of private persons, and sometimes of master manufacturers themselves. There still exist, however, among these latter, many absurd prejudices against the thorough education of their work-people. They fancy that to make these more generally intelligent and refined will be to counteract what they call the " special training," by which they are fitted for their particular mechanical avocations. They are also averse to the encouragement of temperance among their work-people, on the ground that drinking is necessary, to enable these to sustain the fatigue of their occupation, and that the best workmen are generally great drinkers. Some of the more enlightened manufacturers, however, have of late years begun to see the absurdity of these prejudices. The statements of a certain Mr. Fairbairn, one of the principal manufacturers of Manchester, show them to be totally unfounded. This experienced and enlightened man, affirmed that in his establishment, he always selected, for every kind of employment requiring any skill or forethought, those men whose general education had been liberal and thorough, in preference to those whose acquirements were limited to what was conferred upon them by the " special training." He found that it was only the very lowest and most mechanical of the factory employments which were not far better performed by well educated men, than by those more ignorant; and that even in these lowest departments, there would every now and then occur cases, in which superiority of education gave a workman a very great advantage and value. He also maintained that the educated workmen were far more moderate in their demands, and quiet and manageable in their behaviour, than the ignorant ones, who were perpetually actuated by a blind, envious animosity to their masters, which it was very difficult for any kindness or liberality on the part of these to overcome. " In case of any discontents or disturbances among our work-people, when strikes and combinations are apprehended, the best plan is always to collect the more intelligent and well-informed among them, and converse with them for a while in a friendly and sensible way, until they are gained over to sée the folly of their proceedings, and to act as checks upon the turbulence and stupidity of the rest." Mr. Fairbairn also stated, that it was a very mistaken notion, to imagine that drinking really enabled the workmen to sustain fatigue better, and to perform their work with more activity. It might indeed confer a certain temporary stimulus, in cases of great fatigue, but this was more than compensated by the dullness, heaviness, and feebleness which it afterwards brings on. In his own establishment, he was always careful to have a plentiful supply of good drinking-water at all hours for his men, and he found that this refreshed and strengthened them as much as fermented liquor, without the bad consequences of the latter. He referred at the same time to the instance of the boatmen of Constantinople, who are all what would here be called teetotallers, and who are the most powerful, athletic, and handsome set of men imaginable. He also strenuously denied the truth of the belief, that the best and most active workmen were generally given to drinking, affirming that such cases were very exceptional.

It is much to be regretted that the manufacturing population have not a better class of amusements at their command for the recreation of their leisure hours. Gardens and promenades, accessible to the working classes, are very deficient all over England, and particularly in the neighbourhood of Manchester. The taste for the beauties and wonders of nature, which attracts our German labouring classes into the fields and woods on Sundays and holidays, is also, I fear, deficient among the working population of England. The ignorance and want of cultivation, among the wives of the labourers, is probably in a great measure the occasion of the absence of refined and social pleasures among them. Many of the master-manufacturers are now taking great pains to encourage such pleasures and tastes among their work-people. One of them lately gave a great tea party, to which were invited all the labourers with their wives and children, and at which various amusements were provided for them. There was a piano and a large harmonica, and readings and recitations from favourite authors were also introduced. Four hundred persons, men, women, and children, were thus entertained in a very satisfactory manner, at a very trifling cost.

There have been lately set on foot among the manufacturing labourers themselves, various institutions and associations of excellent tendency and effect. There are sick-societies, whose members, by combination, are enabled to procure the benefit of good medical attendance when sick; there are burial-societies, which defray the expenses of funerals for deceased members; and there are the above-named societies for mutual improvement. Then there are the lyceums and mechanics' institutions, by which labouring men may obtain, by the payment of a few shillings every quarter, various advantages for themselves, their wives, and their children; for these include schools, lecture-rooms, libraries, and tea-parties, of various kinds.

There are, besides, other associations of labourers, whose object, sometimes avowed, sometimes secret, is to protect the interests of the members against the real or pretended encroachments of their masters. Upon these the master manufacturers look, of course, with a far less friendly eye. They maintain that such "unions" only promote hostile feelings in the work-people towards their masters, and are far more likely to retard than to promote the objects they have in view. The usual practice of these unions, when they wish to force higher wages from the masters, is to agree among themselves for a general strike, to refuse working on the old rate of wages, and to live upon their own savings as long as they can. On some occasions these unions have exercised a most formidable and tyrannical authority. That of Norwich, about ten or twelve years ago, had not only its regular general assemblies, but its committees perpetually sitting, to watch over the interests of the labourers, under the superintendance of a well-remunerated secretary named Fish. Every proceeding of the manufacturers was watched by these committees, and opposed in various ways if not approved of. Thus if it was resolved by the committee that twenty shillings a week, instead of fifteen, ought to be paid by a certain master to his work-people, the workmen were persuaded and commanded to refuse to work, and spies were appointed to mark those labourers who disregarded the mandate. These lost caste among their companions, by whom they were shunned and despised as traitors and cowards; they were tormented and teazed in a hundred ways; nay, frequently their houses were secretly entered at night, and their work damaged and destroyed. The manufacturers who refused to comply with the demands of the committee were threatened, watched, and annoyed in many ways; and the tradespeople, unfriendly to the union, were deprived of custom and support. The consequences of this tyranny, by injuring the prosperity of the whole city, were eventually as ruinous to the poor as to the rich.

Indeed the consequences of strikes and combinations are commonly far more fatal to the labourers than to their masters. The scanty funds of the work-people are soon exhausted, while the master manufacturers, who have often immense capital at their disposal, can hold out for a very long time. The poor ignorant labourers also, commonly disagree among themselves, while oligarchies are notoriously well united. Generally, after selling their last articles of clothing and furniture, the unfortunate "strikers" are compelled to swallow the bitter humiliation, of returning to their old situations, with unredressed grievances still rankling in their hearts, nay they must be very thankful if they are still permitted to do this. And of course it cannot be expected that the masters should receive back with any very friendly and compassionate feelings those troublesome rebels, who if they could, would gladly have ruined them. Very often too it happens, that in the absence of their usual number of work-people, the manufacturers have been forced to expedients, which have led to inventions and improvements in machinery, by which they are enabled to dispense with a large number of their former labourers. Thus when the latter return to work, numbers find themselves left destitute.

The true interests of both masters and labourers must point to a moderate but sufficient rate of wages. It must be the master's interest that his work-people should be well clothed and well fed, and should enjoy sufficient leisure and rest to keep them in good health; it must be his true interest that they should possess a certain amount of education and refinement, by which alone they can be rendered really valuable and efficient labourers, and a certain amount of innocent and beneficial recreation, by which alone they can be kept cheerful, contented, and satisfied with their situation. On the other hand, it must be the true interest of the labourer that his master should obtain sufficient remuneration and profit for his time and capital, to cause him to prefer the investment of such time and capital in cotton factories, to that of other modes of investment. But while the true interests of both masters and labourers point the same way, passion, prejudice, and avarice commonly contribute to warp the minds of both parties, and to make them prefer their temporary and apparent, to their real and lasting interests.

The master manufacturers, however, are generally enlightened men, who know their own interests, and are experienced and well-informed enough to keep them in sight. The work-people, deficient in all foresight, knowledge, and prudence, are less capable of distinguishing between temporary and lasting interests. Voluntary moderation on the part of the labourers is therefore, perhaps, more uncommon, than voluntary generosity on the part of the masters. The best chance of ameliorating the factory system, will probably be found, rather in acting on the intelligent master manufacturers, than on their ignorant and short-sighted labourers, whose strikes and riots are not only permanently injurious to themselves and their masters, but frequently communicate fatal shocks to the whole system of British industry.

There has been collected in England a good deal of statistical information, of one sort and another, concerning the condition of the labouring classes; yet what has been hitherto brought together is but very inadequate, after all, to the nature of the question, and the degree of information required, to judge of it properly. The science of statistics is yet in its infancy. Tables of averages, which ought to be founded on a thousand, or a hundred thousand different testimonies, are now made out on a few isolated cases; and the collector exults if he can triumph over the suspicion and reserve common to the ignorant and oppressed, when questioned by their superiors, so far as to give the details of the manner of living of a few individuals and families here and there. Yet there are certain facts, which seem to be very well authenticated and confirmed in the various reports and statistical tables published on this subject. Among these I was much struck by the number of instances in which very high wages did not exempt the labourers and their families from misery and discontent. I have myself visited the houses of many families, which I found well furnished, and whose inhabitants were excellently fed, but who yet manifested a stern, gloomy, and deep-rooted discontent. A Dr. Howard, of Manchester, who has written a pamphlet on the evil effects of want of nourishment, declares that there are numbers of families in Manchester, whose members earn very high wages, and who, nevertheless, are living in a state of wretched destitution, bordering on starvation. The following are the wages earned by a few workmen of different classes, every week:

			£.	s.	d.
A machine-printer, with a family of	9 persons earns		4	7	0
A millwright	10	„ „	4	10	0
A watchman	2	„ „	0	15	2
A common labourer	4	„ „	1	2	0
A colourer	10	„ „	2	6	0

Mr. Love mentions the case of a woman, named Hannah S——, who earned, together with her husband, four shillings a week, and received another shilling a week from the workhouse, but who was found one morning dead in her lodging, and had seemingly died merely from want of nourishment. There is probably no other country in the world where five shillings a week could not keep off starvation. Mr. Love also adds, from his own experience, that, in Manchester, numbers are yearly brought to a premature death from want of sufficient food. Dr. Howard gives, in his above-cited work, a detailed account of the expenditure of seven poor families, in the West Riding of Yorkshire, of which each contained, on an average, six members. They earned from twenty to five-and-twenty shillings per week, and had each a cottage, with a little piece of kitchen garden, rent-free, from the masters with whom they worked. With this sum was purchased flour, oatmeal, meat (about four shillings-worth weekly), potatoes, tea, coffee, sugar (a pound a week), milk, soap, coals, tobacco, salt, pepper, and other spices (often six-penny-worth of these every week), rice, and schooling for the children (seldom more than six or sevenpence a week). Four shillings a week for meat! How much meat do our wealthiest peasants and labourers consume in the week? Six-pennyworth of pepper and spice! As much as the schooling for the children.

The extraordinary, and, at first sight, inconceivable fact of great distress prevailing in spite of high and sufficient wages, is to be attributed partly, of course, to the very high rate of prices in England, but partly also to certain peculiarities in the English national character. The English are less capable of finding enough in a little, than any other nation in Europe. If the English could be merry over potatoes and water, and luxuriate in bread only of a Sunday, like the Saxons of the Harz Mountains; or if, like the tee-totallers of Turkey, they could enjoy a carousal over a handful of figs or dates, they would not die of starvation by hundreds, as is now the case. But the English set no value on small pleasures, small gains, and small frugalities; they are always extravagant and wasteful in trifles, and it is only in large matters that they learn to be provident and saving. This feature in the national character, no doubt mainly contributes to maintain that immense disproportion between the rich and the poor which prevails in England. Those who have any chance of obtaining a rank on a footing with the aristocracy, never cease to struggle towards that end; those who have no such chance, scarcely think it worth while to be well off, and squander away their small gains in sheer contempt of their inadequacy. Were the English more disposed to be content with a little, the nation could scarcely, indeed, have attained its present extraordinary degree of wealth and power, but large masses of the people would never have sunk to that deplorable degree of misery and degradation in which they now exist.

The very placards on the walls of the suburbs of Manchester, announce the extraordinary variety and importance of the pursuits in which the population is engaged. Here are the puffing announcements of quack-doctors, who recommend all kinds of life-pills, health-pills, and life-elixirs to the public, and who append divers " cautions to families," in which purchasers are warned to beware of various deleterious compounds, and requested to observe the superscription of the true medicine; here are the dangerous and too often infamous placards of the Socialists and others; here the earnest and resolutely revolutionary announcements of the Chartists, addressed to the " Men of Manchester," or the " Lovers of Justice !" or the " Friends of Freedom;" here invitations to public tea-parties and balls, held in honour of Duncombe or O'Connell, or some other favourite of the people; and here, most important of all, are the bills, addresses, and announcements, of the " Anti-Corn-Law men."

Manchester is the centre of the Anti-Corn-Law, as Birmingham is of the Universal-Suffrage, agitation. At Manchester are held the general meetings of the Anti-Corn-Law League, and here it is that the committee of the League constantly sits. The kindness of a friend procured me admission to the great establishment of the League at Manchester, where I had the satisfaction of seeing and hearing much that surprised and interested me. George Wilson and other well-known leaders of the League, who were assembled in the committee-room, received me as a stranger, with much kindness and hospitality, readily answering all my questions, and making me acquainted with the details of their operations. I could not help asking myself whether in Germany, men, who attacked, with such talent and energy, the fundamental laws of the state, would not have been long ago shut up in some gloomy prison as conspirators and traitors, instead of being permitted to carry on their operations thus freely and boldly in the broad light of day; and, secondly, whether in Germany, such men would ever have ventured to admit a stranger into all their secrets with such frank and open cordiality.

I was astonished to observe how the Leaguers, all private persons, mostly merchants, manufacturers, and men of letters, conducted political business, like statesmen and ministers. A talent for public business seems an innate faculty in the English. Whilst I was in the committee-room immense numbers of letters were brought in, opened, read, and answered, without a moment's delay. These letters, pouring in from all parts of the United Kingdom, were of the most various contents, some trivial, some important, but all connected with the objects of the party. Some brought news of the movements of eminent Leaguers or of their opponents, for the eye of the League is ever fixed upon the doings both of friend and enemy. Others contained pecuniary contributions, from well-wishers of the cause; for each of whom the president immediately dictated an appropriate letter of thanks. Other letters related anecdotes, showing the progress of the cause, and the gradual defection of the farmers, the most resolute supporters of Peel.

The League has now, by means of local associations in all parts of the kingdom, extended its operation and influence over the whole country, and attained an astonishing national importance. Its festivals, Anti-Corn-Law bazaars, Anti-Corn-Law banquets, and others of like nature, appear like great national anniversaries. Besides the acknowledged members of the League, there are numbers of important men who work with them and for them in secret. Every person who contributes 50l. to the League Fund has a seat and a voice in their council. They have committees of working men for the more thorough dissemination of their doctrines among the lower classes, and committees of ladies to procure the co-operation of women. They have lecturers, who are perpetually traversing the country to fan the flames of agitation in the minds of the people. These lecturers, who sometimes earn as much as 600l. a year, often hold conferences and disputations with lecturers of the opposite party, and not unfrequently drive them in disgrace from the field. It is also the business of the travelling lecturers, to keep a vigilant watch on every movement of the enemy, and acquaint the League with every circumstance likely to affect its interests. The Leaguers write direct letters to the Queen, the Duke of Wellington, Sir Robert Peel, and other distinguished people, to whom, as well as to the foreign ambassadors, they send copies of those journals containing the most faithful accounts of their proceedings. Sometimes they send personal deputations to distinguished opponents, in order to tell them disagreeable truths to their faces. Nor do the Leaguers neglect the potent instrumentality of that hundred-armed Briareus, the press. Not only do they spread their opinions through the medium of those journals favourable to them; they issue many periodicals of their own, which are exclusively devoted to the interests of the League. These contain, of course, full reports of all meetings, proceedings, and lectures against the corn-laws; extracts from Anti-Corn-Law publications, repeating for the thousandth time that monopoly is contrary to the order of nature, and that the League seeks only to restore the just order of Providence; original articles headed " Signs of the Times," " Anti-Corn-Law Agitation in London," " Progress of the good work," &c., &c.; and last not least, poems entitled " Lays of the League," advocating in various ways the cause of free trade, and satirising their opponents generally with more lengthiness than wit. Nor does the Anti-Corn-Law party omit to avail itself of the agency of those cheap little pamphlets called " Tracts," which are such favourite party-weapons in England. With these tiny dissertations, seldom costing more than twopence or threepence, and generally written by some well-known Anti-Corn-Law leader, such as Cobden or Sturge, the League are perpetually attacking the public as with a bombardment of small shot. I saw three or four dozen of such publications announced at the same time by one bookseller, Mr. Gadsby. Still tinier weapons, however, are the Anti-Corn-Law wafers, consisting of short mottos, couplets, and aphorisms of every class, grave and gay, serious and satirical, witty and unmeaning ; but all bearing on the one point of monopoly and free trade. These are sometimes taken from the Bible, sometimes from the works of celebrated writers and orators, sometimes from the speeches and publications of the Leaguers themselves, and sometimes are produced by the inventive ingenuity of the editor. Eighteen sheets of these wafers are sold in a pretty cover for one shilling, and each sheet contains forty mottos. Astonishing indeed is the profuse expenditure of labour, ingenuity, wit, and talent, and likewise of stupidity, folly, and dullness, with which, in this wonderful England, the smallest party operations are carried on ! Even in children's books, do both the Leaguers and Anti-Leaguers carry on their warfare, thus early sowing the seeds of party spirit in the minds of future generations.

All the publications of the League are not only written, but printed, bound, and published, at the League-rooms in Market-street, Manchester. I went through the various rooms where these operations were carried on, until I came at last to the great League Depôt, where books, pamphlets, letters, newspapers, speeches, reports, tracts, and wafers, were all piled in neat packets of every possible size and appearance, like the packets of muslin and calico, in the great warehouses of Manchester. Beyond this was a refreshment room, in which tea was offered us by several hospitable ladies, with whom we engaged in conversation for a little while.

I cannot join the sanguine expectations of the Leaguers, that Sir Robert Peel will be the last English minister who will venture to uphold monopoly. It is well-known how long such struggles generally last, and how very frequently, when the longed-for prize appears on the point of being attained, it is suddenly snatched away from that oft deluded Tantalus—the people. The immediate aim of the Leaguers is the abolition of the corn-laws, but they do not propose to stop at the attainment of this object. They will then turn the same weapons which brought down the corn-laws, against all other trade monopolies and custom-house restrictions, first in England and then in other countries, until at length all commercial restrictions between different nations, shall be totally done away with, and trade rejoice in the golden sunshine of freedom all over the world. A tempting object, but alas ! a long and doubtful road.

It was on a cold, damp, foggy morning in December, that I took my leave of Manchester. I rose earlier than usual; it was just at the hour when, from all quarters of the busy town, the manufacturing labourers crowded the streets as they hurried to their work. I opened the window and looked out. The numberless lamps burning in the streets, sent a dull, sickly, melancholy light through the thick yellow mist. At a distance I saw huge factories, which, at first wrapt in total darkness, were brilliantly illuminated from top to bottom in a few minutes, when the hour of work began. As neither cart nor van yet traversed the streets, and there was little other noise abroad, the clapping of wooden shoes upon the crowded pavement, resounded strangely in the empty streets. In long rows on every side, and in every direction, hurried forward thousands of men, women, and children. They spoke not a word, but huddling up their frozen hands in their cotton clothes, they hastened on, clap, clap, along the pavement, to their dreary and monotonous occupation. Gradually the crowd grew thinner and thinner, and the clapping died away. When hundreds of clocks struck out the hour of six, the streets were again silent and deserted, and the giant factories had swallowed the busy population. All at once, almost in a moment, arose on every side a low, rushing, and surging sound, like the sighing of wind among trees. It was the chorus raised by hundreds of thousands of wheels and shuttles, large and small, and by the panting and rushing from hundreds of thousands of steam-engines.

I went out, and traversed the humming and resounding streets, until I arrived at the terminus of the railway, which was to bear me far away from mighty Manchester, with its wonders and horrors, its splendour and its misery, into new scenes, new wonders, and new thoughts.

FROM MANCHESTER TO OXFORD.

The time had arrived for quitting the smoke and steam of busy, wealthy, populous young Manchester, for the learned elegance and leisure of monastic, aristocratic old Oxford. I fled swiftly away on the mighty wings of steam, and very soon the smoke canopy of Manchester, and soon after the whole county of Lancashire vanished on the edge of the horizon. It was not long before the dim blue distance swallowed up the fresh green smiling landscapes of Cheshire. On twenty-two magnificent arches, we glided over the valley of Stockport; and the buildings, manufactories, low steeples and towering chimneys of various populous towns, Crew, Stafford, Wolverhampton, &c., appeared and vanished one after another. In an incredibly short time, we had traversed all Staffordshire from its northernmost to its southernmost point, and we continued our flying march in Warwickshire, until at last we paused at Birmingham, from whence I continued my journey in a stage-coach to Oxford.

The only remarkable object I saw on the road, was a low, antique, picturesque-looking cottage near the village of Stratford-on-Avon, over whose door were inscribed these words: " The immortal Shakespeare was born in this house." But alas! the modern traveller, who flies through the world in railway trains and stage-coaches, has to pass by much which deserves, and would well repay his attention, and I too, was compelled to pass this venerable, this eternally consecrated house, without offering up within the hallowed precincts which echoed the first feeble cries of such an immortal infant, the homage of my fervent enthusiasm. But I shall never forget the glimpse I caught from the stage-coach of this most illustrious cottage. It is a small, one-storied little house, wedged in between two others, and is built in an antique style, of which there are few genuine specimens remaining. Until very lately, it was a butcher's shop, and it is now inhabited by a poor widow, who earns her bread by keeping it in repair and showing it to strangers.

We arrived at Oxford late in the evening, and were met as we entered the city of learning, by a troop of grotesquely attired boys in masks. It seems that there are certain days in the year, when this perambulation of juvenile masques is customary in the streets of Oxford; for what reason I do not know.

OXFORD.

Alfred the Great endowed at Oxford three colleges, which have now gradually swelled to twenty-four. Each of these colleges has its own buildings, its own gardens, its own antiquities, its own magnificent Gothic chapel, its own splendid library, its own peculiar constitution, laws, privileges, and festivals. Yet in spite of this isolation of the several colleges, they are by no means separate schools. The chancellor, masters, and scholars of the University of Oxford, form one united corporate body, who decide all their proceedings in two houses of assembly, called the Houses of Congregation and of Convocation. To detail the respective offices, duties, and privileges of these two houses—their relation to each other, to the university, and to the state, would be here impossible. The constitution of the English universities compared to those of Germany, is that of a complicated Gothic cathedral, to a simple Grecian temple. The supreme power of the university rests, however, with the chancellor, and after him with his representative, the vice-chancellor. These offices are always filled by persons of high rank, generally by distinguished laymen. The two most remarkable chancellors of Oxford I ever heard of, were Oliver Cromwell, who held that office in 1650, and the Duke of Wellington, who holds it at present. The vice-chancellor, however, who is a resident member of the university, is the sovereign

de facto, and to his authority is subject, not only the university itself, but the whole city of Oxford. The mayor of the city does
homage to the vice-chancellor every year; and the authority of the
latter great man is said to be by no means a nominal one. Next in
dignity to the chancellors and provosts of the university, are the
heads of the different colleges, who bear different titles in every
college.

The head professors of the university, are called regius professors,
their chairs having been founded by royal grant. All the other professorships were endowed by private persons and are named after their
founders. These are all remunerated and chosen, according to the
wishes of these founders; so that the manner of their appointment is
often very eccentric and complicated. Thus for instance, when the
Savilian Professor of Geometry is to be appointed, the Vice-
chancellor of Oxford has to apprise thereof by letter, the Archbishop
of Canterbury, the Lord Chancellor of Great Britain, the Bishop of
London, the Chancellor of Oxford, the first Secretary of State, all
the lord chief justices, the first Lord of the Treasury, and the Dean
of the Arches. With this rather miscellaneous assortment of gran-
dees rests the important choice; they are accordingly " conjured"
to search out the most skilful mathematicians of their own or any
other country, and choose among them without favour or partiality,
the individual best qualified for the office in question.

Besides the professorships, there are lectureships, fellowships, and
scholarships, differing from one another in various particulars, which
cannot here be circumstantially detailed. The course of study at the
university is divided into terms, of which there are four in the year.
Every student must have studied for a certain number of terms, before he can take any degree at the university. This taking of degrees is the immediate object of endeavour with all. Those who
have taken their degrees, are called graduates, those who have not,
undergraduates. The students are divided into two great classes:
the members on the foundation, who are supported partially or entirely from the funds of the colleges, and the members not on the
foundation, who pay, and often very enormously, for their instruction and accommodation. This last class has many subdivisions.
There are the " Noblemen," the sons of nobles, who pay the highest
price, and who are accommodated and instructed accordingly; the
gentlemen-commoners, who are the sons of the gentry and poorer
nobility; and lastly, the commoners, the plebeians of the university,
who pay least, and are accommodated in an inferior manner. In
some colleges there are also poor students called servitors, who, although not on the foundation, pay little or nothing for their education,
but perform various services for their colleges.

The richest, most distinguished, and most celebrated of the Oxford
colleges, is that of Christ Church. Here are educated the sons of
the highest English aristocracy. This college boasts of many celebrated names, among those of its former students; among others that

of the present premier, Sir Robert Peel. The students of Oxford are far less liberal in their opinions than those of Cambridge. Cambridge has had the honour of educating many famous Protestant bishops, which it is said " Oxford has had the honour of burning." Oxford is always far more backward than Cambridge, in yielding to the spirit of reform and innovation.

The internal arrangement of the collegiate buildings closely corresponds to that of our old German monasteries. Each college has its own church, its own library, and its own " hall," or refectory, where the members of the college dine, and which is often very splendid. Though the members all dine in the same hall, however, the distinction of ranks is, even here, very strongly kept up. There is the high-table, where the masters, fellows, and gentlemen-commoners sit, and which is a sort of raised platform at one end of the hall; the commoners' table is in the middle of the hall; and there are lower tables at the other end, for the servitors. All the arrangements of the university, are made in the same sternly exclusive spirit. The guest of a student takes rank with his entertainer; so that the parents and uncles of the commoners sit at a lower table, and look up from a respectful distance at the high-tables of the aristocratic youths. Many of the colleges have beautiful gardens, which are open to the public on certain days. I must, however, request my reader, before proceeding further, to accompany me on a short walk through the various colleges of Oxford.

It is Sunday morning. The numberless bells of Oxford are ringing a cheerful yet solemn peal. The streets are filled with elegantly dressed students, masters, bachelors, and doctors. The commoners may be distinguished by their simple but stately black togas, and their square-topped, long-tasselled, black caps; the gentlemen-commoners by the lace, embroidery, and red silk linings of their robes; and the noblemen by the addition of a quantity of gold lace and gold threads, both on togas and caps. The rules and regulations for costume, varied with every degree of rank and every day of festival, are, at the English universities, carried to a most complicated and absurd degree of solemn foppery. How different from the simple rules of the German universities, the chief of which is, " Let each dress as he likes best."

Over the gates of Christ Church towers the belfry, containing the great bell, the pride of the university, commonly called " Great Tom of Oxford," which every evening summons together, by 101 strokes, the 101 students of the college. The colleges are closed at a certain hour, and every student who does not come in at the right time, is subject to a certain penalty. The door-keepers mark the names of all who are not within at the closing, as well as of those who are absent from church, at morning and evening service. The students are generally desirous, if they can, of avoiding this attendance, or, as they call it, of " cutting the church."

Another remarkable part of the college is its kitchen. It is said to be the largest kitchen in England, much larger than that of Windsor Castle, or even than that of the Reform Club. It is, of course, very splendid and complete in all its arrangements. I remarked that it seemed the oldest part of the building. "Yes, sir," said one of the cooks, quite unconscious, probably, of the bitter satire his words conveyed; "they built the kitchen before any other part of the college." Indeed, throughout the university, I could not but remark, that the animal gratifications of the aristocratic students, seemed treated with quite as much attention and respect as their spiritual wants, and that the kitchens and dining-rooms vied with, and often surpassed in splendour, the churches and libraries.

The New College is one of the handsomest in Oxford. Its gardens are splendid, commanding wide and beautiful prospects of the surrounding country. How luxurious must be study and meditation, among the ivy-clad ruins and rich verdant groves of these antique gardens! The church of the New College is very beautiful, and rich in magnificent sculptures, and stained windows. In the church of Magdalen College, hangs a very fine old picture representing "Christ bearing the cross." The origin of this picture is disputed; by some it is attributed to Morales, but whoever the painter may have been, his inspiration can have been of no common order. This church is splendidly decorated with antique stone and wood carvings of the most curious and interesting forms. The reading-desk is in the shape of a great bronze eagle, with outspread wings, upon which the prayer-books are placed; this form, beautifully typifying the upward flight of prayer, is very common in the English churches. In the great quadrangle of Magdalen College, round which run the cloister-walks, the stone arches and pillars are carved with all sorts of grotesque and monstrous shapes, such as those with which the fancy of an old monk might have peopled hell. These were no doubt symbolical figures representing the evil passions and lusts of mankind.

Every thing about the luxurious retreats of Alma Mater, its delicious gardens, its antique libraries, its stately old Gothic churches, its sumptuous kitchens and refectories, the monastic habits of its inmates, all reminded me strongly of the wealthy old abbeys and monasteries on the banks of the Danube; with this difference, however, that the latter are rich in picture galleries, museums, collections of natural history, &c., which are mostly wanting at Oxford. Indeed the monks of the Danube appear to me to take a far more enlarged and liberal interest in art, science, and learning than the students of the English universities.

The lower classes of English society are totally unrepresented at these institutions. How many sons of wealthy peasants and mechanics are to be found at all our German universities; but at Oxford, those whom I questioned had great difficulty in naming to me a single farmer's son. The average annual expense of a tolerably economical student at Oxford, is estimated at 200*l*. We have among our students, many living in a garret, feeding on bread and water, and contriving, by giving lessons in Latin, Greek, drawing, music, or whatever else is required, to work their way arduously to learning and distinction; these are not to be found at Oxford. Here the roads are smoother, and the objects to be aimed at are fixed for every one beforehand. Science is clipped and polished to the semblance of a smooth artificial, well-fenced cloister-garden, into which nothing free, natural, or not according to rule is admitted. Every one knows his road; no one loses his way; but no one cuts new roads, or discovers new points of view for himself. At our universities, science is still a free, graceful, fertile wilderness. Thousands of students plunge into this wilderness. Many follow their own way, and some lose themselves in consequence. But many arrive at new and beautiful scenes and discoveries, and all owe to their own efforts whatever they attain. At Oxford, where every thing is learnt by rote, the students must owe every thing to the ancient mould in which their minds are here cast.

The Oxford students have various associations among themselves for other purposes than those of study, such as archery clubs, hunting clubs, fishing clubs, &c. Their favourite amusement, however, seems to be rowing. They have numbers of beautiful little boats on the Cherwell, and frequently have rowing-matches, or regattas, among themselves. The most important rowing-matches, however, are those which take place on the river Thames, between the students of Oxford and those of Cambridge. During the last five of these, the University of Cambridge was four times victorious, and that of Oxford only once. I was assured however, at Oxford, that this was not so much owing to the real superiority of Cambridge, as to the circumstance, that the rowing-matches took place at the close of the Oxford vacation, and in the middle of the Cambridge term. Whilst the Oxford students therefore came to the match, enervated by a lazy holiday life, those of Cambridge were practising down to the last day. One of these regattas on the Thames must, I should think, be a very agreeable and animated spectacle. The young people prepare themselves as jockeys do for horse-races. They eat sparingly, avoid fermented liquors, and live chiefly on water and roast beef.

I was much surprised by the number of pleasing songs current among the students of Oxford. At an evening party where I met a large number of them, I heard many of these; they were not indeed, genuine student songs, like those of Germany, but treated of miscellaneous topics. Both the music and the words were generally pleasing, and sometimes beautiful. Many of them were martial and naval ditties. I noticed that each student always knew his song through, without stumbling or hesitation, however long it might be. Some of them were songs of satire against the French.

When these were called for, several of the company begged my pardon, as if the singing them was a sort of affront to me. We continentalists are all taken for Frenchmen in England; and though I can hardly suppose that the students of Oxford do not know the difference between a German and a Frenchman, they were, evidently, involuntarily actuated by the common English system of classing us together.

After the colleges themselves I visited the libraries and antiquities. The great Bodleyan library contains, besides great numbers of older works, a copy of every book published in the British empire, during the last hundred years. Access to this library is granted very sparingly, and even the students have to pay an annual sum for the use of it. The division which most interested me was that of British geography and history. Every shire has here its own department, and I was astonished at the minute accuracy, with which the petty history and geography, of every village, hamlet, and parish in England was here detailed. In some cases the history of every family of any importance was given. I found in this library a small collection of German dissertations, but our philological and classical works, such as those of Döring, Müller, and Battman, are best understood and most valued at Oxford. It is, indeed, a curious fact, that although "The Humanities" are so very much prized at Oxford and Cambridge, and although at these universities there is no end to studies and examinations in the Greek and Latin Grammars, yet all the most learned and valuable works of classical philology known here, are translations from the German. It is also strange that, although there have been Hebrew and Arabic professorships at Oxford ever since 1636, and although a knowledge of the Scriptures is the first desideratum for an Oxford theologian, Hebrew is far less generally understood here than at the German universities. With us it is very unusual to meet with a theologian who cannot read his "Old Testament" in the original; here the contrary is the exception.

The Radcliffe library is not so extensive as the Bodleyan, although it is placed in a far more splendid building. It is particularly rich in books of medicine and natural history. The printing-house of the University of Oxford is one of the greatest in the kingdom, and is one of the three printing houses in England which are alone authorised to print the Bible as a church book, without comment; the king's printer at London, and the printer of the Cambridge University being the other two. At this Oxford printing house, they have Latin, Greek, Hebrew, and Arabic characters, but no German or Gothic ones. The theatre of the University is a large and splendid saloon, of which, portraits of the sovereigns of the Holy Alliance form the principal decoration. The victories of the Holy Alliance were nowhere in England received with more exultation than at Oxford. The late victories in China were also hailed here with more enthusiastic rejoicing than elsewhere; but Manchester and Oxford rejoiced in the same event on very different grounds; Manchester on account of its commercial interests, and Oxford on account of the stability thus given to the Tory ministry.

Alma Mater has lately been roughly attacked in a little pamphlet, entitled, "Oxford Unmasked," dedicated, "without permission," to Sir Robert Peel. It is not written with much talent, and does not institute a thorough search into all the abuses existing in Oxford; but it contains some truth, and has gone through a great number of editions. In this pamphlet the monastic customs of the University, the compulsory churchgoings, the long enforced prayers, attended by the young students often only from fear of punishment, and not unfrequently in a state of intoxication, meet with just and vehement censure. Much blame also falls upon the system of overloading the students with dry, fruitless, unmeaning theological studies, and of requiring from them, more urgently, a minute knowledge of the genealogy of Hebrew kings, and the names and dates of Old Testament narratives, than a comprehension of the real spirit and meaning of the Scriptures. The endless examinations in the structure of Greek and Latin phrases, and in the use of prepositions and irregular verbs, is treated with due derision; and the neglect of more profitable studies, such as those of modern languages, modern science, and the fine arts, are animadverted upon. Above all, however, is censured the shameful manner in which, it is said, the heads of the colleges, the governors of the University, the tutors and guides of the youthful British aristocracy, overlook in the young heirs of wealth and influence, not only indolence and neglect, but positive excesses and vices; allowing them to slip easily through all examinations and laws, and encouraging them in the contraction of debts. It must not be forgotten, however, that while much is undoubtedly just in these accusations, party purposes may have led the writer, as they do almost all English writers, into many exaggerations and mis-statements; and that Alma Mater, although guilty of many abuses and evils, may not, really, be quite such a nest of abominations, as some of her opponents describe her. A foreigner will do well, on such questions, to hear both sides, and to be very cautious in accepting, unconditionally, the estimate of either party.

The church of St. Mary's, in the middle of the town of Oxford, belongs to no college in particular, but only to the University in general. Here all religious solemnities are celebrated, and here service is also held twice every Sunday. I went there one Sunday to hear a sermon from Mr. Newman, the most distinguished adherent of Dr. Pusey. This Mr. Newman is, indeed, at present the real head of the religious sect called Puseyites, being a far more eloquent, learned, and sagacious theologian than the founder himself. The doctrines which Dr. Pusey first promulgated in 1833, and which have gained ground chiefly through the exertions of Mr. Newman, are, in fact, nothing but the unqualified assertion of the genuine, orthodox, Oxford divinity. The high churchmen of Oxford were seized with a panic as to the condition and prospects of the Church of England, into which, according to their assertions, false doctrines and irreligious principles had gradually intruded; and they resolved, through the medium of the press, to make an energetic stand, against the prevailing spirit of the times. They published, with this view, a series of pamphlets called "Tracts for the Times," on the government, constitution, rights, and doctrines of the Church, on the authority of the old fathers, and the "standard English divines," and on the errors and truths of Romanism. These tracts were written partly by Mr. Pusey, but chiefly by Mr. Newman. The most famous of all was the important "tract Ninety," wherein Mr. Newman developed the whole system of Puseyism, by giving the Puseyite interpretation of each of the thirty-nine articles of the Church of England.

The Puseyites make a great distinction between Catholicism and Romanism. They maintain that the English reformers sought, not to establish the system of modern Protestantism, but rather the ancient, and truly Catholic church, devoid of those errors and abuses which have deformed the Church of Rome, and which they designate under the name of Romanism. They aim at reconciliation of the Churches of Rome and of England, through a purification of the former, and a Catholicising of the latter; and they call themselves by a name significant of this mixed object—Anglo-Catholics. The obnoxious sectarian name of Puseyites, clings to them, however, in spite of their protestations.

The immediate object of the tract Ninety, which excited an immense sensation at the time, was the explaining away of every thing Protestant in the Thirty-nine Articles; or, as Mr. Newman himself expresses it, the interpreting them " in the most Catholic sense they will admit." The condemnation of the doctrines of Purgatory, of Saint-worship, of Absolution, of Transubstantiation, &c., &c., are all explained away, and slipped over in a subtle, sophistical, truly Jesuitical manner. Yet Mr. Newman wrote this tract, as he declares, " in any thing but an anti-Protestant spirit, and with no partiality whatever, towards the Church of Rome." He desired to prove that English Protestantism is one and the same thing with the ancient orthodox Catholicism, and thus to show that she alone, is fitted to include within herself all Christianity. For this he was greatly applauded by many, and particularly by the Anglican clergy, who love to maintain that the English church is no new establishment, but derives its authority directly from the apostles and early fathers of the Church. On the other hand, a large party in the Established Church, were of course alarmed and offended by finding that Mr. Newman tampered with their thirty-nine articles, and thus, in their opinion, undermined the very foundations of Protestantism. At last his superiors, the bishops, took the alarm, and forbade the continuation of the tracts, which command Mr. Newman, as a faithful son of the church, promptly obeyed.

Whatever may be the truth or error of his doctrines, Mr. Newman is certainly inconsistent in one thing; namely, that while he acknowledges the absolute authority of the framers of the thirty-nine articles, he certainly interprets these in a sense totally different from that in which these framers intended them. He evidently thus " palters with them in a double sense," because, by denying their authority, upon which the Established Church is founded, and by setting up other articles in their place, he would be drawing down upon himself the wrath, and excommunication of his whole church. It is very singular that, in spite of the clear and sharp logical head which he possesses, Mr. Newman's expressions are always vague and uncertain in the highest degree, and seem intended to leave the door open, for slipping out on either side, as circumstances may render most convenient. The tracts seem to have been intended by him as feelers, by which to try public opinion, and learn how far it would be safe for the author to express his own, in an unqualified manner. I say *seem*, for, although such was the impression they conveyed to me, I would by no means deny that it is quite possible, and even probable, that no unworthy Jesuitical caution has been intentionally maintained. Mr. Newman is declared, by all those who know him well, to be not only a man of unexceptionable character and integrity, but to be of a devout, single-minded, and earnest disposition.

In its two immediate professed objects, the lessening of sectarian distinctions, and the retaining in the Established Church of those whose tendencies incline them towards Catholicism—Puseyism has, I think, entirely failed. It has split its church into two hostile factions, and established in fact a new sect of its own; and it has led many over-zealous Protestants into zealous Romanism, by gradual and almost imperceptible gradations. But it is as an *effect,* not as a *cause,* that Puseyism takes its place among the most interesting and startling phenomena of the times; as a manifestation namely of that tendency towards the faith and spirit of the Middle Ages, which is at present stirring throughout the whole Christian world—a tendency, which, however erroneous and unsuccessful in its immediate aims, may not be without its important uses in the revivification and elevation of the prevalent tone of religious feeling.

In one direction the efforts of the Puseyites are certainly of a most laudable and salutary kind; namely, in reforming the arrangements and architecture of the English Protestant churches. Everywhere they are endeavouring to restore churches in the old style, and to enrich them with their former decorations. The costume of their priests they wish also to restore, to something of Catholic pomp and splendour; but the most laudable of their innovations is their energetic attack upon the English system of pews. They maintain that as in the house of God we are all equal, and kneel as brethren in the presence of one common father, the exclusive spirit and distinction of ranks kept up by the pews is highly unbecoming and unchristian. A row of benches without doors or partitions, and all exactly alike, ought to be the only seats in churches; no hiring of seats should be allowed, but rich and poor should seat themselves as they best can when they enter. This desire of reform in church-seats results, however, from a more universal impulse, than that of Puseyism, and is manifested throughout the whole Christian world, puritanical, Popery-hating Scotland not excepted.

As Mr. Newman's sermon added nothing to what I already knew of his doctrines, I was chiefly interested in hearing it, by his manner and appearance. Here, as in reading his tracts, I was quite involuntarily, unexpectedly, and almost unaccountably, reminded of the Jesuits. Mr. Newman, as he appears in the pulpit, is a thin, feeble-looking little man, with a grave, motionless, somewhat inexpressive countenance, in which there is very little either to attract or repel. His eyes are small and rather dull, at least, as far as I could perceive them through his elegant spectacles. The sharp lines of his features seemed to me to mark a clever, and the shape and wrinkles of his forehead, a learned and a studious man. His hair was combed smoothly down, and its straight lines ran parallel with the straight lines of his face, which looked as if it too had been just passed through a comb; yet in spite of all this there was about him a certain repose and dignity, a certain something which might almost be called sanctity, which inspired respect and admiration. He spoke very calmly and soberly, without motion or gesticulation. His arms remained concealed under his desk, and his eyes fixed on his paper. He read without apparent fire or emotion, and avoided all display of enthusiasm or eloquence. I can hardly express the strange effect produced, by hearing him pronounce the most startling and extravagant sentences with the most perfect calmness and indifference. " Newman carefully avoids," said one of his friends to me, " all appearance of zeal, all outbreaks of enthusiasm; he desires that the clear justice of his cause, and the subtle force of his reasonings, shall work on the minds of his hearers without any interference of emotion." I cannot, however, but believe, that this calmness and coldness in Mr. Newman's manner is natural and necessary to him, and is by no means the result of intentional forbearance; and I cannot but think that it is unnatural and unfavourable to the leader of a great religious revolution. Internal conviction, entire and earnest assurance of a truth, produces of itself an enthusiasm like that fire of the Holy Spirit, which descended on the first Apostles of Christianity, and glowed in their lives and doctrines. In default of this holy fire of enthusiasm, the Puseyites are led to rely far too much on church authorities, sophistical reasonings, and Jesuitical subtleties.

FROM OXFORD TO SALISBURY.

Leaving Oxford, I proceeded through the pleasant county of Berkshire, towards the Great Western Railway, in order to be transported by means of the *machinæ vi vaporis impulsæ*,—we had decided at Oxford that such was the best Latin translation for a railway locomotive, into the presence of two interesting monuments of human art—the Cathedral of Salisbury, and the far famed ruins of Stonehenge. Immediately behind Oxford, the landscape began to grow extremely rich and beautiful, and from the first hilltop, there was a magnificent view of the beautiful old city I had quitted.

I travelled towards the Great Western Railway, in company with one of the most wealthy and influential aldermen of the city of London, by whom it was expected that the lord mayor's chair would be filled in a few years. Indeed upon his figure, face, forehead, and bearing, as it appeared to me, had destiny visibly written the title of Lord Mayor of London. I had made his acquaintance at Oxford, and on the journey there, he was very cordial and talkative to me. He informed me that he had been one of the commissioners who sat to regulate the Income-tax in London, and I was delighted to meet with some one who could give me authentic and accurate information, concerning the working of this new and unpopular tax. My alderman assured me that no such difficulties were found in collecting it as the opponents of Sir Robert Peel had prophesied. Each citizen lays before the assessor of his district, his own estimate of his income, which if reasonable, is at once accepted; but should the return appear absurdly below the citizen's manner of living, the assessor makes his own estimate, and it is now the citizen's turn to appeal, if he pleases, to the commissioners. No one whose income does not amount to 150*l.* per year pays any income tax. There are many clerks and others, in Manchester, Liverpool, and London, whose income amounts exactly to 150*l.* pounds a year, these now agree with their employers to deduct a few pence each year from their salaries, so as just to escape the tax. My alderman, who was a friend to Sir Robert Peel's government, insisted upon it that there were no difficulties or objections of any sort connected with the Income-tax; while other Englishmen to whom I have spoken on the subject, being opponents of the premier, were just as earnest and skilful, in proving it to be both oppressive and impracticable. In one respect, I heartily agreed with my present companion, in admiring the just proportion in which this tax falls on poor and rich. On reaching the railway station we parted, he proceeding towards London, and I towards Wiltshire.

The Great Western Railway is now the most perfect and splendid in Great Britain; it is 118 miles long, and its building was accomplished at the astounding cost of 53,000*l.* sterling per mile! The road and the carriages are both as might be expected, of astonishing dimensions. The road is a full third wider than the widest of the other English railways; and the average speed of the gigantic loco-motives employed upon it is twenty-eight miles an hour.

I arrived at the station at Chippenham, at the precise minute fore-told in Bradshaw's Railway Guide, from which town I proposed to continue my journey, in a little gig, through Devizes to Salisbury. It was close to Christmas, yet the whole landscape was covered with the richest, freshest, brightest green. As far as Devizes the country was very beautiful, and was broken up by clumps of green hills and pleasant woodlands, into a series of sweet, verdant little landscapes. Between Devizes and Salisbury, however, lies the tract of country known by the name of Salisbury Plain. This is a cold, bare, tree-less table-land of chalk, without hedges or cornfields, covered only with broad, dreary-looking pasture lands for sheep; it is, however, no plain in reality, but contains many elevations, all of the same barren kind. Here and there it is, however, agreeably diversified by small, fertile, picturesque valleys. There is a tract of country very like this in Wiltshire, called the Marlborough Downs. These " Downs," as they are generally called, are as characteristic of the south of England, as the great heaths and moors of the north; and both are generally used as sheep-pastures. It is rather singular that the word " downs," as applied to treeless, barren tracts of this nature, is likewise used on the northern coast of Belgium; perhaps the word originated with the ancient Belgæ, who once inhabited parts of both countries.

While driving through this steppe-like country, recollections of South-Russian scenery naturally recurred to my thoughts, and I began to reflect what a delightful country this would be for gipsies. Scarcely had this thought occurred to me, than I came across a couple of gipsies, at a wayside public-house, where my horse stopped to drink. I spoke to them, and they answered me in English, al-though they assured me that they were well acquainted with the gipsy language. These, with the exception of two whom I saw in Yorkshire, were the only gipsies I had yet met with in England; and even these, had evidently a great deal of English blood in their veins.

SALISBURY.

The town of Salisbury is one of the oldest boroughs, though not one of the oldest dwelling-places, in England. The old borough of Salisbury, or as it is commonly called for abbreviation " Old Sarum," was situated on a bare chalk hill, of very remarkable shape, not far from the present city. It was formerly fortified ; but the citizens found themselves disagreeably exposed to all the cold winds that raged over the barren downs, and they were also much troubled by want of water, as the barren chalk hill possessed not a single spring.   Thus Camden describes it in the following verse.

" Est ibi defectus lymphæ, sed copia cretæ ;
Sævit ibi ventus, sed philomela silet."

" There is deficiency of water, but superfluity of chalk ; the wind rages there, but the nightingale is silent."

The citizens thus found themselves at length compelled to desert their dreary hill for the fertile and well-watered plain.   Many privileges, however, still adhered to the deserted hill ; and among others that of sending two members to parliament.   Even after all remnants of the fortifications were done away with, the owner of this hill might send two members of his own choice to parliament.   I inquired at Salisbury what kind of election took place for this " rotten borough." I was told that the nobleman to whom the place belonged, summoned together, on the appointed day, the four or five householders who still inhabited " Old Sarum" and named to them the two members whom he wished to send; who were accordingly in due form elected.   Sometimes indeed he did not take this trouble.   He would send for his steward, and give his orders in the following manner, perhaps: " Take care to have my stable whitewashed again ; and then look to it that my two members are properly elected."   I also heard that the noble owner of Old Sarum, hearing upon one occasion that his selection of members had not given satisfaction in the House of Commons, replied : " If parliament are not satisfied with my people, I'll send them two chimney-sweepers next time, and see what they'll say to that."

Salisbury itself has changed very little in modern times.   It is one of the few English towns in which one may still luxuriate in antiquities and antiquarian recollections.   It belongs to the same class of towns with Chester and York, and has long furnished a shelter to 9000 peaceable citizens, without ever exceeding that number.   The houses are built in a very antique style ; some of them are said to be 400 years old.   Salisbury is the only town in England where I saw a large number of houses with thatched roofs ; and the thatch was most plentifully covered with moss.

Salisbury furnishes a very agreeable variety to the traveller, although the inhabitants themselves, modestly call it " a very dull place."   " There is nothing stirring among us.   We have no museums, no trade, no manufactures, and have nothing to show a stranger but our church."

This church, however, is quite a little Gothic bijou.   It is not large and imposing, like the mighty Gothic erections of Paris, Antwerp, Cologne, and Strasburg, or like the cathedrals of York and Westminster in England; but it is so complete and perfect in itself, so beautifully built and preserved, and so admirably situated, that few works of art can furnish the spectator more pure and unmixed enjoyment.   We have here neither to regret occasional barbarisms of taste, nor slovenliness of execution, nor later neglect or injury, nor a disadvantageous situation. It is the neatest, prettiest, completest, and best situated little cathedral in the world. I say little in a comparative sense, thinking of giants like that of Cologne; for Salisbury Cathedral is still a large building, and has one of the highest steeples in England. It is surrounded on all sides by a wide beautiful meadow-ground, which is dotted with large old trees. The cathedral thus stands amid grass and trees, as if in the middle of the lawn of an English park. Even at Christmas, the bright green of the meadow still formed a beautiful contrast to the gray of the old stones. Round this meadow stand the houses of the bishop and prebendaries, hidden among pretty gardens.

The cathedral is said to have as many doors as there are months in the year, that is twelve; as many windows as there are days in the year, that is 365; and as many beams and columns as there are hours in the year, that is 8766. What most struck me in the internal construction of the church, was the extreme slenderness and fineness of the so called "flying buttresses" supporting the steeple. The builders seem here to have spun their stone through the air in some inconceivable manner like the silky thread of a spider. I wondered how these long, thin lines of stone could support themselves in the air; yet they have supported, not only themselves, but the entire steeple, for 600 years. The clusters of round columns which support the roof are also far more light, and less massive, than is usual in Gothic churches. This contributed much to the general effect of lightness and airy beauty, which the whole structure of the cathedral conveyed. After leaving the cathedral, the kind friend, who had undertaken to do the honours of Salisbury for me, introduced me to an aged poet, well known in English literature, but who was now, in mind and body, an entire ruin. It is impossible not to lament, while witnessing such a spectacle, that great poets at least, are not permitted to leave the world at once, when they have lived enough; and that a beautiful mind, like a beautiful body, is permitted to fall, piece by piece, under the murdering strokes of time.

STONEHENGE.

The next day I left Salisbury in order to visit one of the most wonderful monuments on the surface of the British islands. I had to return to the Downs; for it is in the midst of these dreary grassy levels, that the hands of unknown architects have erected the wonderful monument called Stonehenge. It lies six miles from Salisbury, and on the whole of the monotonous road we met no human being, not even one of those shepherds who commonly frequent the neighbourhood of Stonehenge with their flocks.

The first sight of Stonehenge is no doubt disappointing to the stranger. We discover what in the distance appears a small group of closely clustered stones, whose dark colour looks very gloomy against the fresh green of the meadow grass. We must be among the stones themselves to estimate whatever is gigantic and wonderful in these ancient remains.

My first desire was to find out the number of the stones, and I accordingly began to count them. Upon this, an old shepherd, who was watching his flocks close beside the ruins, laughed and said, "That would never do; nobody had ever counted the stones of Stonehenge; it was a peculiarity about the place, that every one miscounted the stones, and if he counted them again, to try his first result, found a different number." I learnt afterwards that this notion was shared by all the inhabitants of the surrounding country.

I found, however, that the counting was indeed no easy matter. I found stones hidden in the grass, of which I could not determine whether they were whole stones or only fragments. I found others lying at a distance, of which I could not decide whether they belonged to the building or not. To the best of my judgment, however, I estimated all the stones, large and small, horizontal and perpendicular, at 140. It seems that this mass of stones was originally arranged in the following manner: There was a circle of about forty very large, long stones, placed upright on end; this outer circle was about forty paces in diameter, according to my measurement, and somewhere between 120 and 130 paces in circumference. Within this circle was another smaller one, of smaller erect stones. About forty paces distant from the outer circle, a low wall and a flat ditch were still distinctly to be traced, which had evidently once encircled the whole.

The stones of the great circle are several feet deep in the earth, and rise twenty-two feet above the surface. They are four-sided, but their shape is rough, and irregular. They are mostly about three feet and a half thick, six or seven feet broad, and from eighteen to twenty-one feet in circumference. These large stones are smooth at the top, and over every interstice between them was originally laid a large cross-stone. The weight of each of the great upright stones is estimated by Camden at 240 cwt., or 24,000 pounds; and of the cross-stones at about half that weight, or 120 cwt. This estimate is far more likely to fall short of the mark than to exceed it, for each of the great blocks must contain 500 cubic feet of stone, and two of these cubic feet probably weigh more than a hundred-weight. In the lower side of each of the cross-stones a hole is bored at both ends, and at the top of each perpendicular stone are two thick projections, fitting exactly into these holes. This is the only fastening between the upright and cross stones. Wonderful must have been the labour expended in knocking away the solid stone at the top of the great blocks, in order to leave these lumps, or pegs of stone, projecting from the top. Still more surprising, however, must appear the feat of raising stones 12,000 pounds in weight, to the top of other stones twenty-two feet high, with the very rude and primitive implements alone possessed by the ancient Britons.

The stones of the inner circle, though likewise forty in number, are only about six feet above the ground, and four or five feet in circumference. No cross-stones now lie over them, though it is conjectured by some that they originally did so.

Let us imagine the building in its original and perfect condition—the centre filled with white-robed priests—the stately stones all decked with fresh boughs and garlands—the smoke of sacrifice, and the streams of incense, passing out among the columns, and the space within the wall, as well as the plain beyond, crowded with gaily-dressed and tattoed Britons—and we may imagine what a wild and impressive scene these ruins once presented.

But now, of the great blocks only about twenty-three are still standing upright, and of the cross-stones only eight still lie in their places. The rest lie prostrate in confused heaps, within and around. Of the stones of the inner circle, twelve only still stand upright. I asked the old shepherd if he remembered when the last great block of stone had fallen. He said he remembered very well that it was several years ago. It had been a very wet year; the ground all around had been very much softened, and one of the great blocks had sunk in consequence a little out of its perpendicular. It was in this position when a violent storm occurred, which brought it to the ground.

But what force can have lifted from their pegs and thrown to the ground those cross-stones whose supporting columns yet remain erect? That human hands should ever have undertaken the enormous labour of disturbing these huge masses is out of the question. Lightning could not have destroyed them, without injuring also the columns. As for storms, if any had occurred since the time of the Druids, capable of actually lifting up masses of stone 12,000 pounds in weight, we should have heard of cities being destroyed, or hills torn up by the same winds. As these are the only destructive agencies to which these cross-blocks of Stonehenge have ever been exposed, we are driven to conjecture that the work of erection was never fully completed; that the Druid architects were either tired of their Herculean labour, or stopped by want of materials, or disturbed by hostile tribes; and that in all those places where two upright columns have no cross-stone over them, they have in reality never had such at any time.

The stone of which Stonehenge is built appears to be granite, but there is not a fragment of granite far and wide around Stonehenge; the whole country is a chalk formation, mixed here and there with quartz, while in the construction of Stonehenge not a fragment of either chalk or quartz is to be discovered. Here is a new wonder of no common magnitude.

Many of the stones are marked with rude carvings, indentations, and marks of lines, rings, &c., which are evidently the work of human hands. The upper parts of most of the stones are covered with moss; and many of the mosses were very large, fresh, and beautiful. I cut several pieces to take away with me as relics.

To what purpose this wonderful monument was erected, appears to be a disputed point among antiquarians. While some believe it to have been a Druidical temple, others maintain that it was a mausoleum erected by Ambrosius Aurelianus to the memory of those Britons who fell here in a battle with the Saxons. According to others again, it was a monument erected by the Britons themselves in gratitude to this Ambrosius.

Neither in the vicinity nor within sight of Stonehenge, grows a single tree or bush. All around is one wide treeless plain. This circumstance, and the dreary leaden colour of the sky which usually hangs over it, render it one of the most melancholy looking places in the world. It is the general rendezvous for all the shepherds of the South Downs, and the tinkling of the sheep bells, almost constantly heard around it, is the only sound that breaks the monotonous silence.

In the August of 1842, the ruins of Stonehenge were the scene of a " dahlia-show." The dreary but solemn old building, must have been very much brightened by the presence of gay company and beautiful flowers.

In the neighbourhood of Stonehenge are several of those small " tumuli," or " barrows," so frequently met with in the Southern Downs.

Stonehenge probably derives its name from the circumstance of the cross-stones hanging upon the columns, which would naturally have appeared to the common people the most characteristic feature in the building.

FROM STONEHENGE TO ETON.

By the time I had seen Stonehenge, the Christmas festival had not only approached, but old Father Christmas was already knocking at the gate; for it was Christmas Eve. At this time all those people in England who are what is called " well off," seek out some place in the country " to keep their Christmas." On Christmas Day, all public institutions have a holiday, and dine more sumptuously than usual. Even the poor vagabonds in the Night Asylums, receive a good dinner on Christmas Day. In many prisons even the criminals obtain some indulgences; and the poorest cottagers receive slices of roast beef and plum-pudding from their wealthier neighbours, that they may enjoy at least one day of plenty in the year.

To the homeless traveller also, the question could not but occur: " Where shall I keep my Christmas?" Luckily the answer was in my case ready before the question, for I had received a kind invitation to spend the Christmas festival, at one of the most beautiful of the neighbouring country-seats, namely at Bowood. I accordingly soon took my seat in the coach for Devizes. The coach was crammed full with Christmas presents of various kinds, among

which numbers of fat capons were the most conspicuous. Our company consisted chiefly of holiday-makers, who were visiting their
friends and relations in town or country. Among them was a
governess, who, as she told me, instructed the children of a " farming gentleman " in the rudiments of the French language; and who
was no doubt glad enough to turn her back upon these " rudiments" for awhile. She had with her, quantities of trunks, band-
boxes, and hat-boxes. She told me that French was now learnt by
almost all the farmer's children. Next to French a knowledge of
Italian was most desired, in a governess among the middle classes.
" And of German?" I asked. " Oh no !" she answered, "not
of German. That is only the fashion among the nobility and
gentry."

I spoke to her of politics, and soon remarked that she was a very
zealous Tory. She expressed the utmost abhorrence of every great
Whig name which I introduced, and she told me that she had spent
her whole life in the families of farming gentlemen, who are all
" out-and-out Tories." She was very lively, and quite as ready for
conversation as any Frenchwoman would have been.

At Devizes I found all the shops decorated with boughs of evergreens, in honour of the Christmas festival. In the butcher's shops,
every fat victim from the South Downs was bestuck with boughs
of holly and laurel. Every sirloin of beef was crowned with a sprig
of holly ; and the ships which passed along the canals, had their
masts and rudders decorated with evergreens.

As I had a few hours to stay at Devizes, before proceeding to
Bowood, I took up the London papers. These journals contained
an immense deal of information, concerning habits and customs
connected with the Christmas festival in England. But, unluckily,
these treasures were so scattered in little scraps and fragments
through the ponderous masses of London news, that it was impossible to make any use of them.

After swallowing a few more of those " curious facts," " dreadful
occurrences," " singular incidents," " horrible accidents," &c., of
which the English newspapers are always as full, as the English
soups are of black pepper—I set out on my way to Bowood.

Bowood is, in every respect, so charming and delightful an abode,
its buildings are so tasteful, extensive, and magnificent; its libraries
and picture galleries so excellent and interesting; and its owner a
man so distinguished, both by his personal character and his great
political influence, that I think it best to leave a description of this
place to abler and more impartial pens ; as I have always shunned
describing to the world that which I most intimately loved and
honoured. After I had shared in the glories of an English " Christmas dinner;" after I had witnessed one of those pretty rural feasts,
which ladies, even of the highest rank, in England, prepare at their
own houses for the children of the poor ; after I had duly admired
the splendid pictures of Ruisdael, El Mudo, Rembrandt, and others,

collected in the breakfast-room; and, after I had amply enjoyed the summer-like Christmas of a great English park, I began to find that my purse was running short, and would soon leave me very uncomfortable, in the midst of every imaginable comfort. I recollected that it was not till I got to Eton, that I should reach any friend to whom I could apply, without shame, for a remedy to this deficiency; and I calculated that I had but just funds enough left, to pay my way to Eton. I accordingly took my farewell of Bowood and its hospitable inmates, and drove over to the Chippenham railway-station.

ETON COLLEGE.

I arrived at Eton at the proper time to make the acquaintance of all the scholars and masters at once. For they were all assembled, 650 in number, in the college chapel, to close their day's work by evening worship. This chapel is the most remarkable building at Eton, and is in some measure the landmark of the place, for its lofty roof is seen on every side, towering out of the lovely plain, through which the Thames here pours its waters. I went up into the organ-choir, which overlooks the whole interior of the chapel. It is 175 feet long, and very lofty. Six hundred healthy and handsome boys, —the flower of English aristocratic youth—were here assembled in prayer. Most of them wore the boyish costume common in England; some, however, dressed in an antique style, which harmonised well with the old Gothic building. Their seats were arranged according to rank. The masters and heads of the college sat upon the uppermost benches; next to them the "noblemen;" below these the "commoners;" and far below these, the poor scholars, supported by the school. To us such an arrangement appears strange and unbecoming. The English see in it only a proper compliance with venerable customs, and the just subordination of ranks.

It is a heart-stirring spectacle to see so many blooming and hopeful youths assembled together; particularly when it is recollected that the past annals of Eton, prove that whoever at any time sees its 600 scholars assembled, sees among them, a great number, whose names and lives will hereafter become interesting to the whole world. How many famous lawyers and authors, how many distinguished statesmen, ecclesiastics, generals, and admirals, have received their education at Eton, and lain on their knees in this chapel, morning and evening? how many future famed and influential heroes, statesmen, orators, and legislators, knelt there at that moment among the rest?

When church was over, the obliging head-master of the school had the kindness to show me round the different parts of the buildings, which are very extensive. The internal arrangement of the school resembles that of an Oxford college. At Eton, also, there is a "foundation," with fellows, choristers, and scholars, belonging to it; but by far the greater number of the members were not upon the foundation. The *original* plan of the college indeed, as at the time of the foundation, in the reign of Henry IV., provided only that a building should be erected, for the reception of " twenty-five poor grammar scholars," and of " twenty-five poor and infirm old men," to pray for the king. This is certainly a curious combination of charities; and at present these twenty-five old men are nowhere to be found at Eton.

At the head of the whole college, stands at present a provost, a vice-provost, and six fellows, resident at the college. These generally hold livings, in different parts of England, at the same time with their college offices. Next to these in dignity is the head-master. He is dependent upon the congregation of provosts and fellows, who decide all matters of general importance to the college. In the management of its internal affairs, however, he is tolerably free and independent. He derives the greater part of his great income, not from the endowments of the college, but from the contributions of the scholars themselves. Below the head-master, there are under-masters and assistants; and besides these there are seventy scholars, seven clerks, ten choristers, and other college officials, who being " on the foundation," are accustomed to earn their board and education, either by serving the college, or by sharing in the duties of instruction. All these people wear the peculiar black college-gown.

These scholars who have nothing to do with the college, beyond receiving its education, and regularly sharing in its church services, do not inhabit the college itself, but the little town of Eton close by, and are accordingly called in the college " Oppidans." There are separate " boarding-houses" in Eton for the accommodation of these young people; and the wealthier among them have their own private tutors, with whom they live.

Very notorious, both, at home and abroad, has been the " fagging system," as maintained among the Eton scholars. It is, namely, the custom for every newly-arrived scholar, to become for two years the " fag," that is the servant, almost the slave, of some older scholar. So far is this servitude often carried, that he must submit, without remonstrance, to the most disagreeable services and tasks, or else he is sure to be exposed to all kinds of insults and torments. A somewhat similar system prevails at most English public schools, but it is said that nowhere has it been carried to so tyrannical and disgraceful an extreme as at Eton.

I asked my friend, the head-master, whether he attempted nothing to stop these abuses. He answered that he did indeed discourage all excesses, but that he did not wish to root out the whole system. For, in the first place, it was an ancient custom, which had attained a certain venerableness by its antiquity ; and in the second place, the system was not without its uses. By fagging, the wild young lads who came to school with no notion of discipline, and had often been

very much spoilt by their parents, were at once broken in to obedience and subordination. This fagging, imposed upon all new-comers,
without regard to wealth or station, was also a sort of antidote to the
general spirit of subservience to rank and riches. The privileges of
wealth and nobility at Eton are not indeed greater than everywhere
else in England ; but as in after life the English aristocracy waive
their claims at times, under particular circumstances, so it is well that
they should learn to do so sometimes at school. The inexperienced
and undisciplined young sprig of nobility, learns, by the system of
fagging, respect and obedience, to those more learned and experienced
than himself. The students of the foundation, or poor scholars,
derive the greatest benefit from the fagging system ; for as they
remain generally longest at college, they are oftener masters ; a fortunate circumstance for them, as protecting them in some measure
from the contempt of the proud and wealthy oppidans.

One of the most interesting old customs of the Eton scholars, is
their famous spring procession to a neighbouring Barrow, called the
Salt-Hill, which takes place every three years, at the end of May or
the beginning of June. They call this procession the " Eton Montem,"
or sometimes simply the " Montem." Teachers and scholars go
together to the Salt-Hill ; the scholars wearing a particular uniform,
and headed by their seniors, who wear the uniforms of marshals
captains, and lieutenants. A standard-bearer carries the college-flag,
with the motto " *Pro more et monte !*" The objects of the procession are, in the first place to have a school festival, and in the second
place, to collect money from the spectators, for the future support, at
Oxford or Cambridge, of the poor scholars educated at Eton. Two
collectors are appointed to carry the money received, these are called
" salt-bearers." They have a number of other boys called " servitors"
to assist them, who are dressed in all kinds of gay and fantastic costumes. They demand a tribute of every spectator and passer-by, and
give in return a ticket with a motto, in remembrance of the festival.
The collection generally brings in from 800*l.* to 1000*l.*; last year it
amounted to 1300*l.* How the heart of many a poor scholar must pant
for fine weather, on the eventful Montem day !

Next to the rowers of Oxford and Cambridge, those of Eton are
the most famous in England. Indeed the greater part of the Oxford
and Cambridge rowers, lay the foundations of their future proficiency
at Eton. It would be a disgrace to the Etonians if they were not
good rowers, since the Thames flows almost through their play-
ground. On two days in summer, which are festivals of the college,
great " aquatic amusements," and " splendid regattas," take place.
But the Etonians practice other gymnastic sports besides rowing.
The games of cricket and football, so dear to the English, are not
omitted. All these exercises for the development and improvement
of bodily strength and agility, which render the school of Eton a
gymnasium, in the ancient sense of the word, are very much encouraged by the authorities. To them, it is frequently maintained,

England chiefly owes the boldness, skill, and courage of her naval and military officers.

Cambridge and Oxford owe more to Eton than skilful rowers. It was a provost of Eton, named Saville, who endowed at Oxford a professorship of astronomy and geometry. Another provost, named William Wayneflet founded the Magdalen College at Oxford. King's College at Cambridge receives all its fellows and masters from Eton; and the provost of that college comes every year to Eton, to attend the examinations. As every thing connected with the English public schools is decided by ancient rules, so each public school boasts of certain great families, who have for centuries had their children educated there, and at no other school. Thus, at Eton, the Dukes of Buccleuch were named to me, as invariably sending their sons to Eton, and to no other school. One family was named to me which had been connected with Eton for three hundred years, and whose male members had always been either scholars, or tutors, or teachers, or fellows at Eton.

I viewed with interest the valuable library of the college, under the persuasion that it was intended for the use of the scholars, as well as of the teachers; and I envied, in secret, the young people who had the run of so excellent a library. To my astonishment, however, I learnt that the library was intended solely for the benefit of the masters, and that the scholars had nothing to do with it at all.

I begged my friend, the head-master, to show me the laws and regulations of the schools. He answered that no printed laws and regulations existed. The whole school was governed, not according to written laws, but according to old custom and usage. Those school arrangements which I had seen, such as the division of ranks in the chapel seats, &c., were all prescribed, not by any written or printed law, but by ancient usage, strictly and closely followed. This does not render the routine of the school less fixed and immoveable. The scholars, themselves, are strongly attached to all their ancient customs; and if the head-master himself were to do any thing contrary to them—were to order, for an instance, an unusual punishment, were it ever so trifling—he would have to encounter the greatest opposition and discontent. Yet a far more severe and disagreeable punishment, would be received without a murmur, if according to custom. The English are everywhere alike, and their schools are governed like their state.

That which I heard of the punishments used at Eton, not only excited my attention, but astonished me not a little. They are all very severe, and all the scholars, except those of the highest class, are liable to corporeal chastisement. Even those of the highest class are liable, for some offences, to be degraded to a lower, and again punished with a rod. It is only the upper masters, who have the right of administering this punishment, and they execute it themselves, after school-hours.

Such a custom is certainly very much in opposition to the spirit of our times, and would not at all harmonise with the principles maintained at our continental schools; and yet I believe upon the whole, the English have the right of the matter. I believe that the abolition of corporeal punishment in our schools, is only a part of the general enervation of discipline, and effeminacy of manners. Three-fourths of human sinfulness, our selfishness, our laziness, our sensuality, are the offences of the body, and why should they not be punished on the body? It is said that this kind of punishment destroys the sense of honour in boys, renders them slavish in spirit, lowers the tone of their characters, &c. But do we see in the Peels, the Wellingtons, the Grahams, the Russells, of English public life, any such effect? They have all passed under the rod or the cane, yet *are* they found wanting in energy, servile in spirit, indifferent to honour, on that account? On the contrary, I believe that they owe much of their energy and greatness, to the strict discipline under which they were brought up.

I was not allowed to be present during a lesson, this being not permitted to any stranger. Even the King of Prussia, I was told, had not been able to obtain this favour. I went, however, through the school-rooms where I found great numbers of names cut with penknives on benches and desks. This is allowed to the scholars, upon condition that the names are to be neatly cut, and are to be done out of school hours. Such a privilege is not without its advantages. Among the names are many, now of great fame and interest, whose presence must be a spur and an encouragement to the scholars.

I found in one place the names of several scholars inscribed in gold letters on a tablet. I was told that these were the Newcastle-scholars; those namely who won the prize, founded by a Duke of Newcastle for certain attainments. The Newcastle prize brings the winner 50*l*. a year for three years; and the name of every winner is perpetuated in gold letters on this tablet. This prize is particularly designed for those who pass most creditably through their parting examination. There are also prizes at Eton for the best declamation, the best piece of Latin prose, &c. Prince Albert has lately founded here a prize of 50*l*. a year, for the study of modern languages, particularly German, French, and Italian. I do not understand why no one among us founds similar prizes in our schools. One would expect to find them at the gymnasiums of our free cities of Bremen, Hamburg, Frankfurt, and Lubeck; but I believe there is nothing of the kind. If some rich citizen, at either of these places were to present 1000 or 2000 dollars to a public school, that the interest might be used as a prize for extraordinary exertions among the scholars, what a benefit would he confer, for an incalculable period, upon the school.

As most of the scholars who distinguish themselves at Eton, play afterwards a distinguished part in the great world, my readers may be interested in learning what young people are at present foremost

in the race, and appear therefore more likely to exercise hereafter a
wide influence upon their contemporaries. In the Eton calendar of
1842, I found three foremost; the names of Rice, Joynes, and
James. The first had been twenty-nine times, the second twenty-
five times, and the third twenty-two times, " sent up for good;"
that is, favourably reported to the head-master and provost. The
first had gained the Verse prize, the Theme prize, the Davie's prize,
the Newcastle's prize, the Essay prize, the Declamation prize, and
the Mathematical prize. The two others had also gained great
numbers of prizes. Are we to see in these boys the future John-
sons, Gibbons, and Humes of England? Or are such rather to be
sought among the neglected and obscure?

The school-room has little that is pleasant or attractive about it.
The present excellent head-master, as I learnt, not from himself, but
from other persons in the neighbourhood, has done much for the external improvement of the school. He has laid out a good deal from
his own purse in collecting a little museum, establishing a singing-
school among the boys, and other similar works. He himself praised
the present provost of Eton very highly, as perhaps to a stranger he
thought it his duty to do. But I learnt in other quarters, that the
provosts of Eton are generally very stingy; regarding the college as
their private property, from which they wish to draw as large an income, and on which to expend as little as possible.

The school-books used at Eton have most of them been put together by masters of Eton, on purpose for that school; they are
most of them now very old. I bought one of these books, namely,
the " Eton Latin Grammar." This grammar is a little curiosity,
and, though printed very neatly on elegant paper, I would not wil-
lingly exchange for it our rational and modernised grammars. The
first division of this Latin grammar contains the parts of speech,
with the declensions and conjugations. It is a master-piece of brevity, and all the definitions are extremely laconic. To this part is
attached a series of hexameters, twenty closely-printed pages long,
in which are sung, the rules and exceptions for the genders, the
irregular verbs, &c. In our grammars these old-fashioned verses
have long ago given way to clear rules in plain prose, addressed
rather to the understanding than the memory. The syntax in the
Eton grammar is written, not in the English, but the Latin language.
After it come other rules, occupying a full third of the grammar,
on prosody, construction, and other matters; and these rules are
written in English and Latin at the same time, and without any
inter-punctuation, in the most confused manner. The following is
an instance:

" Impersonalia (sc. verba) impersonal verbs non habent have not
nominativum (sc. casum) any nominativum enunciatum expressed
(sc. in Latin) ut as taedet me it wearies me that is I am weary or
tired vitæ of life."

It is certain that the thorny paths of the Latin grammar might be far more smoothed for the scholars of Eton than they are. But the English maintain, that this wonderful old grammar of theirs lays the foundations of learning more effectually than any modern compilation could; and the thorns themselves are dear to them, even when they draw blood, and leave ineffaceable marks behind.

The scholars at Eton are almost all English. A short time ago, there were a few Spaniards there, who, however, were obliged to conform to the religious ceremonies of the Established Church. Germans there are none here, unless we count for such, the sons of the Hungarian Count Bathyany. The school appears to be on the increase in its number of pupils. In the year 1836, there were 444 scholars; in 1837, 472; in 1839, 560; 1840, 593; 1841, 635; 1842, 662. It may thus be seen that the system of education pursued at Eton has very far from fallen in the public estimation.

The young people are not overloaded with school hours. Upon an average, they spend only three hours a day in school; but they study much more at their own lodgings, with their private tutors. Their duty at school consists principally in examinations, in repeating the lessons learnt at home, and getting their exercises looked over.

The poorer scholars of Eton mostly go to Cambridge; the wealthiest and highest-born to Oxford; for Oxford, as I have said, is far more aristocratic in its spirit than Cambridge.

In the evening, I went to the singing school, the only Eton lesson at which I was present. This singing-lesson, however, does not belong to the regular course; it is a voluntary exercise in which only a part of the scholars join. It has been very recently established, and was one of the many signs I saw in England of a universal, active, and increasing taste for music.

The cigars which were brought me in the evening at my inn, were wrapped in a piece of a Latin theme, and the bit of twisted paper, with which I lighted them, contained a fragment of a Greek exercise. Indeed almost every thing which I bought in the shops of Eton and Windsor was wrapped in some Greek or Latin composition. The servants of the young students must make quite a little revenue out of the manuscripts of their masters. Indeed, the greater part of the inhabitants of Eton and Windsor live upon these 600 wealthy young students, many of whom spend 400*l.* or 500*l.* a year at Eton.

WINDSOR CASTLE.

The town of Windsor, and that of Eton, are, in fact, one, and the rows of houses stretch, unbroken, on each side of the Thames, to the bridge which unites the two. Thus the youth of the aristocracy grow up under the very eye of the monarch, and the court. Windsor Castle, the ordinary residence of the English sovereigns, stands on the summit of a hill, which begins its rise within the town of Windsor. Its situation and style of architecture are the same as those of a great many other castles in England. But it is larger and more imposing outside, much more splendid and extensive within, and in its situation and prospects also, far more picturesque and beautiful than most others. The principal entrance to the first court-yard is on the townside, and from thence one ascends gradually to the inner court-yards and the principal part of the buildings.

The first conspicuous point observed, on entering the first court-yard, is the chapel of the castle. Near this chapel, we made the acquaintance of one of " her Majesty's Poor Knights;" an old naval officer, maintained at Windsor after becoming unfit for service. These " Poor Knights of Windsor" enjoy a charity founded by Edward III., according to which, eighteen old worn-out officers, were to live at the public expense at Windsor. Six of them were to be naval officers. Formerly these officers wore an old-fashioned uniform, which William IV. exchanged for the modern uniforms of their own ranks. I believe there are not many such institutions in England, for the benefit of officers in the army, and my new friend informed me, that it had cost him no little trouble to obtain admittance here. No less than ninety candidates disputed the vacant post with him; but the Duke of Argyle " got him in." The Poor Knights inhabit a part of the castle, close to the great entrance-gate.

Morning service had already begun in the chapel. We entered and took part in it, as the greater number of the Poor Knights are accustomed to do every morning. We stepped over the graves of many former Poor Knights; and, strange to say, this curious title, which sounds somewhat degrading in our ears, for military men, is inscribed even on their gravestones, which are within the chapel.

This Windsor-chapel is one of those Gothic buildings which one is never tired of admiring. The roof is particularly beautiful. The ribs and grooves of the columns which support it branch out at the top like palm-leaves, in a peculiarly elegant manner, and bend over to meet the branches of the next columns; the roof is supported on these branches. The ceiling looks, therefore, as if woven out of an endless series of bunches of boughs. This decoration occurs so frequently in the English churches, that it might be called an Anglo-Gothic ornament. Nowhere, however, is it carried to such perfection, as in this St. George's Chapel at Windsor. It was built by Edward III., the same king who founded the charity of the Poor Knights. The name of Edward III. is one of those most honoured at Windsor Castle. It was he, also, who founded " the most honourable and noble Order of the Garter;" one of the most distinguished and select orders of knighthood in Europe, and confined exclusively to a few persons of high rank. The arms, and names of the members of the order, are all put up in the beautiful choir of the chapel; and arranged in such a manner that the arms of the sovereign and the princes of the blood hang right opposite to the altar, in front of the organ. I saw that they were already preparing a place for the arms of the little Prince of Wales.

The service was rather long, as is usual with English services. I noticed that the prayer-books were still the old ones used in the times of George IV. and William IV. Since, however, these names with the pronouns " he" and " his" in the prayers would not do for Queen Victoria, the expense of new prayer-books had been spared by pasting everywhere the words " Victoria," " she," her," &c. over the former words. One might have thought that in the royal chapel itself, new prayer-books would have been considered necessary on a change of reigns.

I and the old " Poor Knight" read in the same prayer-book. His sight was now very dim, and he wore gigantic spectacles. I thought of the telescope with which his keen eye was once accustomed to range the furthest horizon. We prayed together out of English prayer-book, not omitting that remarkable clause which I do not think would be found in all prayers for sovereigns, that it might please Heaven to " vanquish and overcome all her enemies." We had even to pray for the Order of the Garter, that it might please Heaven to preserve " this illustrious confraternity !"

After divine service, I took a nearer view of the helmets and arms upon the wall. I found on the list of knights, not one French sovereign, but six German ones, among whom the King of Prussia has now taken his place. The Emperor of Russia, and the King of Belgium, are also members of the order. On the wooden walls behind the seats in the choir, little metal tablets are nailed up, on which are engraved, not in English but in French, the names and titles of former knights; as for instance, " Les armoiries du très-haut puissant et très-noble Prince Henri Duc de Somerset, &c., Chevalier du très-noble Ordre de la Jarretière." The windows of the chapel are rich in old and new glass-paintings; and on each side of the main body of the church stand rows of little chapels, which all have their peculiar interest. They all derive their names from some distinguished English families, by which they were erected as mausoleums; there are the Bray-chapel, the Rutland-chapel, the Lincoln-chapel, &c. Everywhere I found such an extraordinary number of coats of arms, and heraldic signs painted, moulded, chiselled, and engraved on every wall and doorway, that I suppose St. George's Chapel surpasses all other chapels in the world, in that respect. Many words and signs remained entirely enigmatical to me; such for instance as the gold letters: " i h c," upon a blue ground. One chapel wall was covered with painted bunches of flax, another with iron gratings, a third with crosses, a fourth with pelicans, &c.; these being the armorial bearings of the families to whom the chapels belong.

In one of the side chapels stands the Cenotaphium of the Princess Charlotte, which was executed by Wyatt. The body of the princess, covered with a cloth, is represented as lying on a bier. A part of her right hand alone is uncovered, but, through the cloth, the form of the body and the features of the face may be traced. On both sides of the bier kneel or stand, in various sorrowful attitudes, mourning females, all deeply veiled. This is the lower part of the scene. Above is represented the apotheosis of the princess. She rises to Heaven, borne by two angels; another angel bears her child. In the lower department, not a single uncovered face is to be seen; there is nothing but drapery. Nor can I regard it as æthetically correct and pleasing thus to represent the figure of the princess twice in the same group. Is not the body entirely superfluous? I was also displeased that in the apotheosis the infant should be placed in the arms of an angel, and not of its mother. There is another very well known monument—I do not recollect at this moment where—erected, like this, in honour of a mother who died in childbed, in which the artist has placed the child in the arms of its mother, and represented both as bursting out of the grave as blessed spirits. Of course, in this instance, it is the moment of the resurrection from the grave, that is represented, and not the moment of death, as in the monument of the Princess Charlotte.

The whole lower division of the castle is occupied by the dwellings of poor knights, and of ecclesiastics attached to the chapel, and by a great number of towers; the Wardrobe tower, Julius Cæsar's tower, the Salisbury tower, &c. The upper department, entitled "the Upper Ward," contains the real royal residence. Between the two wards stands the inner keep, a massive round tower, which stands on the top of an artificial mound, and overlooks the whole castle. It is the residence of the governors of Windsor Castle. This office has always been regarded as a very important one, because the governor has not only to rule over the castle itself, but sometimes to take charge of state prisoners of high rank, who are, occasionally, placed here. Two captive kings have been imprisoned within the walls of Windsor Castle, King David of Scotland and King John of France.

When the Queen is at Windsor Castle the royal standard is hoisted over the inner keep. When she is absent, as happened to be the case during my visit, the union jack alone fluttered there. There is a printed order in which alone strangers are allowed to pass through the rooms of Windsor Castle. We entered, first, the Brunswick tower, which contains the kitchen-department of the castle. Passing through many dark and many light passages, and leaving behind us the "Confectionary-department," we entered the "Gold-room," which is full of splendid pieces of gold and silver plate. The "yeoman of the gold" led us round the room. This whole department, he told us, is under the superintendance of the Lord Steward. He told us a great deal of the gradations in rank and dignity of the various gold and silver plates and dishes, of which different sets are used, according to the solemnity and importance of the feast.

The following are a few of the most splendid pieces of gold and silver workmanship I saw.

St. George's candelabra, consists of a silver tree, at whose feet St. George is represented in the act of slaying the dragon. Angels with flowers, and wreaths of laurel, are represented hovering among the branches of the tree above the victorious hero.

A silver vase of very beautiful form, which was worked by Burmese silversmiths, and presented by Lord William Bentinck. Although the shape of the vase is as classically elegant as any Etruscan vase, yet the peculiarities of its carving and decoration, show it to have come from an Indian shore. Nor are the circles and lines all drawn with that mathematical precision which would have been preserved by our artists. This is called the Burmese vase.

The largest piece of pure gold to be seen here is the Lion's Head of Tippoo Saib, which is nearly as large as a real lion's head would be. His teeth and eyes are formed of immense jewels. This golden head shows, however, that the country inhabited by the lion, is not that where his portrait is most faithfully taken. A similar piece is the peacock of Tippoo Saib, whose tail is sown with pearls, diamonds, and other jewels. This peacock is valued at 30,000*l*. There are, in all, no less than 200 gold and silver vases, three of which are by Cellini. There is, comparatively speaking, very little plate kept at the St. James's and Buckingham palaces at London ; just as in the town-houses of the nobility, very little of their gold and silver treasures are to be seen, these being mostly kept at their country-seats. Windsor-Castle stands in about the same relation to London that Versailles does to Paris; although inferior, both in size and magnificence, to that palace. Its buildings and apartments are all on a much smaller scale ; they are also less numerous, and less magnificent in their architecture. The stone of which the castle is built, is of an unpleasing and melancholy colour, every building being of the same uniform dark gray. In the walls, however, great numbers of little fire-stones are to be seen imbedded in the stone, which gives it a very rough appearance. Within, the rooms vary of course, very much in size and fitting up ; but while Versailles surpasses Windsor in size and splendour as a building, Windsor is far superior, in the comfort and beauty of its furnishing.

A long corridor running along the series of state rooms, offers a spectacle of peculiar interest to the stranger. It contains a gallery of portraits of celebrated Englishmen, which is probably the most complete in the world. It is a large crescent-shaped gallery, about 250 paces long. On both sides hang portraits, and in front of the portraits stand, in marble or bronze, bust after bust and statue after statue. There is the harmonious and beautiful countenance of Shakespeare, the well-filled head of Bacon, the lean, sickly face of Pope, the round, puffy cheeks of Handel, the bushy eyebrows of Fox, the clever nose of Pitt, the stern, sagacious countenance of Elizabeth, Charles I. in three different attitudes ; and a number of other portraits, beautifully executed, which cannot fail to excite the deepest interest in the spectator.

I question whether there is another royal castle in Europe, so rich in portraits as that of Windsor. There are thirty large and magnificent portraits in the " Vandyke-room" alone. There are full as many by Sir Thomas Lawrence, in another magnificent saloon, called the " Waterloo-room," because it contains only the portraits of men connected, in some way or other, with the battle of Waterloo. I was rather surprised that, among all these portraits of the victors of Waterloo, there was not a single representation of the Great Defeated.

The other rooms, also, are all rich in pictures, old and new, although there are none of such value as some of those at Versailles. The most beautiful work of its kind which I saw, was the immense Gobelin tapestry. This splendid specimen of industry, containing, as it does, a series of pictures going through the whole story of Jason and Medea, and that of Esther, is certainly the grandest needle-and-thread epic ever produced. A rich collection of bronze statues and groups, about two feet in height, which goes through several of the Queen's private rooms, is also well worthy the attention of the lover of art.

In the " Guard-chamber," I observed two small banners hanging over the statues of the Dukes of Marlborough and Wellington; and I learnt that these banners were presented every year to the Queen by the two dukes, as tokens of vassallage, in return for the fiefs of Blenheim and Strathfieldsaye. On this annual act of homage depends the tenure of each estate.

My readers will understand that it is impossible for a sketch like this, to name, in the very briefest manner, half the interesting and curious particulars to be observed at Windsor Castle. This is, of all royal country residences of Europe, the most ancient. The French Versailles, the Spanish Escurial, the Austrian Schönbrünn, the Prussian Potsdam, the Russian Zarskaye-Selo, all are new in comparison with Windsor. It has been inhabited almost uninterruptedly by sovereigns. Here resided all the famous Edwards; here the Stewarts expended immense sums upon their favourite abode; and here George III. made himself as comfortable as he could, during the whole of his long reign. The parliament of 1824 voted the sum of 300,000l. for its decoration; and its embellishment has cost the nation, since the beginning of the nineteenth century, nearly a million sterling!

It was a gray, misty winter's day, when I stepped out of Windsor Castle upon its beautiful terraces; the fog hung heavily round, and the trees were bare of their foliage. Nevertheless, these terraces, the gardens, the green landscape around, with the old Thames winding through it, the venerable tree skeletons·on their rich green turf; and lastly, Eton, with its ancient college, its splendid church, and its lovely play-grounds, presented altogether so attractive and beautiful a prospect, that not even the fog and cold could damp my delight. This Windsor terrace has some resemblance to that of Richmond, although it is far superior. A new tall building, which is rising just in front of the Eton Chapel, will unluckily, however, mask a part of this beautiful prospect.

"Time and tide wait for nobody," says the English proverb. In this age of railroads we ought to add, "Time, tide, and train, wait for nobody." We hastened away from the lovely landscapes of Windsor, and the evening train bore us away, with a thousand fellow travellers, to be merged like an insignificant drop in the ocean of human life that surges for ever on the shores of the Thames.

CHRISTMAS PANTOMIMES IN LONDON.

All London was wrapped, on the day of our arrival, in one of those dense impenetrable fogs, of which it is commonly said in England, that " you could cut it with a knife." In spite of the brilliant gas-illumination of the London streets, we often saw literally nothing but the melancholy glimmer of a lamp, and this only when we had fairly hold of the lamp-post. The brightest gas-lights looked like expiring night-lamps.

Such a veil of fog must really be a source of great embarrassment to all the inhabitants of London. You cannot make two steps in the streets, without risking the embrace of a lamp-post, or the running butt up against some other passenger. Particularly dangerous are those streets paved with wood, where the carriages roll very softly. It must be fine weather for pickpockets and other scamps, who can be out of sight in a moment. It is, probably, owing to the admirable skill of the English coachmen, that such a state of the atmosphere does not occasion more frequent accidents.

The next day, the air was no clearer. We burnt candles till eleven o'clock; at which time a sort of daylight made its appearance. The sun shone, but I know not how many miles above the heads of the Londoners. Around them all was twilight; and in many shops and offices, lights were burning all day long. Strange to say, this London fog is not like that of other countries, but of an unnatural blackish yellow tint. When you look up to the sky, during one of them, you seem looking into a boundless sea of blackish yellow fluid. I believe it is the coal-smoke which gives the London fogs this peculiar colour.

In ancient Rome, the month of December was distinguished by the celebration of the Saturnalia. In Franconia and Thuringia, the village children were formerly accustomed to go in fantastic disguises from house to house, collecting, amidst songs and jests, presents and money, which, however, they also again distributed.

In France there were, at this time of the year, diversions of a similar character; and there, also, a dignitary was chosen to preside over them, called L'Abbé de la Malgouvernée, in England, the "Lord of Misrule," and in Oxford, "Imperator et Præfectus ludorum." Thus, all over Europe, Christmas formerly brought in his train the same mummeries, pantomimes, and games. Nowhere, however, were they more abundant than in England, where even at the courts of the kings, Christmas pantomimes were produced; and nowhere else, we may add, are there at the present day, so many traces of old Christmas observances to be found. In the capital, pantomimes are presented in a more brilliant manner than they ever were before, as the extraordinary resources of the principal theatres are lavished upon them. In the country, and at the seats of the gentry, the peasants are still the usual actors in them. I happened to pass, at this season, through several little villages of Wiltshire, and almost in every one, we encountered a band of boys in fantastic and comic disguises, going from house to house, and representing a kind of dramatic performance. The most usual Dramatis Personæ are Old Father Christmas, St. George and the Dragon, Maid Marian, Beelzebub, a Giant, the Dumb Daughter of the King of Egypt, &c., &c., and the dialogue is pretty much the same in all.

Shakspeare, in his youth, had, doubtless, witnessed, and assisted in such performances, in the little village of Stratford-on-Avon, and his classical and humorous weavers, carpenters, tailors, and bellows-menders, in the *Midsummer Night's Dream* were probably suggested by them.

The disorders which frequently, in former times, attended these masquerades, and their unquestionably heathen origin, brought them into bad odour with the clergy, and they were often forbidden under severe penalties, but they have not the less maintained themselves up to the present time—nay, they have, as I have said, assumed a more splendid form, since they have been taken up by the theatres, where, every Christmas, is presented a "New Grand Musical, Romantic, Historical, and Tragi-comical Pantomime," in which the conjurations and enchantments of Fairyland are mingled with all sorts of jests on politics and the topics of the day, seasoned with a liberal distribution of kicks and cuffs among all the male personages of the drama.

FROM LONDON TO WINCHESTER.

By the time the Christmas festivities are fairly over, the members of parliament, who are for London the earliest messengers of spring, return to town, and gradually, as the beautiful parks and squares· begin to assume their verdant robes, they are followed by a crowd of pleasure-seeking ladies and gentlemen. This season of the year, when the bees begin to find their narrow dwellings insupportable, when worms and birds, and all creatures, seek the open air, and when the people of all nations feel an impulse to leave the crowded abodes of cities, for the beautiful scenes of nature—at this very time an un-accountable kind of instinct seems to lead the English gentry to hurry into London—which they quit again on the approach of autumn. This " London season" furnished me with such copious materials for observation, that it would lead me too far away from my present subject to enter upon them at all, and I must therefore reserve them for a future work expressly devoted to the metropolis of England.

Of three great roads which led from London to—the Antipodes, the one by the railroad to Folkstone, Boulogne, and Picardy, another down the Thames to Calais, I preferred the third, over Southampton and the Isle of Wight to Havre-de-Grace. It is perhaps the most interesting of all, and I was already acquainted with both the others.

The railroad leading to Portsmouth and Southampton, is called the South Western, and leads, first through the county of Surrey, which, after the English Paradise, Kent, is the principal hop country —the hop gardens, as is well known, taking the place of vineyards in England, as beer may be said to do that of wine with the English population. The " picking season" is as animated a time as is the vintage, on the banks of the Rhine. The poor but merry Irishmen come over in swarms for this work, and the owners of the hop-gardens erect long barns or sheds in the fields for their accommodation, or sometimes leave them to bivouac like gipsies under the hedges. Maidstone and its lovely environs I have seen, but from what I have heard, I think Farnham, in Surrey, must carry off the prize of beauty even from it.

A handsome young lady, who sat opposite to me in the railroad carriage, informed me also, that to the other attraction of Farnham, besides the best hops, must be added that of a great number of young unmarried ladies. My informant, who, with the exception of an old gentleman, who did nothing but cough, was my only companion, was going down there to visit her friends, during the temporary absence of her husband.

We Germans have such exaggerated notions of the reserve and stiffness of the English ladies, that I hesitated some time before venturing on a remark. As, however, the above-mentioned coughing old gentleman, who began the journey with us, got out at Wimbledon, and I had contrived in two or three manœuvres, to advance from the distant end to the opposite seat of the carriage, I took courage at length to observe that it was " a very fine day." " Indeed most beautiful," was the answer, in a soft flute-like voice, and as the ice was now broken, we proceeded from observations on the weather and the country, to a lively conversation, in the course of which she informed me that she had been five years married to a barrister, that she lived in the neighbourhood of London in a pretty cottage in the Hampstead-road, and that she looked forward with much pleasure to returning to her native place for the " picking season," with which so many recollections of her childhood and youth were associated. Her husband was to take her back with him on his return from the sea-side, whither he had gone for his health. She had one child, a boy of four years old, whom she said the father had taken with him. I could not help thinking that with us or in France so young a child would have been left with the mother; but this is not the only occasion I have had to remark the attention paid by Englishmen to their children.

I must confess also, that the simple natural manners of English-women of the middle as well as the higher classes, are exceedingly bewitching, and that I felt much annoyed when the cry of " Farn-ham station, Farnham station," gave the signal of separation from my new and charming acquaintance. I assisted her out of the carriage, and delivered her over to the care of her waiting-maid, and at parting we shook hands in the most friendly manner; she even recommended me to stop also at Farnham for a few days, to see the hop picking, and then continue my journey. I do not believe that many of our continental ladies would have done as much.

Resisting, not without a struggle, the temptation to follow this pleasant advice, and warned by the vile whistle of the locomotive, I resumed my place, which now appeared so unsupportably lonely, that I took the first opportunity of changing it for one in a second class carriage, where I could again enjoy the society of human creatures. Chance would have it that I should again find an opportunity of observing the relations of the sexes in England. I found myself now placed opposite to a pleasant-looking girl, whose modest though neat costume declared her to be a London maid-servant. I soon learned that she had been some years in service with a merchant in London, and that she was going to Winchester to see her mother and her brother. She had with her several pots of flowers, which she had purchased in London for her brother, as, she said they were not to be had so good or so reasonable in Winchester. A young man who was seated beside her, and who looked like a clerk, politely offered to carry some of these for her, as he perceived they were rather troublesome to her, and I, although somewhat late, followed his example, and relieved her from the remainder of her burden.

When we reached the station, we found that she had such an endless list of goods and chattels to get collected, that the omnibus drove off and left us; the clerk and I, however, divided her baggage between us, and placing our maid-servant in the middle, marched in this order into the renowned city of Winchester. We had to drag the luggage quite to the other end of the town, where dwelt the relatives of our protégé, and our way led us past the celebrated cathedral, whose magnificent outline was visible even through the darkness of the night. It is surrounded by a large churchyard with fine old trees, and we crossed its lonely paths, and wound our way through a series of crooked narrow streets, unenlivened by a single lamp, through which our young companion seemed perfectly to know her way, but none of which I could recognise on the following morning.

We arrived at length at the house of her mother, delivered our flower-pots, carpet-bags, baskets, and hat-boxes, and after receiving many hearty thanks in return, set off to seek out our inn, and our own effects, which had been carried off by the omnibus aforesaid. This was not the only time when an Englishman had been beforehand with me in attention and politeness to the weaker sex; I could relate many little adventures of a similar character, which all go to prove that in England, even among the lower classes, women are usually treated with much attention and delicacy. I may add that in England also, I have met with maid-servants, waiting-maids, cooks, and nurses, whose deportment was such, that it seemed to me impossible for men to treat them with any thing but respect.

On the same evening I found myself in company, in a comfortable and antique mansion, the residence of a clergyman of the established church, but I did not till the following morning become acquainted with its beauties.

The " Baronial Halls of England" are paradises, and many magnificent works have been devoted to views and descriptions of them; but not less charming are many of the residences of the clergy, the rectors, vicars, curates, and especially of the deans and chapters— When I run over in my memory the parsonages I have seen, I bring before my mind's eye a whole series of picturesque and interesting buildings, one of the time of Elizabeth, another in the old French taste; a third resembling, externally, a castle of the middle ages, but fitted up with every modern comfort, and almost all draperied with luxuriant ivy, and surrounded by rich flower-gardens and smooth shaven lawns. Even the ecclesiastical residences in the cities, as for instance, the palace of the Archbishop of Canterbury, at Lambeth, have usually a rural and villa like air about them.

When, on the morning after my arrival, I accompanied my clerical friend into his beautiful grounds, I was really enraptured with the place; it seemed to me as if I could live there for ever, but the owner spent little of his time in it as he had several other residences in which he spent a part of the year. We had also from these gardens a very fine view of the cathedral, but we did not remain long in the contemplation of it, as I was eager to enter this magnificent edifice, one of the finest and most ancient of the English cathedrals. Winchester, as is well known, was the place of residence of the kings of England down to Edward I., in whose reign London began to rise in importance, and Winchester, as well as its neighbour, Salisbury, to decline.

I will not attempt here any description of this building, since I have already spoken of those of York and Salisbury, which it much resembles, but one remark I cannot avoid making, with respect to its situation. The Cathedral of Rouen, the Dom of Cologne, the Minster of Strasburg, indeed all the fine old Christian temples of the continent, lie in the very midst of the bustle and uproar of town life. They are mostly surrounded by market-places, and all the busy traffic of the most crowded streets. They rear their lofty spires out of the thickest throng of houses, which are sometimes built so closely round as almost to conceal them.

Not so the cathedrals of England. Smooth lawns, parks, stately old trees, and a solemn cloistral silence, seem to throw around them a perpetual sabbath. At a little distance from them lie the quiet dwellings of the clergy attached to them; thus at least it is with Winchester, Salisbury, Durham, partly with Westminster Abbey, and, in short, with most of the cathedrals all over England. The English plan is certainly the most pleasing at a first glance, but there is something to be said also for that of the continent. The English churches often convey the idea of being in some sort the property of the clergy; and of not belonging to the town. Our cathedrals, on the contrary, seem seated like mothers among their children, or like pillars or rocks of refuge, in the midst of the troubled tempestuous ocean of worldly business.

Since the royal palaces of Winchester have fallen to decay, its most celebrated institution is the old college, on account of its school, which rivals Eton, Westminster, and Harrow. It was founded in the 14th century by the renowned prelate Wykeham, whose name, by the establishment of this and a college at Oxford, has become familiar to the students, and through them to the whole population of England. The seventy poor scholars of Winchester, are called after him Wykehamites, and are educated gratuitously from his endowment; but besides these, there are many wealthy scholars who study here at their own expense. The whole arrangement of the buildings, churches, and school-rooms, resembles in many particulars those of Eton and Oxford, but I still observed much that was peculiar. In one room a figure is shown to strangers, which is meant to represent the ideal of a trusty servant. It is compounded of a stag, a hog, an ass, and a man—the ass symbolising the patience, the stag the swiftness, and the hog the contentedness of a good servant with what is given to him to eat and to drink.

On the wall of one of the school-rooms I observed the representations, first of a bishop's cap and staff, with the words " Aut disce;" secondly of an inkstand and a sword, significant of expulsion, with the words " Aut discede;" and finally, of a rod with the superscription " *Manet sors tertia cædi,*" that is to say, " Either stay and learn, or leave the school, or, as a third choice, stay and be flogged."

Touching this third point of the rod, a foreigner has some difficulty in understanding its niceties. A little treatise might be written upon it, entitled " The Rod in the Public Schools of England," for in every gymnasium the customs respecting its distribution are somewhat different. In some, the culprit receives it in the presence of the other scholars, in others, after their departure. In some of the buildings a room is set apart for this recreation—known to the boys as the " brushing-room." In one school which I visited, I was told that the boys formerly had to make the rods themselves, in their leisure hours, but as it was found they played too many tricks over this employment (probably they thrashed each other beforehand with the dreaded implement), the custom has been abandoned. Such of these instruments as came under my observation were generally rather more than a yard long, very solid in their construction, and with the appearance of having seen service, although I was told they were seldom used more than two or three times.

One of the most remarkable documents was the code of laws for the discipline of Winchester School, inscribed on the walls of the school-room. They are so singularly characteristic of English school life, that I shall here transcribe them, from a printed copy for the year 1840, which I purchased in Winchester.

TABULA LEGUM PÆDAGOGICARUM.

IN TEMPLO.—*Deus colitor. Preces cum pio animi affectu peraguntor. Oculi ne vagantor. Silentium esto. Nihil profanum legitor.*
IN SCHOLA.—*Diligentia quisque utitor. Submisse loquitor secum. Clare ad præceptorem. Nemini molestus esto. Orthographiæ scribito. Arma Scholastica in promptu semper habeto.*
IN AULA.—*Qui mentas consecrat clare pronunciato. Cæteri respondento. Recti interim omnes stanto. Recitationes intelligenter et apte distinguuntor. Admensas sedentibus omnia decora sunto.*
IN ATRIO.—*Ne quis fenestras taxis pilisve petito. Ædificium neve inscribendo neve insculpando deformato. Neve operto capite neve sine socio coram Magistris incedito.*
IN CUBICULIS.—*Munda omnia sunto. Vespere studetor. Noctu quies esto.*
IN OPPIDO AD MONTEM.—*Sociati omnes incedunto. Modestiam præ se ferunto. Magistris ac obviis honestioribus. Capita aperiuntor. Vultus gestus incessus componuntor. Intra terminos apud Montem præscriptos quisque se contineto.*
IN OMNI LOCO ET TEMPORE.—*Qui Plebejus est Præfectis oblemperato. Qui Præfectus est legitime imperato. Is ordo vitio careto. Cæteris specimen esto. Uterque a pravis omnibus verbisque factisque abstineto.*
Hæc, aut his similia qui contra faxit, si quando deferantur judicium damus.
Feriis exactis, nemo domi impune moratur. Extra collegium absque venia exeuntes, tertia vice expellimus.

In many old institutions and colleges among us, the number twelve has been regarded as holy, because it was that of the apostles.

This appears also to have been the case in England; and in Winchester the number of the various classes seems also to have been regulated by some sacred or biblical signification. The warden and the ten fellows who are appointed for life, represent the apostles, with the exception of Judas Iscariot, who is of course not represented;— the head and second master, and the seventy scholars, represent the seventy-two disciples, and the sixteen choristers the four great and twelve lesser prophets.

At the close of the school year the scholars break up, after having solemnly sung, in the presence of the assembled clergy and gentry of the neighbourhood, the hymn of Dulce D mum, known throughout England, and said to have been composed by a poor Wykehamist, condemned as a punishment to remain at school during the holidays. The story goes that after composing this song and the melody to it, he continued singing it incessantly, till languishing more and more, in vain longing for his home, he fell sick and died. The æsthetic value of the composition is of course not great, but it is so expressive of the feelings which animate millions of hearts, that it has spread from Winchester to Eton, Harrow, Westminster, and all public schools, and is everywhere sung with enthusiasm. The mail coaches used formerly, at Christmas and other holiday times, to be filled with boys, singing this favourite ditty, and holding in their hands little banners, on which Dulce Domum was inscribed in great letters. Now, that mail coaches have been driven out of fashion by railroads, this has gone the way of many good old customs, and these well filled coaches are only to be seen in the pictorial representations of the well known " Christmas book."

There were few things in England that interested me more than these ancient foundation schools, intimately connected as the history of most of them is with that of the country at large, and I made a point of seeing them all, and of examining the annals of most, in which are faithfully recorded the names of all who have received their education in them.

The city of Winchester is a clean and pleasant place, as most English country towns are, which have nothing to do with trade and manufactures, steam, smoke, or sea-coal. In this respect they contrast most agreeably with the provincial towns of northern France, which are usually dirty and disorderly, and surrounded by gloomy old walls and fortifications, whilst those of England are seated among trees and blooming gardens, connecting them with the open country. The French towns show nothing but walls and stones, but the English are full of shrubs, grass, and foliage; and such a thing as dirt or rubbish is scarcely to be seen in them. This is especially remarkable in Winchester, which, though so old a city, shows nothing of the wrinkles of age, but looks as fresh and gay as a city of yesterday. I have frequently mentioned the market-halls, erected during the present century in most of the English towns. Winchester also possesses one, where the market-women sit in long rows, a more convenient, but by no means so picturesque an arrangement, as when they sat with their butter, and eggs, and vegetables, on the steps, and around the old market-cross, a beautiful memorial of former days. Thus do our times, even in the smallest things, daily grow more rational, but less interesting.

In the Netherlands, and in the north of France, there are many of these crosses.

From Winchester, I made a little excursion to the neighbouring poor-house of St. Cross, an ancient and beneficent institution, dating from the beginning of the twelfth century. England swarms with such, and they, as well as many of the schools, have much that is monastic in their arrangements. Frequently the school and the poor house are connected together, as in the case of the celebrated " Charter House" of London, where there are apartments for the reception of the aged and the care of the sick, in the same building as the school-room.

The poor of St. Cross wear a peculiar costume, which resembles that of monks—a long black robe with a silver cross round the neck. They call each other " brother," and are called so by the world, and the building in which they reside has quite the air of a convent. It consists of three sides, enclosing a spacious court, and opposite to the entrance lies the magnificent old church of the establishment. Each brother has his cell, or rather his three cells, in which if he is married he lives with his family. Behind his cell lies his garden. In this, as in many convents, there is on certain holidays, a distribution of provisions to the poor of the neighbourhood. There is also a daily " dole" at the gate, of bread and beer, which is given to all who apply for it. I have already had occasion to speak of such a one, in describing the seat of the Duke of Sutherland; and though this of St. Cross is only the second I have seen, there are in England many such. The porter receives, every day, a certain number of cans of beer, and loaves of bread to distribute. The beer I found standing in metal vessels near the door, and the bread, cut in pieces, lay near it. The porter informed me that he not only always gave away what he had, but had frequently not enough for the applicants. I was myself there at eleven o'clock in the morning, and there was but little of the daily portion left, so that I fear the guests who arrived in the evening would have been badly entertained.

It seems to me that a certain part ought to be set aside for the weary wanderers who might arrive towards the close of the day. In the middle of the day the distribution might with more propriety be discontinued; but the early morning, when the wayfarer may be preparing for a journey, or the evening, after the fatigue of the day, appear to be the times when such a gift is most needed. To many a one it may be a consoling thought, on a long and weary way, that he is sure to find refreshment in the evening at St. Cross.

These English " doles" at the gates of castles and colleges are certainly among the most beneficent of charitable institutions. They seem to imitate the kind providence of God, which everywhere, in field and forest, scatters the sweet refreshment of fruits and berries. Were there a few of these charitable doles in the streets of London, some unfortunate creatures might be saved from dying of starvation; and had I the means, I would gladly establish such on all the roads of the world.

SOUTHAMPTON.

After passing Winchester the railroad divides into two branches, one leading to Portsmouth, and the other to Southampton. The latter, to which I now hastened, is, decidedly one of the handsomest towns in England. It is beautifully situated; encircled with gentle slopes covered with wood, and sprinkled with charming country seats. Coming from the interior of the country, we discover the beautiful waters of the Bay of Southampton, or " Southampton Water," as it is called, close on the shores of which lies the town, while beyond it stretches the largest forest in England, called the New Forest. It has the air of a happy and prosperous place, and I believe this appearance is not deceitful, the trade of the town having nearly doubled within the last ten years. The completion of the railroad to London, and the consequent facility of transmitting goods in four hours, instead of by a long day's journey, has of course opened many new prospects for it, and one of its most immediate consequences has been the removal to Southampton of the East India packet station.

Considering its many advantages of position, the wonder is that Southampton has not long since risen to much greater importance. It has always been a harbour of the second or third class, the duties paid in Liverpool amounting to eighty, and those of London to two hundred times those received in it—indeed it could by no means pretend to rival the commerce even of Hull, Bristol, or Newcastle. The town has a pleasant fresh appearance, but possesses some antique remains, which harmonise very agreeably with its more modern edifices, as I have noticed the new and the old usually does in English towns. One of its most interesting antiquities is an ancient gate, called " Bargate," at the beginning of the principal street of the town. It exhibits two great coarsely executed figures, very much like the Gog and Magog of Guildhall in London. These two of Southampton are said to relate to the romantic history of the warlike knight, Sir Bevis, of Southampton, the hero of many legends, who slew two giants, one of whom called " Ascapart," he had previously retained for a considerable time in his service.

I took a particular interest in this last-named giant, because he was baptised at Cologne on the Rhine, whither Sir Bevis had arrived from the East, with his beautiful heathen bride, Josyan. This beauty received the rite at the same time, and demeaned herself, of course, in a becoming manner; but the giant, for whose christening a whole tun of water had been prepared, behaved very ill, and took the cold bath very much amiss.

> "The people had good game and laughe,
> But the Byshoppe was wrath enoughe."

Southampton was a town as early as the time of the Romans, by whom it was called Clausentum; but it did not then include the whole area of the present town, but lay to the side, on a peninsula, around which winds the river Itchen. On this spot stands one of the delightful country-houses I have so often alluded to, "Bittern Manor," the property of a Scotch lady, and the residence of the celebrated oriental traveller, Urquhart. It was my agreeable fate to pass several sunny autumn days in this, in so many ways interesting spot, among persons in every way worthy of it.

There is really something heavenly in this English country life. In the morning one finds oneself at breakfast with all the great London newspapers; the day is spent in excursions, and in the evening, purified from the soil of travel, by the help of soap and brushes, and clean linen, one enjoys the society and conversation of ladies and gentlemen, while lounging in luxurious arm-chairs, at the tea-table or over the fire; and should there happen to be found among the company two travellers, one of whom has seen the whole East, and the other a considerable portion of it, these two can go out together at night into the park, and, kindling a fire in the Roumelian or Tatar manner, wile away, in stories of strange lands, a part of the time which others are passing, in oblivion on soft feather beds.

NETLEY ABBEY.

My first excursion from Southampton was to the ruins of Netley Abbey, from the sight of which I promised myself so much the more pleasure, that I had neglected to see many other beautiful and celebrated ruins of English monasteries.

The ruins of Netley Abbey lie on the shores of the bay, and the road to them passes between a number of parks and country-seats. The rich profusion with which these are scattered all over the country really amazes a foreigner; in these is seated the real marrow of the country, the most opulent, influential, and cultivated classes of the English people. With this abbey many interesting historical recollections are associated. It was in possession of the Cistercian monks down to the reign of Henry VIII., who drove them away, and presented the abbey to Sir William Paulet. This remarkable man raised himself to be Marquis of Winchester, and Lord High Treasurer of England; and, what is more, maintained himself in this post thirty years, through all the stormy times of Henry VIII., Mary, and Elizabeth. He maintained himself at this elevation, according to his own confession, by having in his composition more of the willow than of the oak; and he was not taken from it by death till he had had the satisfaction of seeing one hundred and three of his lineal descendants.

Netley Abbey became subsequently the residence of several Earls of Hereford, till at length, in the year 1700, it appeared to be in so decayed a state, that he sold a part of it for building materials. The person who bought it, began immediately to take down a part of the building, but was, according to the story, stopped one night by a dream that appeared of evil import. He dreamed that while he was taking down the arch of one of the abbey windows, a stone fell on his head and killed him. His friends begged him to desist from the destruction of the building, but he paid no attention to their remonstrances; and one day while he was endeavouring to loosen a plank from a wall, a huge stone was shaken from its place, and falling on his head, struck his skull. The wound was not dangerous, but it happened that while the surgeon was endeavouring to remove a splinter of the bone, his knife slipped, and caused the instant death of the patient.

One principal cause of the beauty of English ruins is the dampness of the climate, which covers them so immediately with a mantle of verdure. At Netley Abbey, the court-yards, chapels, halls, and chambers are all filled with trees, the edges of the walls covered with plants, and the ivy has hung its rich garlands round every elegant column and window-frame. In the centre of the largest space within the ruins, some speculator has established a table where the traveller may obtain ginger-bread, and ginger-beer, soda-water, and biscuits, and the vendor of these dainties has set up his tent in the cell of one of the monks. The trees and bushes seem here as if they were representing the scenes in Ovid's *Metamorphoses*. A thorn covered with its red berries, seems to be looking out of one of the windows at the Southampton Water, as once the young daughters of the Earl of Hereford, or some among the 103 descendants of the Marquis of Winchester may have done. Instead of porters and tall lacqueys, two tall trees keep watch at the gate; and instead of horses, we find in the stables, fine specimens of the stately ash. For the aged crones who may once have tenanted its chimney corners, we find there knotted and gnarled trunks, and the church is filled with plants and shrubs which seem like a metamorphosed congregation of devout worshippers. Beyond the abbey, the ground rises a little, and thence I had the view of the sea through its arched windows.

During the excursion which I made on the following day from Bittern Manor, I saw many more extraordinary and fantastic decorations of walls, also of vegetable origin. I had been told of a wine-cellar in Southampton, from the vaults of which the fungi had formed enormous garlands and tassels. I wished to see it, but as it was a bonded warehouse I could not be admitted without the concurrence of so many of the official persons, that I almost repented a request that seemed to occasion so much trouble. The sight, however, was really such as to make amends for it. The whole extent of the vaults was thickly hung with tassels, composed of a countless number of small mushrooms, and varying from a foot to a yard and a half long. Some hung perpendicularly down, others across from one wall to another. Sometimes they were shaped like round balls, and strung like beads together. Most of these wreaths were of a dark gray colour, but some were snow-white. The whole was suspended in a mass over our heads, and the cellar had something the appearance of a stalactical cavern, with only the difference, that every breath of air that rustled through it, set the whole in motion.

The people would not allow me to take down one of these mouldy garlands, saying that the owner of the cellar was so jealous of them, that he would not have them touched. The whole had indeed so pretty an effect, that it seemed a pity to disturb them, but it was certainly the first time in my life, that I recollect to have seen dirt and dust turned into an article of luxury, and made an object of jealousy. My inquiries were vain as to how this cellar came to be so especially decorated, as I was told there was no other like it in Southampton.

THE NEW FOREST AND ITS GIPSIES.

The most interesting scene in the neighbourhood of Southampton is, perhaps, the New Forest, which lies opposite to the town. It includes an area of 66,000 acres—more than half of the extent of the whole of the royal forests in England, of which there are but ten, Dean Forest and Windsor Forest being among the principal. This New Forest is said to owe its origin to the barbarous tyranny of William the Conqueror, who laid waste the country far and wide, destroying the dwellings, driving away the inhabitants, and not even sparing the churches, of which some assert that he destroyed no less than thirty-six, though other historians limit the number to twenty-two. All this was in order to form, from their fields and homesteads, a hunting-ground, convenient for his neighbouring residence at Winchester.

The highest officer appointed to the care of the New Forest is the Lord Warden, and under him there is a numerous establishment of official personages—some for the " venison," and others for the " vert"—an old Norman French word signifying any bush large enough to conceal a deer. As we seldom hear among us of English forestry, my German readers may, perhaps, wish to know something of the distribution of these officers. The whole forest is divided into fifteen walks, and for each of these is appointed a " keeper." The trees stand under the special superintendence of the " Woodward," who has under him twelve regarders. There is a particular tribunal for all matters connected with the forest, composed of four verderers, who are usually men of property and interest in the neighbourhood. Besides these, there is a forest surveyor, whose business it is to mark the wood which is fit for the use of the navy.

The New Forest is, however, not quite an unbroken stretch of woodland, as it is interrupted in many places by fields and villages. Some of its most interesting inhabitants are the gipsies, who abound more within its limits than anywhere else in England ; for which reason most of the attempts towards the reformation and Christianising of these people, have proceeded from Southampton. A Committee has been formed there called the " Southampton Committee for the Improvement of the Condition of the Gipsies," and there is a clergyman here who has made these wanderers his especial study, and published a little book concerning them. I paid a visit to this gentleman, and made an excursion for the express purpose of meeting some gipsies, but was not successful, the inhabitants of the neighbouring huts telling us that they had gone away the day before. From what I have had other opportunities of seeing and hearing, however, concerning English gipsies, I do not believe they are a much more civilised race than those of Hungary and South Russia, although they are by no means so purely oriental in their exterior, as in those more eastern parts of Europe. Many who pass in England by the name of gipsies, appear to have scarcely a trace of their Hindostanee origin, but others again with their dark skins, black eyes, Indian features, and language, sufficiently indicate the part of the world whence they have proceeded.

As in England in the New Forest, so they have in Scotland their head quarters in a wildly romantic region in the Cheviot Hills, near the village of Kirk Yetholm close to the English border, whence they roam over all the neighbouring countries. From the New Forest, they visit principally the fairs round London. In some letters concerning the gipsies written by a Scotch preacher, near the above mentioned establishment, (the metropolis of the gipsy kingdom, as it is sometimes called,) there are many remarks which strikingly coincide with what I have myself seen of this singular people among the South Russians and Tartars. The extraordinary suddenness and violence of their quarrels, for instance, the fantastic and terrible curses they heap on each other, and their equally sudden reconciliations. The pride also which they have in their race, outcasts as they are, is a point in which the Hungarian gipsies appear closely to resemble those of Scotland. Among the former I have often heard the remark that their people was the oldest and most distinguished in Europe. Attachment to their children is a marked characteristic of both, but the Scottish gipsies form an exception to almost all others, in desiring that their children should be instructed. The majority of them can read, and many possess a Bible, so that even among these eccentric people the love of learning, so general in this country, manifests itself.

The gipsies in Scotland commonly profess to belong to the Presbyterian church, as in Liefland and Courland they do to the Lutheran, in Hungary to the Catholic, in Moscow to the Greek, and in Tartary to the Mahomedan religion. In South Russia I recollect being particularly struck by the exquisite development of the figure, and a certain air of elegance often observable among the gipsy women ;

the Scotch preacher says the deportment of the gipsy women is often so graceful, that one might sometimes fancy they had been brought up at a European court.

Crabb, the "gipsies' advocate," as he has been called, has sometimes such extraordinary notions concerning the reform of the gipsies, especially on the subject of religion, that I must confess he does not appear to me to be building on very solid ground. It is said, indeed, that he has been very unfortunate in his "reformed gipsies," as they have mostly turned out more criminal and more unhappy than their wild brethren.

In illustration of the difficulty of reforming a gipsy, a story was told me, which, strange and romantic as it sounds, was undoubtedly true in its principal circumstances.

A lady of rank and fortune, who happened to have no children, and who lived in the neighbourhood, had taken so great a liking to a beautiful little gipsy girl, that she took her home, had her educated, and at length adopted her as her daughter. She was called Charlotte Stanley, received the education of a young English lady of rank, and grew up to be a beautiful, well-informed, and accomplished girl. In the course of time a young man of good family became attached to her, and wished to marry her.

The nearer, however, this plan approached the period of its execution, the more melancholy became the young Hindostanee bride, and one day, to the terror of her foster mother, and her betrothed husband, she was found to have disappeared. It was known that there had been gipsies in the neighbourhood; a search was set on foot, and Charlotte Stanley was discovered in the arms of a long, lean, brown, ugly gipsy, the chief of the band. She declared she was his wife, and no one had a right to take her away from him, and the benefactress and the bridegroom returned inconsolable. Charlotte afterwards came to visit them, and told how, as she grew up, she had felt more and more confined within the walls of the castle, and an irresistible longing had at length seized her to return to her wild gipsy life. The fellow whom she had chosen for her husband, was said to be one of the wildest and ugliest of the whole tribe, and to treat his beautiful and delicate wife in the most barbarous manner. He was some time after, condemned to be hanged for theft, but his wife, through the influence of her distinguished connexions, procured the commutation of his sentence to that of confinement in the hulks. During the time of his imprisonment, she visited him constantly, and contrived in many ways to improve his situation, without the savage manifesting in return the smallest gratitude. He accepted her marks of affection as a tribute due from a slave, and frequently even during her visits ill treated her. She toiled incessantly, however, to obtain his liberation, supplicating both her foster mother and her former lover, to use all their efforts in his favour. At the very moment of his liberation, however, when Charlotte was hastening to meet him across the plank

placed from the boat to the shore, the savage repulsed her so roughly
that she fell into the water. She was drawn out again, but could
not be induced to leave him, and returned to her former wild way of
life, in the New Forest and the fairs of London. I saw the portrait
of Charlotte Stanley, which was preserved by the friend of her
youth. Her story is a kind of inversion to that of Preciosa, and
might make an interesting romance. The Southampton committee,
it is said, have not been more fortunate with the gipsies, whom at
different times they have put out to service, than was the benefactress of Charlotte Stanley, for they all return, sooner or later, to
their wild wandering life.

The number of all the Scotch and English gipsies is estimated
by Mr. Crabb at 18,000—a number which I should be inclined to
think even overrated.

A MAGAZINE OF ENGLISH SEA STORES.

In the morning, before breakfast, I usually placed myself on the
lawn before the house at Bittern Manor, and sent up the incense of
a cigar, from the altar of a Roman divinity, to me unknown, the
Goddess Ancasta. The altar was in excellent preservation, and the
words "*Deæ Ancastæ*" were perfectly legible, as well as some letters which looked like "*Tetricus.*" This deity, I found, was not
known to any of the mythologists of Southampton, and was, probably, one of the innumerable little local goddesses, which abounded
within the wide limits of the Roman empire, and which the amazing
religious liberality of the Romans, was always ready to receive into
their Olympus. Tetricus was, perhaps, the person who erected the
altar to her. Many others had been dug up in the park, and many
Roman coins found on the site of the ancient Clausentum. A line
of circumvallation was also shown to me, which extended from water
to water, and cut off the peninsula on the land side.

A lovely garden, stretching across these memorials of a time past
away, and a seat by the altar of an unknown goddess, were of course
sources of enjoyment to a lover of antiquity, such as he does not
often meet with. After this morning sacrifice, I betook myself to
the town to admire the handsome and interesting shops in the High-
street. This looking into shop windows is a favourite amusement
in England, and I met with many, even of serious, middle-aged men,
who acknowledged to taking great delight in it. The variety and
elegance of the wares to be found in this rich country, where the
American, African, East Indian, and Chinese goddesses of plenty
pour out the abundance of their horns, is really astonishing. But
among all the shops, none interested me more than those called ship
chandlers, and which include almost all imaginable things wanted
for ships or sailors. Not only the English seaport towns in general,
but also all the little ports on the Thames—Woolwich, Gravesend,

Chatham, &c., swarm with these shops, but those of Southampton excel both in the quantity and quality of their wares, from the circumstance that the Southampton waters are filled with the yachts of noblemen and gentlemen, lying at anchor, several of which I visited, and found them, in every respect, patterns of beautiful and solid construction.

In these shops the elegant looking sailors that one sees about Southampton, with fine blue jackets and snow-white trousers, and who, on inquiry, we find to be Lord This and Colonel That, purchase what they require for the fitting out of their vessels, and the goods kept in them are, consequently, of the best quality. Since we know little of such shops among us in Germany I will endeavour to describe the nature of their contents.

In the first place we find all kinds of astronomical and marine instruments—sextants, quadrants, telescopes, barometers, compasses, &c., of the greatest variety and the most costly construction, for instance, sextants of the finest steel, with their scales marked on silver gold, or platina, and placed in mahogany boxes lined with velvet, with ivory handles; telescopes from a foot and a half to seven feet in length; drawing implements of every description; lanterns adapted to all kinds of weather—signal lanterns, deck lanterns, captains' lamps, illuminators, concave, convex, flat and prismatic lamps and lanterns, some of which could be fired under water; compact heating and cooking apparatus; "patent concave cabin stoves;" improved safety fire hearths, for crews of from 8 to 135 men; and fishing tackle for every kind of fish to be found in the world.

Further, there are machines for filtering water of a most ingenious construction, and which cannot be excelled, for the perfection and rapidity of the process, the dirtiest water coming out as clear as crystal; and there are wine-coolers and butter-coolers, "on the most improved scientific principles," in which butter is preserved in the hottest climate as well as in the coldest winter in Germany. Then we find an immense collection of maps and charts of the eastern, western, southern, and northern seas, besides an interesting collection of what are called nautical books, a branch of literature of which we Germans know little or nothing. Among these are works in which the flags of all the nations in the world are represented, and "codes of signals" for merchant ships and ships of war, and "Rhodes' Universal Signals for Day or Night at Sea." Treatises on British and French lighthouses; collections of novels, tales, and songs for sailors; nautical miscellanies; and sailors' prayer-books. One of the richest classes of these marine books is that of the "Sailing Directions" for the Northern Ocean, for the coasts of England and Scotland, for Brazil and South America, for the Mediterranean, to and from the East Indies, &c. To a Humboldt or a Ritter such books as these, containing the most exact observations on the formation of the coasts, the variations of weather, and all other phenomena of those seas, would be of the greatest value; but the cost of a collection of them would be so great, that I fear we cannot expect our Royal German Libraries to be enriched with them, for the benefit of our geographers and men of science.

There is an immense variety in the size and form of the account-books for ships kept in these shops, and the arrangement of many of them is admirable; and there are besides, flags, and stuff called "bunting," used for this purpose, sails, anchors, chains, from "quarter-inch link chains," up to "sixteen-inch best proved link chains," a whole catalogue of sporting tackle, and things never seen before under the title of "miscellaneous articles." As the yacht which I have mentioned, and many other vessels, generally take some guns on board, these also belong to the list of the chandler's goods, and their doors are generally decorated with cannon of various calibre, from one to two-and-thirty pounders, with the necessary ammunition. Our peaceful German *Krämers* would little think of dealing in such warlike articles; but the English have also boarding swords, scimitars, boarding pikes, and even toma-hawks. Among their ordinary articles of trade, also, are fire-works, serpents, crackers, pin-wheels, Jacks-in-the-box, French squibs, gold rain, air balloons, &c., &c. One chandler, whose shop I visited, said he was always ready to execute any order for fire-works, " up to the value of 500*l.*"—an expression which may give some idea of the sums sometimes consumed in this way in one evening by a rich Englishman. In London, of course, the trade in all the articles I have enumerated is carried on on such an extensive scale, that it is not possible to include so many in one shop as at Southampton, but there exist separate establishments for each branch.

PORTSMOUTH.

One of the most interesting excursions I made from Bittern Manor, was that to Portsmouth and the Isle of Wight, and, by the help of steam and post-horses, it only occupied a few days.

Portsmouth forms a remarkable contrast with Southampton; it is an ugly, ill-built town, consisting of a great heap of small, insig-nificant houses. It neither exhibits any thing old, nor any thing new, which could be of the smallest interest in an architectural point of view, and the inns are so bad, that one might fancy oneself in the most out-of-the-way corner of England. All, indeed, that Portsmouth offers to interest a stranger, lies partly on, and partly under the water—namely, the great ships of war, the marine arsenals, and what is contained in the dock-yards. I have visited all the celebrated dock-yards of England—Deptford, Woolwich, Chatham, and Portsmouth, and each presented so much food for observation, that were I to attempt to give any thing like a complete description of them, I should run the risk of doubling the size of my book. I will, therefore, merely mention some particulars that have remained on my memory. I began my inspection of Portsmouth dock-yaid, by partaking of an excellent breakfast on board the Excellent, an English ship of war, where all the young artillerists of the fleet practise manœuvring. I had arrived with the governor in a beautiful eight-oared boat, and we were received with all military honours, the captain coming to meet us, and along with him a lovely little antelope from Syria, brought from Egypt by one of the officers of the expedition. This charming little animal sported round the breakfast-table, eat pieces of bread, and seemed as full of life and health as the officers and crew of the ship, which is saying much. A slight mist which had hung over the surface of the water, when we began breakfast, dispersed just as we rose from table; the morning sun shone out brightly, and all prepared for the experiment in gunnery which we had come to see. Some new kinds of shell were to be tried, each winged by ten pounds of gunpowder, and having in the centre a tube containing fire, and closed by a wooden peg, which required it to strike against wood or stone before it could explode. Out of thirty-eight bombs which were tried, fifteen burst on striking the water, or before reaching their destined point, so that the experiment was not considered successful. It seemed to me, however, that I should explode myself at every shot, and I really could not refrain from sundry convulsive starts. I remained near the cannon, that I might observe all the operations, and I found the concussion much stronger on the deck above than immediately behind it. The ricochetting of the balls on the smooth, mirror-like surface of the sea, was beautiful, and when they struck the water a powerful shock was felt, even at the distance of the vessel. They threw up high fountains at every stroke, out of the midst of which they rose, and then struck the water again, twelve or fourteen times, raising each time a dashing column of spray. The shells were not thrown out of mortars, but from large cannons, about each of which more than a dozen men were busied like ants, each, however, keeping exactly to his own department. The bombs were filled in a particular apartment, and for the necessary illumination of the magazine, a long corridor was parted off, and separated from it by strong glass windows, behind which were placed the lamps, so that the rays of light could pass through, but no spark.

Among the manœuvres which I witnessed, no one interested me so much, as that of firing with a cannon placed on a moveable plate, made to represent the motion of a vessel on the waves of the sea. It swayed about forward or backward, to the right or the left—in short, with that pleasing variety of movement, so well known as occasioning sea-sickness. The gunner, however, by drawing a small cord, can regulate the whole machinery and bring it to a stand-still in a moment. This he does at the moment when he thinks he sees, exactly before the cannon's mouth, the object at which he is supposed to aim, and the officers can then judge whether that would have been the proper moment to fire the gun.   Another interesting vessel which I visited at Portsmouth, was the Victory, well known as that in which Nelson breathed his last.   The little cabin into which he was carried, from the deck where he received his mortal wound, was, when we visited it, illuminated with six lamps, as well as the between decks, where there was a small arsenal of the arms of marines.   This vessel is the residence of the captain of the harbour, who has under his superintendence all the hulks and ships lying in ordinary.   His apartments were admirably fitted up, but really after I had heard so much of the effects of cannon-balls, upon these wooden dwellings, they no longer appeared to me very attractive.   I was told by many experienced sailors, that the balls, when not fired from too great a distance, generally go right through plank and copper sheathing, and every thing living or dead that comes in their way. I should feel in a sea-fight, like the princess in the fable, who, in her glass-house under the sea, could nowhere feel herself safe from the goggling eyes of the great fish, her husband.   Sailors are, however, it is said, not so often wounded by the balls themselves, as by the splinters of wood which strike and often kill them.   It appears, therefore, that their wounds and mutilations must be more various and complicated than those of land troops.

There were few other ships, than those in ordinary lying at Spithead, and of these there were about thirty lying at anchor in a long row, extending three or four miles; they were without masts, and each had a sort of roof or shed erected over it for its protection, and a few men are left on board of each; and this motionless fleet is commanded by a lieutenant, whose business it is to watch all that goes on, on board these vessels, to inspect them from time to time, and to report upon their condition.

Of the machinery which I saw in the dock-yards of Portsmouth, none appeared to me more remarkable, or more truly admirable, than what is called the " Block machinery," constructed by the celebrated engineer Brunel, to see which alone it is worth while to go there.   Blocks are, as is well known, the sheaves of the pulleys which receive the ropes or tackle of a ship, and every vessel requires some hundreds of them.   These were lately manufactured for the English, as they still are for every other navy, by a very crude process, with the help of the common turning lathe, and the object was to produce a machine, by which a great number could be made at a time.   Mr. Brunel found means to overcome the difficulties of this task, and invented a machine, worked by steam, which fully answered the purpose.   The most remarkable circumstance connected with this invention is, however, that it was produced at once in complete perfection—like Minerva springing fully armed from the head of Jupiter.   I was told it was more than twenty years since it was set up, and that when lately it was visited and inspected by the inventor, he declared he could find nothing in it to alter or improve. This is, perhaps, unexampled in the history of human inventions.

It would be impossible by description to give any idea of the construction of this machine, and, indeed, it is not always perfectly understood even by those familiar with the subject.

The wood of which these blocks are made is peculiarly hard, and this it was that formerly rendered the work so toilsome, and the application of the irresistible steam-power so very desirable. The wood is cut, by ever-revolving circular saws, into cubic masses; and twelve of these are placed at a time on the spokes of a wheel, which in its evolution presses them against a sharp knife. This operation is afterwards repeated, with a finer cutting instrument. The blocks are then bored through to make room for the pulleys, and the difficulty of these operations is great, as the block has not a cylindrical, but an irregular form. The whole is then polished, and this, as well as all the other operations, is so perfectly executed by the machine, that it might be thought the work of the most careful and skilful turners. The same machine also makes the metal rollers and pulleys, and fixes them firmly in the sheaves—in short, it is a perfect wonder, and had Mr. Brunel never done any thing else than invent this block-machinery, he would have rendered his name immortal. It is used only, however, for the English ships of war, and I cannot understand why the government does not allow such to be manufactured also for the use of the merchant navy.

Among the other interesting operations which I saw here was also, the making of copper bolts, used in such large quantities in shipbuilding, and the forging of a great anchor for a man-of-war, the most tedious, toilsome, and difficult of all the operations of the smithy. Powerful men, wielding vast hammers, strike the glowing mass of iron for a quarter of an hour together, every stroke seeming enough to shatter a rock, without producing any visible effect upon it. Every time, after having received a few blows, it cools again to a degree of unconquerable obstinacy, and must again, with incredible toil be placed in the fire, and heated for half a day before it is capable of being worked any more. If it is necessary to strike the iron on the other side, the turning takes so much time, that it is sure to cool during the operation, and must then be again placed in the fire for a quarter or half a day, and I believe weeks or months elapse before any thing like an anchor is produced. One's heart is really torn to witness such never ending toil.

The collection of anchors here at Portsmouth is I suppose the largest in the world, and there are hundreds of them with such mighty arms, that it is inexplicable and inconceivable, how the power of wind and water can ever avail to rend their giant grasp.

As the anchors consist of a great number of bars of iron forged together, so do the masts, of many trees, fastened together by bolts and braces. In walking in the forests of Russia and Poland, I have sometimes admired the gigantic firs I saw there, and wondered how it was possible to use such a tree for the mast of a ship, but here at Portsmouth I learned that for a mast of the largest size, almost a dozen such trees are required. The centre or kernel of the mast is cut square, and is made of one particular kind of tree, and the side pieces, which have all their separate names, are taken from other trees. Even if the whole could be found at once as long and as thick as required, a mast composed of several pieces would be preferred, as it is considered to be more elastic and to stand better in a gale. It must also be more easily replaced, at least it appears probable that in a storm a part might give way without the whole being destroyed. When a mast is struck by lightning also, I am told, the injury is more partial, in the case of a mast of this description, than it would be with one made of a single tree; and how important this consideration is, may appear from the circumstance that, during the forty years of the present century, no fewer than a 120 British ships of war, in various parts of the world, have had their masts partially or wholly destroyed by lightning.

The various establishments connected with the navy, lie on both sides of the water, and our boat, rowed by eight " jolly young watermen," shot across from one to another like a trout. Clarence-yard is a particular division of the docks, occupied only with the victualling of the fleet, and one of its most remarkable departments is that employed in biscuit-baking. The dough is there, like the wood, iron, and copper, on the other side of the water, worked by steam. It is kneaded, rolled out, cut into six-sided pieces, and pierced with holes, (to assist in its preservation by letting the air through,)—all by mighty steam-engines. In the baking-house, which put me in mind of a great cotton-spinning establishment in Manchester, are fabricated no fewer than nine tons of biscuits daily— about 18,000 pounds,—a magnificent provision of food for the hungry stomachs of the English sailors, and unfortunately also for the worms, for the preparation of biscuit has not yet reached such perfection, as to preclude the ravages of these unpleasant companions at the feast. The English sailors, however, look on them as quite in the ordinary course of things, and have thus acquired a habit of always knocking their biscuit on the table before they eat it, with a view to shake out the worms. Indeed this is so constant a practice with them, that they do it involuntarily, even when they eat biscuits on shore.

Near this baking-house lies that where the beef is prepared, and near this, immense stores of rum, tea, cacao, and other articles, of which the enormous quantity of cacao especially struck us. This excellent, nourishing, and not intoxicating beverage, plays a very important part in the English navy, and, with the present zeal against rum and brandy, it is daily becoming more so. English sailors are always abundantly provided with it, and considering the greatness of the navy, it may be imagined that the quantity consumed is very large. The tanks for water, which are made of iron and lined with tin, keep it in excellent preservation. Some was given me to taste which had been kept no less than fourteen years, and yet tasted as sweet and fresh as if it had just been fetched from a spring.

Early on the following morning I set off for the Isle of Wight, crossing to reach it, the famous roads of Spithead, the best and most spacious in the kingdom, which, as well as the harbour of Portsmouth, is deep and wide enough for the whole British fleet to lie at anchor in perfect safety. It is narrow at the entrance, but spreads out to a great breadth within, the Isle of Wight lying like a protecting dam before it. A thousand ships of the line might lie behind like a flock of ducks. It seems, indeed, as if people considered themselves quite too safe here, for it is well known that the Royal George, a great ship of war of 100 guns, sunk in this harbour in the finest weather. The ballast of the vessel had been thrown all on one side, in order to lift the other partly out of the water, for the sake of some necessary repairs; the operation was unskilfully performed, and some guns probably rolled suddenly over, so that the lower port-holes on that side touched the surface of the water, and as these were all open, the water rushed in and filled the vessel, so that it sunk in a few seconds with all that it contained. Probably some of the crew may have jumped overboard, and been drawn down afterwards with the vessel, but 600 persons lost their lives by this accident, which took place only about 100 yards from the shore. I was told by an eye-witness of the scene, that the waters closed over the spot with a peculiarly hollow sound, and there arose from it a column of water almost like a water-spout, and the great waves occasioned by the sinking of such a vast body, spread all across the harbour, and set every vessel in motion. This took place in the year 1782, and down to the present time, during a period of more than sixty years, the divers have been employed in bringing up from the wreck, treasures and curiosities buried in her. We sailed close to the spot, and saw two vessels lying at anchor there, between which heavy burdens were drawn up, such as two cannons lately recovered. I was told the work would now soon be finished, but it is likely that many an object, much coveted by man, is lying there buried under slime and sand. A whole library of books has been written concerning the melancholy fate of this vessel, and all the attempts to raise it, either wholly or in parts, which have, from time to time been made.

ISLE OF WIGHT.

The beautiful little harbour of the Isle of Wight, opposite to Portsmouth, called Ryde, has, during the last ten years, risen from an unimportant village to a town of 5000 inhabitants, and I had occasion to make the same remark, with respect to perhaps a hundred places on the English coast, which, lying on rivers or arms of the sea, have been indebted for their increase to the vast facilities afforded by steam navigation. Let any one cast a glance at the map of England, and consider the numerous openings of this kind, and the innumerable points, whence it is necessary to cross, and he will be able to make something like an estimate of the number of such little harbours which are rising into importance by the aid of steam.

The Mole at Ryde, which is thrown out into the sea, is 2000 feet long, and forms, as an Englishman said to me, one of the finest marine promenades in the kingdom. These marine promenades, on the moles of their harbours, on the ramparts of their coast fortresses, and on quays and breastworks, form a class of walks peculiar to England; and they are usually seen covered with promenaders, inhaling the fresh sea breeze, till the sun has sunk beneath the waves.

The promenaders of Ryde, from their mole, look with especial satisfaction on what they boast " is the finest piece of water in the kingdom." I remained twice standing there looking over at Portsmouth, and the Swedish and French as well as English ships that were lying there; and each time some old sailors, or other idlers, who are always lounging about, made the observation to me, " I dare say, sir, no country can boast of such a fine piece of water," and both times I heartily concurred in their opinion. From Ryde I travelled in the very agreeable company of a good-humoured native of the island, round to its southernmost point, and then crossed it through the centre. The little towns of Newport, Brading, and Cowes, have delightful situations, and the sea-shore presents the most beautiful views of rocks and sea. The road leads sometimes through meadows, sometimes through lovely groves, and is almost always sprinkled, on both sides, with villas and country-houses. The climate of the island is so mild, that there are places on the south coast, where ice and snow are unknown. The myrtles bloom here the winter through, and many invalids desiring a warm climate, yet unable or unwilling to go further, live constantly in the Isle of Wight. Almost in every place where we stopped, we were told of some such lady or gentleman, who had come for the benefit of the air. Yet though the climate is so extremely mild, the vine does not flourish here, although it is said that it formerly did as well as in many other parts of England, where it is never cultivated at present. It is likely, however, this is not so much to be attributed to a change of climate any more than in America and Prussia, where the same observation has been made, as to the increased means of communication, by which it has become easier to procure good foreign wine, so that it has no longer been thought worth while to make bad wine at home. There is in the Isle of Wight, not sun enough to ripen grapes, although there is no deficiency of warmth, but the heat is distributed through the whole year. There are many plants of southern origin which grow in England, and will not grow in Germany, because the severity of our winter kills them; whilst, on the other hand, there are a great number which do well with us, and would not live in England, because there is not heat enough in the summer.

The Isle of Wight has the form of a lozenge, having two sides turned to the south, and two to the north, and differing widely in their aspect. The former are rocky and abrupt, and the sea often undermines the cliffs, so that large masses fall down into it, and these falls have occasioned many bold and singular configurations, of which the most celebrated is the so-called Needles, a group of precipitous crags on the western point of the island. The waters which break from its centre also, have, in forcing their way through the rocks, gnawed out many steep valleys and ravines, here called " Chines." This word signifies in fact, the part of the back near the spine, and is not used to signify a valley anywhere in England but in the Isle of Wight; but there we have Luccomb Chine, Franklin Chine, Brooke Chine, and Black Gang Chine, which as England swarms with lovers of the romantic, and travellers in search of the picturesque, are extolled to the skies for their beauty and sublimity. The whole island is intersected from north to south by a valley, watered by a river with a Spanish name, the Medina, and the town of Newport, lying about in the middle, is its capital. It is beautifully situated, is an ancient town, and sent two members to parliament before Manchester and Birmingham were heard of there, and has besides, in testimony of its antiquity, the fine old Castle of Carisbrook, rearing its stately front from a rock in the neighbourhood. The whole way is beautiful to Cowes, the celebrated little port, where the Queen of England is now about to establish her residence. The whole harbour was full, when we arrived, of the elegant yachts of the " Royal Yacht Squadron," which has a house here for the reception of its members; and we cast many a " longing lingering look" behind at the lovely scenery around, as the steamboat carried us swiftly away on our return to Southampton.

I remained only one day longer in the neighbourhood of the Goddess Ancasta, and the next evening, when the dinner cloth was removed, and the ladies disappeared, took the opportunity, sorely against my will, to utter my farewell to England. One of my last recollections of it, is of the interesting physiognomies of a well-known amiable English traveller, and a renowned admiral, as they kindly stood on the steps of the hospitable threshold to see me off. Without, all was darkness, and when I reached the pier of Southampton, I could only distinguish the steamer that was to take us to Havre, by the lanterns at her mas head. The wind was very high, every body was muffled up, and I could only just perceive some shadowy forms, which deposited my luggage, and some outstretched hands which held a lantern, and demanded a remuneration. I crept into my favourite corner near the bowsprit; all the beautiful objects on the shore were veiled in murkiest night, and towards twelve o'clock, when we were dashing across the channel, my thoughts of England gradually faded into confused dreams.